The "Why" Behind Classroom Behaviors, PreK-5

The "Why" Behind Classroom Behaviors, PreK-5

Integrative Strategies for Learning, Regulation, and Relationships

Jamie Chaves
Ashley Taylor

Foreword by Tina Payne Bryson

FOR INFORMATION:

Corwin

A SAGE Companyy

2455 Teller Road

Thousand Oaks, California 91320

(800) 233-9936

www.corwin.com

SAGE Publications Ltd.

1 Oliver's Yard

55 City Road

London EC1Y 1SP

United Kingdom

SAGE Publications India Pvt. Ltd.

B 1/I 1 Mohan Cooperative Industrial Area

Mathura Road, New Delhi 110 044

India

SAGE Publications Asia-Pacific Pte. Ltd.

18 Cross Street #10-10/11/12

China Square Central

Singapore 048423

Acquisitions Editor: Jessica Allan

Senior Content Development Editor: Lucas Schleicher

Associate Content Development Editor: Mia Rodriguez

Project Editor: Amy Schroller

Copy Editor: Integra

Typesetter: Hurix Digital

Proofreader: Tricia Currie-Knight

Indexer: Integra

Cover Designer: Scott Van Atta

Marketing Manager: Olivia Barrett

Library of Congress Cataloging-in-Publication Data

Names: Chaves, Jamie, author. | Taylor, Ashley (Pediatric psychologist) author.

Title: The "why" behind classroom behaviors, PreK-5 : integrative strategies for learning, regulation, and relationships / Jamie Chaves, Ashley Taylor.

Description: Thousand Oaks, Califorinia : Corwin Press, [2021] | Includes bibliographical references.

Identifiers: LCCN 2020022953 | ISBN 9781071816103 (paperback) | ISBN 9781071816158 (epub) | ISBN 9781071816141 (epub) | ISBN 9781071816134 (ebook)

Subjects: LCSH: Problem children—Education (Early childhood) | Problem children—Education (Elementary) | Behavioral assessment of children. | Classroom management.

Classification: LCC LC4801 .C43 2021 | DDC 371.93—dc23 LC record available at https://lccn.loc.gov/2020022953

This book is printed on acid-free paper.

SUSTAINABLE FORESTRY INITIATIVE

Certified Chain of Custody
Promoting Sustainable Forestry
www.sfiprogram.org
SFI-01268

20 21 22 23 24 10 9 8 7 6 5 4 3 2 1

Table of Contents

Foreword

"Kids are different from how they used to be." This is a refrain that, over the last few years, I've heard repeated by seasoned educators all over the United States. They mean a variety of things when they say this, but in general, the message is typically something along the lines of more kids being more dysregulated more often in response to the typical demands of the school day, and that more children struggle when it comes to attention, behavior, and mood, all of which obviously impact learning. I'm consistently told by teachers that they don't feel that they've been trained to work with so many kids with such varieties and intensity of needs, and they don't feel supported enough to do this demanding work well. Add in a generation of parents who are sometimes less trusting of teachers, and the job, in many ways, really is harder than it's ever been.

If you're like many educators these days, you're feeling tremendous pressure to do more in shorter periods of time and with a larger number of students in your classes—many of whom have higher needs. Understandably, you feel that despite (or maybe partially because of) your desire to be a great teacher who loves your students and wants to champion them, you experience toxic levels of stress. You feel desperate for tools and perspectives to help you make sense of and address the most challenging behaviors you see in your classrooms, and you want ways to reach parents so that they partner with you and support you instead of blaming you. You may be a gifted teacher who's even considering leaving the field because the challenge feels too great. You're inspired by the idea that you can do hard things, but you're tired of doing those hard things *day after day* without the tools and support and time to manage classroom dynamics more effectively. For years I've wished that committed educators like you could find powerful, practical tools to help you be more effective in dealing with these challenges.

Now, Dr. Jamie Chaves and Dr. Ashley Taylor, both of whom have spent countless hours in classrooms observing students, providing support to teachers and administrators, and working as consultants and collaborators in school settings, are making that wish come true. They both bring a tremendous wealth of knowledge to the table, and I'm so proud of them, of the work they've done and of how many schools and families have been transformed by having worked with them. And I'm excited about this book, which brings you incredibly interesting, meaningful, and relevant knowledge from their fields which will help you face the pedagogical and behavioral challenges before you.

Working from their respective fields of expertise, Jamie and Ashley take what's crucial in order for children to learn, and make it accessible and readily applicable. In this book, they'll guide you in how to approach situations with curiosity, allowing you to work from a deeper awareness of a child's nervous system and internal landscape. After reading *The "Why" Behind Classroom Behaviors, PreK–5*, you'll be in a strong position to begin to make transformative changes, particularly for the most difficult children who need the most help. You'll discover how to create a sensory-aware environment, as well as how to honor individual differences and learning capacities, and make sense of and change behavior. You'll have new analogies, examples, and language to encourage parents to see what's really happening with their child, and to join with you in doing what it takes to help their child learn. This book offers you a toolbox that will allow you to problem-solve in whole new ways and be more effective in navigating the challenges you face daily.

Let me give you a little background to help you see why I can so wholeheartedly endorse the authors of this book. I've known and worked with Jamie and Ashley for years. They've both served in leadership positions at The Center for Connection (CFC), an interdisciplinary clinic I founded and direct, where we've gathered a team of experts from various fields such as mental health, neuropsychology, educational therapy, occupational therapy, and speech and language therapy. Jamie and Ashley have made enormous contributions to the success and vision of the CFC, where we ground everything we do in the science of interpersonal neurobiology (IPNB), an integrative field that looks at the findings of many fields of science—neuroscience, psychology, education, etc.—that help us understand how we function in the world. One of the primary foundations of the framework of IPNB is a concept called integration, which describes the process of different parts becoming linked together while maintaining their distinctiveness. For example, different parts of the brain that are specialized to perform specific processes are also functionally linked with one another, so the student can function with a whole brain instead of just responding in a moment from only part of the brain. Integration matters, because when students are in states of integration, they are more flexible and adaptive. They can then be more regulated and stable, making better decisions and more effectively addressing obstacles that appear before them. Being in states of integration leads to well-being, receptivity to learning, and many other positive outcomes. Therefore, we want to promote integration in our classrooms.

Integration is actually a great way to think about mental health, whether we mean a healthy mind, a healthy relationship, a healthy classroom or school community, or a healthy world. With this information, along with another big foundational concept of IPNB—neuroplasticity, the process by which experiences change the brain—we can begin to examine whether a particular type of intervention might be promoting integration within a student in a specific way or getting in the way of integration, and whether there might be a more effective way to help a child regain balance—in a particular moment, and in her life overall.

Guided by the principles of IPNB, everything we do at the CFC proceeds from this unique, integration-based way of viewing individuals who are facing obstacles in their lives. Traditionally, adults who have worked with struggling kids have focused on symptoms and behaviors, diagnosing a problem and then creating the appropriate interventions. That makes sense from a certain perspective, but the problem is that too many times, this process occurs without deep attention to the "why"—what's *causing* the symptoms? The way I talk about it, and the way Dan Siegel and I explain it in our book *No Drama Discipline*, is that it's important to "chase the why."

Chasing the why changes how we work with kids and the kinds of outcomes we achieve. For example, I once worked in therapy with a third-grader who was experiencing a lot of anxiety. He felt paralyzed any time he was asked to speak in front of his small class, made up of kids he'd known since preschool. He was also having trouble sleeping and was experiencing almost daily stomach aches, and every day he would cry, not wanting to go to school, even though he loved his teacher and had been primarily happy at school before third grade. As I began to explore his individual anxiety experience—its severity and frequency, when it started, what triggered it, what gave relief, how his parents amplified or calmed his states, and more—I also talked with his teacher and asked his parents about his daily schedule. I was chasing the why.

I discovered that while his teacher and parents were suggesting that he "try harder" because he wasn't completing much work during the school day, he was actually working harder than any other student, spending as many as three to five hours after school each day trying to complete his homework. My mental health lens helped me understand the issue from the anxiety disorder theory and see that as anxiety would go up, it was harder for him to concentrate and complete his work. But I needed more than that knowledge: I needed curiosity. I wondered about anxiety as evidence that a nervous system is in hyper-arousal, and that led me to ask the next question: What's *causing* or at the source of that hyper-arousal? Why was his nervous system sending out threat and reactivity signals, when all the other kids were experiencing his classroom as a safe environment?

The thinking that he experienced anxiety because he had an anxiety disorder seemed like circular reasoning. But worse, where did that diagnosis leave him? It wasn't very helpful to me, either, as I sought to help him. Sure, I could work with him using "top-down" interventions, where I would give him experiences that would activate the top parts of his brain, like his prefrontal cortex, to encourage insight and problem-solving. And I could also work with him using some "bottom-up" interventions, where I would give him experiences to regulate and calm the more reactive, lower structures of his brain, his nervous system, and his body through movement, rhythm, guided breathing, or sensory input. Those were helpful strategies, but they didn't really address the issue.

As I chased the why, I began to wonder what was preventing this child from managing the demands of his classroom. Luckily, at the CFC I worked with and learned from neuropsychologists and brilliant educational therapists, and as a team we explored some possibilities of some learning challenges. Could he have an attentional regulation challenge, maybe? Or perhaps a significantly slower processing speed, compared to his other cognitive skills? After a psychoeducational evaluation, and a diagnosis of attention deficit hyperactivity disorder (ADHD), inattentive type, and a processing speed percentile in the teens, along with the rest of his cognitive profile in the 80–90th percentile, it became clear that *the anxiety was communication*. It was telling us, "Something isn't working here for me. Doing well is unachievable for me, and I keep feeling like a failure. I try really hard, and still I can't keep up." He wasn't articulating that message with his words, but his behavior was definitely telling us. *Of course* he felt anxious! Anxiety was an *appropriate* emotion, given the discrepancy between the demands and expectations of his classroom and his current capacity. The anxiety was a symptom, and one that should not have been seen as pathology, but rather helpful information, leading us to a deeper understanding that would allow us to better support him so he could thrive.

Peeling back the layers to get to the why led us to discover some really important things that allowed him to realize that he wasn't "dumb" like he thought he was. On the contrary, he simply had a powerful brain that had strengths as well as challenges that made parts of school more difficult. With the right accommodations in the classroom, combined with working with an educational therapist for a period of time to learn how to capitalize on his gifts and find work-arounds for his areas of difficulty, and eventually going on a low-dose stimulant, everything changed. The adjusted perspective turned out to be transformative for this kid, who, I'm happy to report, thrived, achieved, and even spoke in front of the whole school the next year without much trouble. That's what chasing the why can do for us.

For another student, years earlier, I was asked to observe and make some suggestions for a first grader—I'll call her Lila—who refused to walk, but would instead stomp everywhere she went. She would not sit on the rug but would hide under her desk with her hands over her ears, sometimes plugging her nose. She had such intense emotional storms that at times she looked almost dissociated. She was very smart, yet she couldn't get ideas down on paper if she had to use a pencil to write. At times she was a model first-grader with lovely collaborative social interactions, then the next moment she'd be oppositional, dysregulated, and inconsolable. Her experienced teacher's strategies that were consistently effective for most students didn't make even a tiny bit of difference in changing how Lila behaved day after day.

There was no trauma history, and Lila was fortunate enough to have engaged parents who were both providing her with secure attachment. Her environment seemed "just right" in terms of providing developmentally appropriate stimulation and challenge. She lived in a safe neighborhood, and after ruling out pervasive developmental disorders, the only way I knew to view her actions was as evidence of some sort of mood or behavioral disorder, neither of which really fit. I could see that her nervous system was experiencing a threat response, but I couldn't figure out what was going on.

Chasing the why, I went down the rabbit hole of researching and reading about what I was seeing. That's when I discovered the phrase "sensory processing" and learned about the world of pediatric occupational therapy. This student had a sensory processing challenge that, as we discovered with the help of an occupational therapist (OT), activated a threat response in her nervous system, and it impacted many areas of her functioning. The stomping was in part because she had under-responsive sensory processing in one domain, and the forceful march she used to walk allowed her to get enough sensory input to make sense of her movements and the world. It wasn't an act of defiance. And in other areas, she had *over*-responsive sensory processing, particularly to sounds and smells. Her behaviors were a result of her nervous system activating the threat alarms. Once Lila was evaluated by a skilled OT, who was then able to cultivate an experience of safety by creating playful moments, building a trusting relationship with her, and providing individualized sensory input to integrate how her brain processed sensory information, things began to improve for Lila. In partnership with Lila's school, the OT offered guidance on how to meet her sensory needs in ways that allowed her to feel safe and to learn. Over time, Lila learned how to meet her own sensory needs and to ask for what she needed, allowing her to be an active, engaged learner who became skilled at regulating her emotions and behavior.

Notice that in both of these cases, the community of people who cared for these children chased the why, trying to get to the root of the problem. We had to get to its source. Just as it would be ridiculous to repeatedly prescribe an antihistamine for a person getting hives every day, without working to discover what the person was allergic to, it didn't make sense to treat symptoms without examining the cause of what was going on.

This is what we aim to do at CFC—to look not only at behavior, but at what's causing the behavior in the first place. From the beginning, our foundation has been built on the science that regulation and safe relationships go hand in hand; that we can harness neuroplasticity to change the brain by utilizing the power of regulated relationships; and that by chasing the why as an interdisciplinary team, we can provide specific, repeated experiences that will allow the brain to fire and wire in ways that build integration, allowing the child and the family to more fully thrive.

And it was through building our team at the CFC that I came to have the privilege of knowing, working with, and learning from Jamie and Ashley. First I met Jamie. Within minutes of meeting her (over breakfast burritos), I knew she was the one to build our OT program, to teach the rest of us how to think from a sensory-savvy lens. She could help us go beyond our too-differentiated points of view and introduce us to concepts and interventions that became game-changers: processing, attention, regulation, social communication, and more. Jamie had the IPNB lens and was ready to learn more to layer complexity into her own work. She talked about how mental health and occupational therapy needed each other. She used the magic words of "regulation" and "relationships" and "the use of self" to create safety in order to create the best chance for neuroplasticity. I'm grateful for all that Jamie has taught and continues to teach me and our team, and for the stellar OT program she's built at the CFC that has changed the lives of so many families, and also so many classrooms and teachers.

With Ashley it was much the same. From the moment she joined our team, she began building our assessment division, founding everything on a quality, relationship/regulation-based approach to assessment. She also began our 0–5 program, and soon she was in high demand throughout our community. Ashley's brilliance, deep clinical discernment, kind heart, and ability to hold complexity while joining with parents and teachers in ways that don't overwhelm them are inspiring. Our team and I are better for having worked with her and learned from her.

As you'll see in the coming pages, a key concept for Jamie and Ashley is the importance of understanding not only a child's behavior, but the context as well. As they'll explain, they often see, in homes and in mental health offices and in schools, that compliance- or obedience-based behavior modification is enforced without understanding where the breakdown is for the child. Without exploring the appropriate interventions or skills that need to be enhanced, a child often experiences not just tolerable stress, but toxic stress. Chronic states of stress can lead to more dysregulation and more behavioral problems, making things worse. Many of these children experience what I don't think is too dramatic to call "educational trauma"—they undergo overwhelmingly terrifying or intensely stressful experiences because they have repeated experiences of getting in trouble for things they cannot help and cannot change, and this leaves them feeling helpless, afraid, and angry. No wonder their nervous systems are so reactive.

But when *regulation* is cultivated, created, and built, the problematic behaviors typically take care of themselves. Regulation emerges over time as development unfolds and as the prefrontal cortex develops and strengthens its ability to down-regulate, or lessen reactivity and threat signaling. As Jamie and Ashley will explain, regulation is also something that can be built through various types of therapies, medications, safe relational experiences, and more. When adults co-regulate, by being the calm, safe harbor in the storm, and by *helping* children calm and become regulated, they achieve feelings of safety and comfort. Repeated experiences of co-regulation become internalized both in terms of mental models, where children expect that someone will show up for them and help, but also in terms of neural wiring so that they can develop the capacity to regulate themselves.

It's sometimes easier to go with our assumptions and decide that a child *won't* behave or that she has some character flaw like being lazy, or that the student's parents are too indulgent and don't ask enough of him. But we want to do better than that in our interpretations of a situation. Many children are punished, criticized, or told scary things about who they are as learners and humans because a parent or a teacher assumes the child is *choosing* to not do well, when it often turns out that the child has a learning challenge or a trauma history, and in fact the "right" behaviors were something the child is not yet able to demonstrate.

Instead, we need to recognize that unwanted behavior is often communicating that something isn't working for this child, and she's likely experiencing intense stress. Instead of saying, "This kid is so rude," or, "Why is he making bad choices?" or "Why doesn't she try harder?" our question should be, "What's causing that threat response?" Then we can more compassionately *and effectively* respond and intervene to change what's happening in our classrooms.

This book and the ideas in it come at an important time, and I so admire its two authors. With intellect and clarity, Jamie and Ashley have taken crucial concepts from beyond their field of expertise and applied them in their own professional domains, offering a gift to educators everywhere, just when we need it. The focus on regulation and a felt sense of safety as the essential beginning for learning and accessing content, which may look and feel different for different students, is crucial if we're going to shift to meet the needs of students today. One of the most powerful paths to cultivating regulation and safety is simply the relationship between student and teacher. You, as an educator, hold tremendous power to change students' brains, minds, and behaviors, simply in how you build relationships with them. Connected relationships lead to connected, integrated brains.

Teachers—what you do matters. Through your relationships with students, and the kinds of repeated experiences you provide, you're not only influencing their abilities, skills, knowledge, behaviors, and minds, you're also changing how their brains fire and wire. You are brain architects and sculptors. With 40 percent of children not having secure attachment with their parents, you are a safety net for so many children, helping them feel safe, seen, soothed, and secure, showing up for them so that they can learn and become their best selves. We thank you for the gifts you give our children, mostly by who you are, and how you build relationships with them.

My hope is that this book is a gift to you—to fuel your own journey of curiosity and innovation; to give you a wider, richer lens that leads you to more compassion for yourself and your students; to help you understand more about the mechanisms behind what you already do that works, and why other things don't work; to give you practical strategies you can implement to help students be more successful and regulated; and to empower you to effectively do the work you feel passion and purpose to do so that you find deep meaning in being the teacher you aspire to be.

—Tina Payne Bryson, LCSW, PhD

Preface

Over the years we've interacted with countless educators who are seeking new ways they can support their students. We've observed how being an educator can often take a toll—physically, mentally, emotionally, and financially—in a way that inadvertently impacts students. We have witnessed the dedication, passion, and love that you have for your students. We have also seen your pain, frustration, and sadness when things do not go as planned. Through this book, we hope you feel our dedication and love for you. We are in this with you and are here for you, hoping to move through challenging times toward success together with each teacher and student.

The IPNB framework and other relational lenses that we discuss and expound on throughout this book have guided us professionally as therapists and personally as parents for years. We hope that you will find the strategies, as they relate to IPNB and other regulation-based frameworks, to be healing not only for your students but also for you. We hope to take a supportive, accepting, and reflective stance throughout this book where mistakes are valued, questions are expected, and both are used as tools toward growth for teachers and students.

Throughout the book, we have integrated some of the latest brain-based research. We've done our best to remain true to the concepts in the research without bogging you down with all the nitty gritty details. At the rate research continues to emerge regarding the brain, it is likely that in a handful of years we will know even more about how our brains grow, learn, and develop through relationships with others. We recognize that we can only respond to the knowledge that we have at any given time, and that as our knowledge grows, so does our ability to apply that information.

Whether you are an educator just starting out, someone who has been in education for a decade, or you have dedicated the majority of your life to education, we hope that the ideas in this book will be illuminating and formative, providing you with the opportunity to ask questions and reflect on what practices will work best for you and your academic setting. We don't claim to have all the "right answers" and are not pretending to know the specifics of your classroom dynamics. We aren't saying there is one "right way" to teach, or that you must do all these things to be "successful" as an educator. We are hoping that the information in this book will provide you with a starting point to ask questions. There is no "right way" or "one size fits all" to learning, regulation, or relationships. There are some foundational pieces that make it easier, however, and if we are able to stay curious, ask questions, and better understand what is underlying the behaviors in ourselves and our students, we can create better outcomes for both.

It seems that as soon as children learn how to talk, they begin asking questions. Why is the sky blue? Why do we have to wear seatbelts? Why do frogs jump? Why do we need to eat broccoli? The questions at times seem never ending, and some may be more difficult to answer than others. However, the emergence of asking questions in early childhood marks an important and exciting developmental milestone. Questions represent our door to discovery. There is not yet an expectation that a young child should know the answer to their questions. Somewhere along the line, as we enter high school, college, and the workforce as adults, there seems to be a shift—we are *supposed to* know it all. For some, asking questions may feel anxiety provoking or a way of admitting they don't know something they should already know. But we cannot stop asking questions. In this book, we hope to help re-define success from "knowing it all" to knowing how to ask the right questions.

As we've mentioned, research is always changing—especially when it comes to the brain. It is *impossible* to know everything. We hope, through this book, you can reconnect with your inner child and rediscover the magic necessity of curiosity and asking questions. We hope to foster an environment of acceptance, openness, and support for all educators—to create a community where we can come together to support each other, ask questions, and search for the "why" behind some of the struggles you may encounter within your schools and classrooms.

We need each other now, more than ever. The development of a connected community is more important than it was even a few months ago. As we write this book, the world is changing, education is changing, and the way we are able to connect with others is changing due to the COVID-19 pandemic and subsequent global health crisis. In the upcoming wake of the pandemic, even more challenges will be presented. Teachers, you have been put in the daunting position of creating Distance Learning Programs essentially overnight, and we have been in awe of your ability to rise to the challenge! Your resilience and perseverance in the face of uncertain circumstances is inspiring. While there are so many unknowns in the world right now, including the way in which we are able to educate children, the concepts and ideas throughout this book remain the same. The foundation of regulation and the teacher-student dyad as precursors to learning are now more important than ever. Teachers and students need to feel safe to engage in academics, yet we are all currently experiencing a threat to our safety. As a result, you may see more students experiencing outbursts, meltdowns, disengagement, distractibility, or withdrawal. The necessity of digging a little deeper to search for the "why" is becoming more essential every day as you consider how to best support yourself, your own regulation, and the regulation of your students (and parents!). Resilience is how we adapt in the face of adversity. Teachers, you will remain on the front line for many years of providing a safe, co-regulated environment for *all* of your students. We are here to help you through this process.

Acknowledgments

FROM JAMIE

I would like to acknowledge the support of my family, friends, and colleagues throughout this process. In particular, my husband Francisco not only has provided encouragement and affirmation but also has entertained our toddler so I could carve out time to write. I have been surrounded by positive, co-regulating relationships that have influenced me at every stage of my life. To my mom and dad, Lynn and Keith Olsen, who always show up. To my siblings, Geoff, Laura, and Jennifer Olsen, who embrace their nerdy sister. To the handful of teachers who inspired my love of learning: Mr. Robert Ludwigsen, Mr. Earl Kyle, Mr. Jim Anderson, to name a few. To my mentor, Freddie Berger, who took a chance on a new grad. To countless friends and colleagues who engage in conversations that spark curiosity and keep me grounded. To a faith community who reminds me that a relationship with Christ serves as the ultimate model of how to see others and myself.

I am particularly grateful for my co-author, Dr. Ashley Taylor, who helped to bring balance to the language and content of the book. I have learned a tremendous amount from Ashley over the years, and learned even more when writing this book. Thank you, Ashley, for your knowledge, expertise, compassion, and collaboration—you made this process enjoyable and motivating. Let's do it again soon!

FROM ASHLEY

It has been an honor to partner and collaborate with my co-author Dr. Jamie Chaves. Her passion, vision, and plan made this idea into a reality! Thank you, Jamie, for your patience, dedication, organization, and diligence in getting this done. I really enjoyed partnering with you on this journey!

I want to thank my family, my two sweet boys, Jackson and Henry, who have cheered me on and encouraged me every step of the way. To my husband, Hunt Dougherty, I could not have done this without your patience and support. You always believe in me, which helps me to believe in myself—thank you! To my parents, Claudia and Allen Taylor, and my sisters Amanda Taylor Nava and Samantha Taylor Suehiro, thank you for always being there for me.

I want to especially thank so many who have been my teachers, mentors, and educators through the years—those of you whose inspiration, calm, and knowledge have guided me in my professional journey and allowed me to continue my path toward growth and development, including Dr. Esther Chon, Dr. Barbara Stroud, Dr. Mona Delahooke, Dr. Shireen Sonefeldt, Dr. Joy Malik-Hasbrook, and Dr. Daniel Franklin.

JOINT ACKNOWLEDGMENTS

We would like to thank Hunt Dougherty for his creative contributions in the production of the images throughout the book. Thank you for your patience and artistic eye.

We both are incredibly grateful and would like to give a special thanks to Dr. Tina Payne Bryson for her knowledge into the IPNB framework, and for her vision of creating a multidisciplinary therapy practice informed by IPNB. Without The Center for Connection, we would have never met. Tina, you have been an inspiration to us for many years. Thank you so much for your guidance, wisdom, and generosity of spirit. Your dedication and passion for bringing people together is amazing, and we are truly so appreciative and full of gratitude for your support throughout this process!

We are grateful for the families and teachers we have worked with over the years who have helped shape us as clinicians. As a general note, all the names and identifying details in the vignettes and scenarios have been fabricated, and edited to protect the privacy of individuals and families.

PUBLISHER'S ACKNOWLEDGMENTS

Corwin gratefully acknowledges the contributions of the following reviewers:

Tamara Daugherty
Third Grade Teacher
Zellwood Elementary
Orlando, FL

Hope Edlin
Teacher
Bethel Elementary
Simpsonville, SC

Pérsida Himmele
Associate Professor
Millersville University
Millersville, PA

Marcia LeCompte
Former Teacher
Baton Rouge, LA

Kellee Oliver
Coordinator of Pupil Personnel Services
Hopewell Area School District
Aliquippa, PA

Stephanie L. Turner
4th Grade Teacher
Bradley Academy
Murfreesboro, TN

About the Authors

Jamie Chaves, OTD, OTR/L, SWC, is a pediatric occupational therapist with over 8 years of experience working with children who have sensory processing differences and learning differences. She received bachelor's degrees in health science and psychology from Bradley University, and a doctorate of occupational therapy from Washington University School of Medicine in St. Louis. Dr. Chaves is the division leader for the occupational therapy department at The Center for Connection in Pasadena, CA—a multidisciplinary clinic that provides an array of services rooted in the IPNB framework. She recognizes the importance of a play-based, relationship-based approach to therapy that is rooted in regulation. She does contract work with various private schools in Pasadena, CA, particularly delivering teacher in-services and parent education on a variety of topics including promoting positive handwriting, sensory integration strategies in the classroom, how diet and sleep influence learning and regulation, and the impact of screen time on development and learning. Dr. Chaves lives in Pasadena, CA, with her husband and two young children.

Ashley Taylor, PsyD is a licensed clinical pediatric psychologist with a practice in Pasadena, CA. She is endorsed in California as an infant-family and early childhood mental health specialist. Dr. Taylor received bachelor's degrees in psychology and Spanish from the University of Vermont in Burlington, VT, and attended the Wright Institute in Berkeley, CA, for her graduate training. She has worked in Vermont, Massachusetts, and California supporting children, families, and educators for over fifteen years. She specializes in providing comprehensive pediatric evaluations assessing for developmental delays, autism, trauma, ADHD, and learning disabilities. She also provides parent–child dyadic mental health therapy as well as educator and parent trainings and workshops. She has provided evaluations and mental health services for the pediatric population across multiple settings, including intensive day-treatment programs, medical settings, schools, community mental health, and private practice. She believes in the power of building healthy relationships to build healthy brains! Dr. Taylor is also the mom to two fun and active boys who are always ready for the next big adventure!

Please visit the companion website at
resources.corwin.com/ClassroomBehaviors
for downloadable resources.

"To raise new questions, new possibilities, to regard old problems from a new angle, requires creative imagination and marks real advance in science."

—Albert Einstein

CHAPTER 1

Searching for the "Why?"

"When we begin to know ourselves in an open and self-supportive way, we take the first steps to encourage our children to know themselves."
—Dr. Dan Siegel, M.D.

Most teachers and early childhood educators enter the field because they love children and are passionate about providing them with a learning experience that will benefit each child throughout his or her life. Many educators beautifully orchestrate the 25+ students in their classrooms while operating within the curriculum standards provided by each state. Teachers not only instruct children about how to write their name and execute multiplication tables but also are there for students in many different ways. They make a child smile who is having a bad day, put a Band-Aid on a child's knee after she's fallen down, give up their snack when a child forgets to pack one, and spend their nights tailoring lesson plans to motivate children to learn. They foster curiosity, empathy, friendships, and help students to learn who they are and who they one day hope to become. Parents entrust their children to a teacher's care for the majority of each day. Parents "expect" that teachers are "doing their job" to help prepare their children for the next stage of education and the next stage of life. Teachers have an enormous job of preparing the next generation for success; however, many may feel overwhelmed by their responsibilities and experience the frustration of being underpaid and not supported.

Nowadays, teachers are tasked with increasingly more responsibility for fostering development within the school environment. The burden often falls on them to establish foundational skills that children previously had when entering school: things such as postural stability (i.e., the ability to sustain an upright position in a chair), shoulder and hand strength, the ability to identify and express how they are feeling, as well as the ability to enter play with peers appropriately. Moreover, according to the Center for Disease Control, the rates of neurodevelopmental diagnoses, such as autism spectrum disorder, attention deficit hyperactivity disorder, and sensory processing disorder (SPD), continue to increase, resulting in a more diverse population in every classroom.[1] In fact, the National Center for Learning Disabilities (NCLD) estimates one in five children have a learning difference.[2] With the lack of training and educational opportunities around how best to teach to a wide variety of learning needs and develop a foundation of emotional and relational safety, teachers often feel overwhelmed and underequipped. They may occasionally feel at a loss about how to best support the children they so clearly want to help. Oftentimes the strategies they use to manage challenging behaviors may seem ineffective, short-lived, or perhaps even detrimental to the student's progress.

At times, children with unique learning needs engage in behaviors that look oppositional, defiant, lazy, or disengaged. In fact, a 2017 NCLD report revealed "that children with learning and attention issues are as smart as their peers and can achieve at high levels but too often are misunderstood as lazy or unintelligent."[2] They are assigned a behavior plan that may have good intentions but does not actually address the underlying cause of the negative behaviors. In order to optimize a learning environment that accommodates all children, it is necessary for teachers to explore "why" a child is displaying certain behaviors. As the "why" begins to be uncovered, better supports and systems can be put in place to address the underlying cause rather than put a Band-Aid on the behavioral symptoms. *It's not that teachers don't want to discover "why," because most teachers do want to understand the underlying cause when a child is having a difficult time. It's that many teachers don't feel equipped to ask the right questions, don't know there's a different way of addressing behaviors, don't have the resources with over 20 children in the class, or do not know how to work against a system that has been doing the same thing for decades.*

There is hope! With the advancements of brain research, we now know more than ever before that the nervous system can be changed over time. We also know more about the interconnectedness of the brain and interconnectedness of people than ever before. This is good news not only for children with learning differences and social-emotional difficulties but also for adults who are learning new ways of interacting with and responding to the needs of all children. Our brains and relationships can change, too. This is due to exciting research about the brain's neuroplasticity. **Neuroplasticity** is the brain's ability to change over time with certain repeated experiences. This concept underlies the statement "neurons that fire together wire together," which we use frequently throughout this book. This means that the more frequently you practice a certain skill set, the more likely those neuronal connections in the brain will be created and solidified, making it easier for us to do new things over time. We all have certain strengths as well as areas where we struggle. This is likely tied to certain areas in the brain that aren't fully developed, or integrated, which we will discuss more in Chapter 6.

Our students do too, and as we will explore throughout this book, children's disruptive behaviors are what we see on the surface. Underneath those behaviors are likely certain vulnerabilities, possible skill sets that are lagging, or certain areas of the brain that aren't fully integrated that we need to uncover and better understand. It all starts with slowing down, and asking, "Why?"

Neuroplasticity: the brain's ability to change over time with certain repeated experiences.

Reflective Activity

Asking "why" a student is displaying a certain behavior allows you as a teacher to optimize a learning environment that accommodates all children. As the "why" is uncovered, better supports and systems can be put in place to address the underlying cause. Rather than putting a Band-Aid on the behavioral symptoms, we can address the underlying vulnerability. We know that most teachers want to understand the underlying cause when a child is having a difficult time, but many teachers don't feel equipped to do so. The National Center for Learning Disabilities (NCLD) estimates one in five children have a learning difference, meaning in a classroom of 30 you are likely to have

(Continued)

(Continued)

at least five to six students who require more support. Take a moment to think about those students and start to uncover the "why."

Student with unique learning needs	Assumptions I make about him/her	Questions I can ask to gather more information

A BRIEF INTRODUCTION TO INTERPERSONAL NEUROBIOLOGY

Throughout this book, we will discuss some concepts related to brain science that will help us to better understand the "why" underneath children's (and our own) behaviors. One framework that we, the authors, have valued in our personal and professional lives is interpersonal neurobiology (IPNB). We will use this framework as a starting point, but will also integrate other ideas, research, and theories throughout this book. Some of the other frameworks we used as inspiration to the ideas and activities in this book include the Neurosequential Model of Therapeutics (NMT); Developmental,

Individual-Differences, & Relationship-Based Model (DIR); the Neu-rorelational Framework (NRF); and Ayers Sensory Integration (SI). All of the frameworks we draw on have the theme of supporting brain-based regulation, development, and understanding of behavior through the lens of co-regulating relationships. *This means that our brains grow and develop from and through relationships with other people. Through safe co-regulating relationships, we can support the brain development of our students, ultimately allowing for optimal learning environments for all. We aim to give strategies to educators that you can use within your classrooms that are informed by this research.*

IPNB is a framework developed by neuropsychiatrist and author Dr. Dan Siegel that serves as a starting point for asking "why" a child is behaving in a certain way and for intervening once the "why" is uncovered. In this book, we will discuss some of the principles of IPNB, and other relational frameworks, and help apply them to the classroom setting.

IPNB posits that human functioning, well-being, and regulation is a product of integration among and within three separate systems.[3] This is known as the "triangle of well-being."

1. *The brain/body* includes our brain, nervous system, and body functions. If certain aspects of these are not functioning properly then we may see an impact on empathy, insight, resilience, or physical health.
2. *Relationships* include how we navigate building connections with others as well as how our brain grows through relationships with people in our lives. If we lack the skills to build relationships or do not have safe, trusting relationships with those around us then we may see an impact on communication and social engagement.
3. *The mind* includes mental processes, thoughts, feelings, and experiences. It is the subjective experience of how we regulate, understand, and organize our physical experiences and our relationships with others. Dr. Seigel describes the mind as "the process that regulates the flow of energy and information." This flow of information within our bodies and between people actually has the potential to shape and change our minds. He goes on to explain how mindful awareness can help us all live more fulfilling lives, become better teachers, and become more engaged students.

Each of these three systems must be integrated in a way that promotes "linkage" and "differentiation." "Linkage" refers to the connectedness of areas in our brain, relationships with others, and integration of mental processes. "Differentiation" refers to the unique functions and aspects of our brain, self, and mental processes. In this way, everything has its special role and works together to create something whole. The end result, as Dr. Dan Siegel puts it, is an "integrated brain, empathic relationships, and coherent mind." If one system is not well integrated, it can result in the feeling of chaos (feeling "out of control" or unstable) or rigidity (being inflexible or controlling). When chaos or rigidity takes over, it becomes difficult to self-regulate, engage in complex thinking, or participate in social activities. Many times, this is what happens with children who are "acting up" or "misbehaving" in school— they are communicating that something is out of balance in their brain, relationships, and/or mind.

Another important aspect of IPNB, as well as other brain-based relational frameworks, explores the organization of the brain and how this relates to our ability to function and engage with the world around us. The brain develops over time and is structured to promote integration, or connectedness. There are many different types of integration, and we will focus on a few in this book. One of the ways integration occurs in the brain is horizontally (i.e., right hemisphere and left hemisphere) and vertically (i.e., top part of the brain and lower part of the brain). Let's first explore the two hemispheres of the brain—or the "horizontal brain." The horizontal brain is organized into a right hemisphere and a left hemisphere. Research shows us that each hemisphere is responsible for different functions despite the fact that both hemispheres are in close communication with each other. We need to rely on both hemispheres in order to function in a regulated and integrated way. More research is developed all the time on how interconnected the left and right hemispheres really are and how closely they work together. While this is the case, it is helpful to have a general understanding of the differences between each side of the brain:

- The right hemisphere is traditionally recognized as the creative, imaginative, and intuitive hemisphere.[4] It detects and makes sense of emotions. A child who has strong right hemisphere functions and is experiencing less integration with the left hemisphere at a particular moment might need help putting language to his feelings and

understanding his emotional states in a more logical and
linear way.

- The left hemisphere is traditionally recognized as the
logical, linear, verbal, and literal hemisphere. A child who
has a strong left hemisphere mode of processing but is
experiencing less integration with the right hemisphere at
a particular moment may appear rigid or have difficulty
discerning nonverbal cues. She is not being intentionally
defiant; she just needs help developing flexibility,
processing emotions, and doing things "out of order"
without becoming overwhelmed.

You may see yourself as being more logical and detail-oriented or as
being more connected with your emotion and intuition. Do you find
yourself processing information in more of a language-based way, or
through more visual, nonverbal means? While we all have certain
modes of processing that we rely on, our brains have *hopefully* developed the ability to function in a well-rounded, regulated, and integrated way throughout most of our days. However, when we enter a
situation where we feel stressed or dysregulated, our brain becomes
less integrated, and we tend to fall back on a less integrated way of
approaching the world—which may be from either a more emotional
or a more logical way. In this book, we simplify this concept by refer-
ring to certain situations and activities as being more "right-brained"
or "left-brained." We also hope to provide you with information
and activities to help build an awareness into when we may fall into
moments of chaos and rigidity and how to move through this.

When we have appropriate linkage between the two hemispheres,
the brain is considered well integrated. This allows us to step back in
highly emotional situations and implement logic, feel what we are
feeling, verbally express our feelings, and figure out what steps to take
to solve the problem. The integration of the horizontal brain emerges
primarily from development and experiences. This means, for example, that in toddlers and younger children, we can expect them to
approach situations with a more emotional, "right brained" mode of
processing until the flow of information from the logical, linguistic,
"left brain" allows for integration.[4]

In addition to the "horizontal" organization of the brain, there is a
bottom-to-top organization of the brain—this is called the "vertical"
organization of the brain. The vertical brain is a product of our evolution, whereby the lower levels of the brain are more primitive, quicker

to process or respond to information, and instinctual, while the higher levels of the brain are developed over time, are slower to process information, and allow us to have conscious control of our bodies and minds. Here are a few examples of vertical brain organization:

- At the lowest level of the brain is the *brainstem*, which is responsible for our most basic involuntary functions: heart rate, breathing, blood pressure, motor reflexes. Think about a newborn baby who is beginning at the most basic level.
- The next level is comprised of sensorimotor processing, which takes place in the *midbrain*. Think about an infant's motor development and sensory exploration through the first year of life.
- Then there is the level of the *limbic system*, which is responsible for emotional regulation. Think about a toddler who is wrestling with her emotions and trying to gain more self-regulation.
- Finally, there is the level of the *cerebral cortex*—all of our higher-level thinking, attention, and engagement. Think about a school-age child who is cognitively engaged in learning.

As you look at the vertical organization, you can see that the lower levels of the brain are also responsible for the fight, flight, freeze response (discussed in Chapter 2), memories of sensory experiences (discussed in Chapter 4), strong emotions, and impulsivity (i.e., acting before thinking). The higher levels of the brain are responsible for decision-making, learning new things, problem-solving, self-understanding, insight, empathy, morality, impulse control, and developing regulation.

Children (and adults) must first have their needs met in the lower levels of the brain in order to engage in more complex processes at higher levels of the brain. For example, a child who is hungry cannot complete his multiplication table because his brain is focused on meeting that basic need for food. Once that child eats a snack, he will be much better regulated and engaged in academic demands. A child who is experiencing anxiety cannot use higher-level thinking to "push through" the situation because her brain is communicating fear and threat. After that child is comforted and calm, she can then return to the situation and problem-solve a way forward. In both situations, it is a matter of "can't," not "won't."[4]

As we mentioned above, science has shown that the brain is "plastic" or has "neuroplasticity," which means that the brain can be changed

Supportive Diagram

Our brain is organized vertically, from bottom to top, whereby the complexity increases as you move up. The needs of the lower levels of the brain have to be established before skills in the higher levels of the brain can develop. Co-regulating, safe, consistent, and secure relationships are an important part of this process, every step of the way.

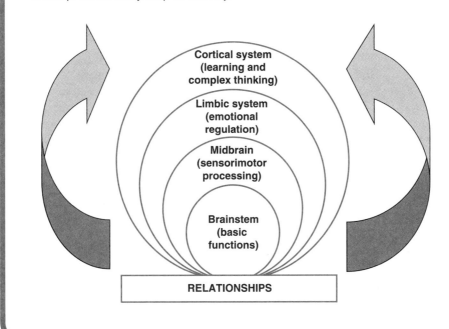

through rewiring the neurological system.[5,6] This indicates that the brain actually learns to respond to different situations, tasks, and activities through experience and repeated exposure. Eventually, through a lot of practice, the brain translates this into an automatic response. For example, when we learn to tie our shoes, we must concentrate on the task and practice it the same way over and over before the brain learns the specific motor pattern. After a while, we don't even have to think about how to tie our shoes, and we can do it with our eyes closed. However, if someone taught us a different way to tie our shoes, we would be teaching the brain a new motor pattern that requires more conscious thought and rewiring of the neurons being fired.

This concept is true for our emotional responses as well. If a child repeatedly has negative emotional experiences when completing math computations, then the brain will start to wire in a way that signals distress when any type of math problem is presented. If the child can remain regulated while facing the challenges of math computations, through positive co-regulating relationships with those around him, by using mindfulness strategies, and by skill-building, his brain will start to wire in a way that no longer triggers a stress response.

As you can see, the integration between the horizontal (right and left) and vertical (top and bottom) parts of the brain is critical. This integration happens slowly as a child develops and is a result of the experiences and relationships she has throughout her life. The need for an integrated brain to promote regulation is true for every child regardless of his or her learning needs. When children are regulated, they can be curious, engaged, focused, and responsive. When a child is not regulated, we as parents, educators, and clinicians need to look a little deeper, try to figure out where disintegration is occurring, and better understand "why" they are having difficulty regulating. We will continue to unfold these concepts throughout the book.

Oftentimes, children need someone to co-regulate with—someone to come alongside them and say, "I understand you're having a hard time. Let's figure it out together." However, the response often heard by the child is, "You're giving me a hard time. You need to do what I tell you." **Co-regulation** requires a positive relationship with that child—someone she can feel safe with and trust. Co-regulation and safe relationships are where the heart of teaching lies. This is where regulation is developed. This is where learning begins. By identifying brain-based responses to common triggers in the classroom setting, we can use what we know about the brain and relationships to identify ways to help each student and teacher fulfill his or her full potential. These concepts are explored more in depth in Chapter 2.

APPLYING A BRAIN-BASED, RELATIONAL LENS TO THE EDUCATIONAL SETTING

Co-regulation: attuned and responsive interactions between child and adult that allow them to reach a state of regulation together.

The research is clear in that our brains grow, develop, and change through relationships and experiences with others.[4] Children who have sensory-enriched, relationally safe, consistent, and predictable environments have larger, better developed, and more integrated brains.[7-9] It is therefore important to focus on the quality of relationships with each student. As a teacher, you have the power to form, change, and mold each developing brain in your class, and help your students form a positive association with learning. By engaging in healthy, stable, foundationally safe relationships as well as sensory-attuned learning environments, teachers have the power to positively impact brain development, brain integration, and overall body and brain-based regulation, ultimately enhancing each student's ability to learn.

Strategy I: Engage in Positive, Regulating Experiences

The same concept of brain development, integration, and regulation is true for all of us: parents, professionals, and teachers. Just as children who have relationally safe and sensory-attuned environments are better able to regulate and learn, teachers who are regulated have a larger capacity to connect with students, engage in the joys of students' learning, and feel energized about what they do. In this way, the IPNB framework and other relational models serve as a form of self-care, support, and understanding for educators. In order for a teacher to effectively co-regulate with a student, the teacher must first be regulated. Oftentimes, dysregulated adults cause a child to be more dysregulated as well, resulting in a cycle of co-dysregulation. This is why it is important that teachers feel supported and equipped to take on the daily challenges they face in the classroom. Teachers must be engaged in positive relationships with those around them every day, as well as engaged in regulating experiences throughout the day.

When we engage in positive, regulating experiences, this helps to facilitate an "integrated brain, empathic relationships, and coherent mind." These regulating experiences can be small moments throughout the day, such as sitting with a cup of coffee in the morning, walking around the block on your lunch break, eating lunch with a favorite colleague, or writing in a journal a night. When chaos or rigidity takes over, it can negatively impact the way you interact with those around you—especially your students. If you start to experience more chaos or rigidity in your life, particularly related to teaching, it is likely that the integration of your brain/body, relationships, or mind is obstructed.

In his book, *The Mindful Brain,* Dr. Siegel states,

> The human connections that help shape our neural connections are solely missing in modern life. We are not only losing opportunities to attune to each other, but the hectic lives many of us live leave little time for attuning to ourselves.[10]

It is therefore important that we not only focus our minds on ways to engage, attune, and connect with our students but spend time sending the flow of energy into connecting, engaging, and attuning with ourselves. By allowing ourselves this space, we will open the door to the endless potential of human capacity for compassion, empathy, and love, feel more successful in our lives but also support the next generation in becoming empathetic, compassionate, and loving adults.

Reflective Activity

Now it's your turn to complete an IPNB triangle for yourself. Think about your relationships, brain/body, and mind. Write a + next to the things that help facilitate the integration of each system or a – next to the things that hinder the integration of each system.

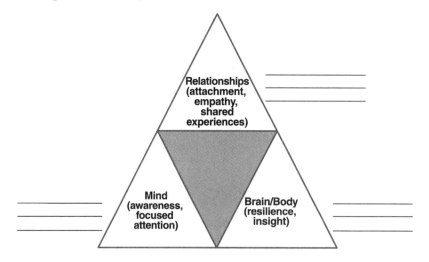

Consider: What areas of your triangle are more integrated than others? What areas are less integrated than others?

_____

_____

_____

Strategy 2: Reflect Often

Reflection helps cement learning.[11] One of the exciting things about life and our brains is that there is no end to self-discovery. Because of this, we will provide opportunities throughout the book for you to integrate the left and right side of your brain by understanding this information in a logical way and also having the opportunity to reflect and "feel" the information on a more experiential level. The "reflective activities" in each chapter will help you, as teachers, to consider various aspects about yourself and your teaching approach in order to better connect with your students' experiences and enhance your ability to utilize the information in this book.

In his books, Dr. Dan Siegel talks about the foundational importance of COAL: curiosity, openness, acceptance, and love.[3,10] We hope to foster this tone throughout our book, as well as provide opportunities for us to use this as a starting point to allow a safe place to reflect together. Here are some questions that you can use to reflect about yourself as you get started. You can keep these questions in mind as you continue to read.

- What can I do to regulate myself throughout the day?
- What are signs of dysregulation that I notice in myself?
- How can I create patterns of empathy, understanding, and trust with even the most challenging students?
- Who can I talk to or be with in order to process the events of my day or week?
- What areas of teaching are restorative and which areas are draining? Why?
- Which of my personal relationships are restorative and/or draining, and how do they impact my teaching?

Next, consider these questions regarding your students. Again, keep these questions in mind as you continue to read this book.

- Why might this student be demonstrating this behavior?
- Are there patterns of dysregulation that I notice in this student?
- How can I come alongside and join with, rather than penalize the student?
- What can I do to help this child co-regulate in this moment?
- Is there something I am doing that is contributing to a cycle of co-dysregulation?

- Am I making false assumptions about this student's behavior?
- What are the strengths of this student, and how can I capture those strengths?
- With which students do I need to build stronger relationships?

Not only is it important to use the brain to help our students develop integration, but it is also important to remember how to use the power of the mind in moments of stress and dysregulation. As we get to know ourselves better, and reflect more often, this will help us to have more integration in our brains and our lives. We will then be better able to maintain a regulated stance when confronted with overwhelming situations. *Once this happens, we will be better able to use a right hemisphere to right hemisphere connection[11] between teachers and students to portray a regulated, safe, meaningful message of connection and comfort to the other person.*[6,11] This means connecting emotionally, using mostly nonverbal communication. We will discuss how to do this in moments throughout the book, especially when we talk about attending to our nonverbals. This type of "right to right" connection between people, if done correctly, can help to develop a powerful, protective relationship or "teacher-student dyad," between a teacher and the students in her class.

Strategy 3: Identify Vulnerabilities and Reframe Triggers

We often hear teachers say they want to help particular students who are struggling, but they don't know how or where to start. We hope this book will serve as a resource for you, as teachers, to empower, equip, and engage students. As a result, we will see students thriving who once were failing; students engaging who once were withdrawing; students supported who once were penalized; and teachers who feel successful, empowered, and ready to take on new challenges.

Trigger: an event or behavior that occurs causing teachers and/ or students to enter a state of dysregulation.

Vulnerability: an underlying area of functioning that is not yet fully developed or integrated.

As teachers, you likely spend so much time thinking and worrying about your students. Wondering what triggered certain behaviors, and how to help them navigate certain situations better next time. You likely don't have too much time to think about yourself, what **triggers** you, and how to better support your **vulnerabilities**. We hope to be able to provide you with the opportunity to care for yourself and reflect with the activities in this book.

It is therefore important to spend a few minutes thinking about your triggers and vulnerabilities as well. You may notice that there are certain students, parents, or particular stressful situations that trigger you to become more dysregulated. Identifying such triggers can allow you to better explore "why" you may be triggered and what vulnerabilities underlie your triggers. Vulnerabilities may include a sensory sensitivity, a learning difference or disability, a traumatic memory, or a skill that has not yet been fully mastered. We will explore individual differences as well as additional potential underlying vulnerabilities in Chapter 6. In this way, your triggers can be reframed as a learning experience and your vulnerabilities as an opportunity for growth. When you feel yourself becoming triggered, it is important to be more conscious about how you can regulate yourself so that you can then co-regulate with a student to prevent both of you from entering a heightened state of dysregulation together. Keep these triggers and vulnerabilities in mind as we move through the principles and strategies in this book.

We all fluctuate between different states of arousal and regulation throughout the day. In the fast-paced classroom environment with over 20 students, it can be difficult to identify what the trigger was, let alone what vulnerability may be underlying the trigger that is causing the particular student to become upset. This can also happen to us as adults, since it is sometimes hard to know why we are triggered or overwhelmed. By building insight into your own states, warning signs, and vulnerabilities, you can better maintain your own state of regulation and ultimately model this for your students. Likewise, it is important to remember that a student is not doing certain things *to* you or the behaviors aren't directed *at* you. At times, a student's challenging behavior may feel manipulative. It might feel as though they are doing something intentionally to push your buttons or get on your nerves. Most of the time, however, challenging behaviors from students are a cry for help, and an attempt on their part to connect with you. However, they likely do not know how to connect with you or ask for help in an adaptive way. When you find yourself feeling as though a particular student is doing something on purpose to intentionally make you mad, remember, it is not your fault—try not to take it personally!

While you've likely spent time thinking about your students' triggers, we invite you look even deeper. What might underlie the triggers? How can we identify what vulnerabilities may be hiding underneath the behavior, and even underneath the trigger to the behavior? Students who frequently experience triggering events at school may

Reflective Activity

You can use the chart below to help identify student behaviors that are triggering for you, warning signs in your body, changes in your nonverbal communication, or ways that you can tell that you are becoming frustrated, overwhelmed, as well as the underlying vulnerability:

Triggering student behaviors or environmental stressors:	Identify warning signs in your body:	Underlying vulnerability	What can I do in this moment to calm myself?
Students talking, and/or noisy environments are very overwhelming for me.	My muscles get tight, I clench my jaw, my heart beats quickly, I start thinking thoughts that I can't take this anymore!	Maybe I have an auditory sensitivity that makes noisy environments unbearable to me.	Take a deep breath, ask for help from my teaching assistant, get a glass of water, model for my students how to calm down when upset.

need extra support through co-regulation and brain integration. Asking "why" a student might be triggered is the starting point to better understand the vulnerability underneath his behavior. There are many reasons and potential vulnerabilities why a student may be triggered. From individual differences, sensory preferences, learning styles, temperaments, learning disabilities and SPDs, there are many reasons why students may enter a state of dysregulation. Let's take a moment now to think about a student who may be particularly challenging and hypothesize why this might be.

Reflective Activity

Think about students who are particularly challenging or who need extra support. Complete the chart below for those students. You can revisit these students as you progress through the book.

Why might the student be struggling? What vulnerabilities might they have?	Are there patterns/ triggers of dysregulation?	What can I do to co-regulate?	How can I help support the student?

We will continue to explore the various ways teachers and educators can integrate the principles of IPNB and other relational theories into their classrooms for the sake of their students as well as for themselves. The demands of the school environment make it even more important for students to stay regulated in order to optimize learning—from the academic workload to the sensory stimulation to the social environment. Therefore, the relationship between the teacher and students, along with the teacher's understanding of the students' behaviors, is an integral piece of the student remaining regulated. This is called the *"teacher-student dyad"* and will be expanded on in Chapter 3. While this strategy may take more effort to begin than some other teaching strategies, it can yield more engaged learners, more rewarding relationships, and more successful experiences for both teachers and students in the long run. First, we need to further explore regulation and understand why it sets an important foundation for learning.

CHAPTER 2

Regulation as the Foundation for Learning

*"When awareness is brought to an emotion,
power is brought to your life."*
—Tara Meyer Robson

Jane was an active, curious, and full-of-life first grader at a public school in a large city. She was eager to engage and play with other students but had difficulty sitting still, listening to the teacher's directions, and following along with classroom expectations. At times, she got up in the middle of the teacher's lesson to dance the "floss" or point out the window and exclaim, "Look! There's a peacock!" Some students laughed and engaged with Jane, while others became frustrated that she was interrupting the teacher, Ms. Sperry. This was often disruptive to the whole class and bothersome to her teacher. At other times when she was completing written work, she became frustrated and fell down on the floor or threatened to hit others. Some of the school staff commented that Jane was just trying to get attention, while others felt that she was being manipulative and attempting to get out of completing her schoolwork.

Ms. Sperry initially responded to Jane by focusing purely on her behavior, telling her she was being disruptive or inappropriate, and commenting that she should sit down and listen like the other students. Ms. Sperry had a large class with over 20 students and she was often triggered, becoming frustrated, and overwhelmed by Jane's behavior, often not knowing how to respond. Every day Ms. Sperry moved Jane's "behavior clothespin" down the behavior chart, which resulted in Jane's behavior pin being in the "parent contact zone" on most days. However, this didn't seem to resolve the problem—the next day Jane was back at it again. Jane began to feel as if she *was bad,* and her behavior became increasingly worse. Jane began to hate school and make comments that no one liked her. This resulted in a difficult cycle with Ms. Sperry as well as Jane feeling unsuccessful and disconnected. It was, quite frankly, exhausting for Ms. Sperry.

When we simply focus on the surface behaviors, we miss an amazing opportunity to look underneath the surface to figure out what might be causing those behaviors. When we take time and use the tools outlined in this book to search for the "why," we can better know how to support students' success moving forward. When Ms. Sperry looked a little bit deeper into Jane's story, she found out that Jane had been adopted at the age of 5 and spent her early years in foster care. Jane struggled overall with knowing how to connect and build relationships, which often resulted in her engaging in silly or inappropriate behaviors as a way to get others to like her. Jane wanted to learn and complete the given schoolwork, but she was unable to do so in an environment where she didn't feel safe or regulated.

When we look at behaviors as a form of communication, we can then take a few moments to figure out what the behaviors are trying to tell us.[1] Over time, Ms. Sperry connected with Jane in a positive way, helped her to feel safe, and removed the behavior chart clothespins, which was causing Jane to feel a sense of shame. She reframed Jane's behaviors as an attempt to connect, and she provided opportunities for Jane to build a positive relationship with her during recess and breaks. While this took additional time, it was far more rewarding and far less exhausting for Ms. Sperry. This teacher-student connection increased Jane's sense of emotional and relational safety, decreased her fear, and improved her behavior, which ultimately increased Jane's ability to learn.

This chapter will look closely at the importance of building positive relationships in the classroom setting, and how the *relationship* in and of itself can serve as a way to increase a student's regulation and ultimately improve learning.[2] A teacher may feel overwhelmed with a large class of students who all bring their own histories, strengths, challenges, and needs. It may seem almost impossible to know the individual needs of every student in the class. Through the framework of interpersonal neurobiology (IPNB),[3] and other brain-based relational models we can understand that there are some basic regulation and relationship-building skills that every teacher can use in class that work to build protective relationships with all students. These strategies also serve to increase students' and teachers' sense of safety, overall regulation, and feelings of contentment and success in the classroom setting.

WHAT IS "REGULATION"?

Regulation is a term thrown around a lot in today's vernacular. Since we will be using the term quite a bit in this book, it will be helpful for us to identify what we mean by regulation and how to identify different states of regulation in ourselves and in our students. Regulation can be defined in many ways—from nervous system arousal and regulation, to emotional regulation, to body-based regulation, to co-regulation between and within a dyad such as the teacher-student or parent-child dyad. Regulation is also defined as "behavioral organization," defined as achieving an optimal arousal level in order to effectively handle the demands placed on us. Regulation is actually a very broad term, but we will use it to describe an individual's ability to manage his or her internal emotional and physical state in order to stay calm enough to communicate, solve problems, learn, connect with others, sit and focus, follow directions, complete school assignments, and make decisions. This fundamental regulation is necessary if any teaching or learning is going to occur.[2,3]

Regulation of the body is when we feel at ease in our bodies.[4] More specifically, it is when the sympathetic and parasympathetic branches of the nervous system stay relatively in balance. Some activation of the sympathetic and parasympathetic nervous system is good and protective, but when either branch is activated too much it can result in maladaptive responses.

> **Regulation:** an individual's ability to manage his or her internal emotional and physical state in order to stay calm enough to communicate, solve problems, learn, connect with others, sit and focus, follow directions, complete school assignments, and make decisions.

- The *sympathetic nervous system* helps activate us and arouse us into a state of action. If the sympathetic nervous system is too engaged, then we can get easily overaroused, anxious, hyperactive, or angry. If something happens to trigger a fight or flight response, the sympathetic nervous system is activated. This is when a child experiences something as threatening, and she may yell, scream, fight her way out of it, or run away.[4] For example, Jane is feeling frustrated and "on edge" about completing her writing assignments. Her teacher tells the class it is time to pull out their workbooks and complete the sentences. Jane looks at the workbook and becomes overwhelmed, not knowing where to start. Because her sympathetic nervous system is overly activated, she yells, "I hate this!" throws her workbook on the ground, and threatens to hit the student sitting next to her.

- The *parasympathetic nervous system* helps slow us down and prepares us for rest. If the parasympathetic nervous system is too engaged, then we can get easily underaroused, depressed, sluggish, or passive. The freeze response can be triggered by something that is perceived as threatening, but it is activated by the parasympathetic nervous system. This is when a child wants to shut down, hide under a desk, or not talk.[4] If, in the example above, Jane's parasympathetic nervous system was overly activated, then the same writing assignment may trigger her to clam up, hide in the hallway, or cry in the bathroom. Jane could also say she's too tired or bored to complete the assignment.

When the autonomic nervous system is out of balance, we tend to become either more rigid or chaotic, as we talked about in Chapter 1. There are many things that can trigger one of these responses, such as challenging new academic tasks, certain uneasy social situations, or particular tones of voice. Overwhelming sensory information can also trigger such a nervous system response. Sometimes students with learning and attention challenges are triggered by reading or writing. Students with an autism spectrum disorder, attention deficit disorder, or slower processing speeds may be triggered by certain social interactions. We will explore each of these nervous system triggers in subsequent chapters.

It will be important for us to learn how to recognize different "states of regulation" and what they look like in our students and ourselves.[5] Various research models talk about regulation in different ways: the idea of "green zone" regulation used in *The Whole Brain Child*, the "just right zone" of the How Does Your Engine Run? program, Dr. Dan Siegel's "window of tolerance," or the "Goldilocks zone." Whichever you decide to use, the idea is that our brains need to be in the "just right" zone of regulation in order to focus, attend, learn, and complete work. It is therefore very important for teachers to know how to recognize when their students are in this "just right" zone, when they are not, and what to do to get their students back into the "just right" zone before trying to teach new or challenging concepts.

When the sympathetic nervous systems take over too much, then we can go into a "red zone" or fight or flight state of arousal. This is when we become angry, fearful, outwardly anxious, or overly excited. On the way to the "red zone" we pass through the "yellow zone," which

Supportive Diagram

Understanding the "states of regulation" can help you determine which state you or a student might be in at any particular time and help you better understand his behavior. It is important for teachers to know how to recognize when their students are in a "just right" zone, when they are not, and what to do to get their students back into the "just right" zone before teaching a new or challenging concept. It is also important for teachers to recognize when they are moving through different states of regulation themselves so that they can help themselves get back into the "just right" zone for teaching.

Red Zone	• Sympathetic nervous system takes over and causes fight or flight response. • Emotions: Angry, fearful, outwardly anxious, overly excited, stressed.
Yellow Zone	• Heighted sympathetic nervous system response that has not yet reached fight or flight. • Emotions: Frustrated, somewhat stressed, somewhat nervous, silly.
"Just Right" Green Zone	• Balance between the sympathetic and parasympathetic nervous system that allows for social interaction and higher cognitive engagement. • Emotions: Happy, calm, engaged, focused, social.
Blue Zone	• Parasympathetic nervous system takes over and causes a freeze response. • Emotions: Sad, disengaged, bored, tired. Sometimes feeling mad or angry can also result in a blue zone response.

is a heightened state of arousal that is usually more manageable than the "red zone." This might be when we become frustrated, somewhat stressed, a little nervous, or silly. On the flip side, when the parasympathetic nervous system takes over too much, then we can go into a "blue zone" or "freeze" state of arousal. This is when we become sad, disengaged, bored, or tired. It is notable that some people will actually go into a "blue zone" when they are angry or overwhelmed. For this reason, it is important not only to pay attention to disruptive behaviors but also to students who are disengaged, shut down, or oddly not disruptive at all.

Emotional regulation comes with greater brain integration; this allows us to keep our feelings from going to extremes—or to help us remain regulated and feel "just right." When we feel ourselves getting dysregulated, we can activate our sympathetic or parasympathetic nervous systems, respectively, to stay regulated. If our sympathetic ("fight or flight") nervous system is activated, we need to engage in an activity that feels safe, quiet, calm, repetitive, and regulating. It often helps to decrease the sensory input in the room (e.g., turn off the lights and remove loud noises) to create a sense of safety. If the parasympathetic ("freeze" or "rest") nervous system is activated, we may need to engage in something that gets our body moving such as jumping jacks, stretching, going for a walk, or getting a glass of water. As this capacity to engage in regulating activities strengthens, emotional responses more quickly reflect a return to a balanced automatic nervous system, even in the face of stress. This takes practice and requires establishing positive patterns.

Throughout the day, children *and* adults move through different states of regulation. We may be calm, relaxed, happy, and ready to focus at one moment, or stressed, angry, and frustrated at another. We often have strategies to move back into a state of calm when we get dysregulated. For example, a student may be focused on completing a math worksheet until another student comes over and knocks the pencil box off her desk. While this is frustrating and may result in an exchange of words, she can calm down by taking a deep breath, picking up her pencils, and re-engaging with the math worksheet. If teachers are not in a calm, regulated state, students will pick up on that and it will be very difficult to teach them because they will sense that something is "off." If students are not in a regulated state, they will not be able to focus, sit still, attend, or learn. Likewise, if we as adults are not in a calm, regulated state, it will be much harder for us to focus on our jobs and complete our work to the best of our ability.

Interactive Scenario

Considering the following narrative of Lilliana's school day, plot on the chart how her regulation fluctuates throughout the day. Take note of how these fluctuations may impact her ability to learn.

Lilliana sluggishly enters class and typically lies on the floor during morning meeting. She often does not raise her hand to participate in math class and seems bored with the material. When Lilliana comes in from recess, she seems engaged and eager to learn in social studies. By the end of social studies, she is clearly ready for a break. You frequently get reports that Lilliana does not eat her lunch and has a difficult time remaining seated in the cafeteria. When she comes back from recess she, again, seems engaged in learning and is eager to start language arts class. Her music teacher reports that Lilliana is disruptive and has difficulty following directions. By the time she returns from recess to get ready for home Lilliana is again sluggish and needs more reminders than other students to write her assignments down and pack her bag.

Lilliana's Regulation During the Day

Red Zone

Yellow Zone

Green Zone

Blue Zone

Morning meeting · Class #1 · Recess · Class #2 · Lunch · Recess · Class #3 · Class #4 · Recess · Class #5 · Pick-Up

Lilliana's regulation is as follows:

Blue → Blue → Green → Green/Blue → Yellow → Green → Green → Red → Blue

As a note, it seems that movement (i.e., recess) is regulating to Lilliana, and loud noises (i.e., the cafeteria and music class) can cause her to become dysregulated.

In the introductory vignette, when Jane became dysregulated, she engaged in silly, disruptive, or "attention-seeking" behaviors. She did this because learning, connecting, and engaging with others was threatening to her due to early childhood traumatic experiences. She felt unsafe in relationships—one of the important pieces for an integrated brain that we will explore in Chapter 3. She fluctuated between sympathetic nervous system and parasympathetic nervous system responses, at times threatening to hit others and at other times hiding under her desk. She was rarely in the "just right" zone where

Reflective Activity

Think back over the events of your day today. Can you recall moments when you were in the "just right" zone? What was happening in that moment? What interactions were occurring between your students and yourself? What was going on in the environment? Use the tools below to think back over your day and identify when you were "just right," when you felt yourself move into the "fight or flight" zone, and when you might have felt yourself fall into the "freeze zone." Can you recall a situation in which you were "co-regulated" with a student you were working with?

Fight or Flight Zone Moments	Just Right Zone Moments
_____	_____
_____	_____
_____	_____

Co-Regulation Moments	Freeze Moments
_____	_____
_____	_____
_____	_____

she was able to connect, learn, attend, and engage with others. Over time, as she realized she was no longer going to get in trouble for her dysregulation, she slowly started to build a safe, protective relationship with her teacher, Ms. Sperry. Little by little this sense of safety in relationships changed the neural pathways in her brain and helped her associate relationships with safety. With safety, consistency, and regulation being modeled to her on a daily basis, over time she was able to begin to use the same skills.

REFRAMING THE DEVELOPMENTAL EXPECTATIONS OF REGULATION

Before we dive into strategies to promote regulation in the classroom, it is important to recognize and reframe the developmental stages of regulation. It is easy for us as adults to stretch our expectations of children, especially as society is pushing for children to mature more quickly. If we take a step back to ask ourselves if our expectations match what is developmentally appropriate, then we can better come alongside the student. It is also important to acknowledge that even if a child "should" have certain self-regulation skills, he or she may still require some degree of guidance from a trusting adult figure in order to calm down or solve problems. At certain times children may "regress" in their ability to regulate, especially if a child has gone through a traumatic or stressful life event.[6] As the demands in our environment increase, our ability to remain regulated often decreases—such as when introducing new learning concepts.[7] This is because the brain is funneling resources to different parts of the brain in order to facilitate motor, language, or cognitive development.

Emotional regulation tends to develop in a stepwise manner that includes identification, integration, building coping skills, and practice.[8,9]

1. *Identification* includes building an awareness of what the feeling is and how to identify it. Pre-K students will need more assistance in identifying their emotions than a third grader. However, that does not mean that a third grader will not need assistance at certain times or under certain circumstances. After you have helped a student identify a particular felt emotion, you can move into the integration phase.

2. *Integration* as we discussed in the introduction helps connect the language and logical processing parts of the brain to the emotional and intuitive parts of the brain. You start to hear 2- and 3-year-olds exclaim, "I'm mad" or "I'm sad," which is a good indication that they are beginning to integrate their internal felt sense of the emotion with a logical, language-based understanding of what it is that they are experiencing. This becomes more complex as children get older. For example, 4- and 5-year-olds have the capacity to understand that when we get mad, our muscles become tight or our hearts start to race. And 6- to 7-year-olds can better understand the connection between thoughts, feelings, and behaviors. For example, "When I get mad, my muscles get tight, and I think that I hate the world," but "When I'm happy, I feel like dancing and singing, and I think that I can do anything."

3. *Building coping skills* involves the teaching of strategies to facilitate improved "emotional regulation." It is important to realize that you cannot actually "teach" self-regulation. It's a process that we all move through as we develop and mature. However, you can equip children with tools and provide modeling so when they are ready, they have resources available. Know that teaching regulating coping skills will be more effective *after* you have achieved the identification and integration phases, even though our inclination is to jump right to "fixing" the problem as soon as possible.

4. *Practice, practice, practice!* Be aware that these coping skills take a lot of practice and modeling in order to reinforce and make into an automatic pathway (similar to the example of tying shoes in the introduction). It is also important to know that students need to practice these skills when they are in a regulated "just right" state. Just as learning any new skills, if we are not in a regulated state, we will not be able to learn or practice such skills. If we wait to tell a student to take a deep breath when they are already in the red zone, they will likely yell, "No, that never works! I'm never breathing again."

While emotional regulation develops over time and we progress through different stages of development as we grow, it is important to remember that our brains do not always develop in a stepwise or linear fashion.[10] *There will be occasions when we see a child achieve a certain developmental milestone, complete a task well, or demonstrate*

Supportive Diagram

Emotional regulation typically occurs in a stepwise manner that is reliant on modeling from adults and consistent co-regulation. It is not possible to "teach" self-regulation, but it is possible to equip students with the foundational skills to flex their emotional regulation muscles through the following process. The adult's ability to monitor and maintain their own state of regulation and model a regulated state is very important in the development of regulation skills in children. Remember that setbacks for all of us will occur and are an indication that the brain is changing!

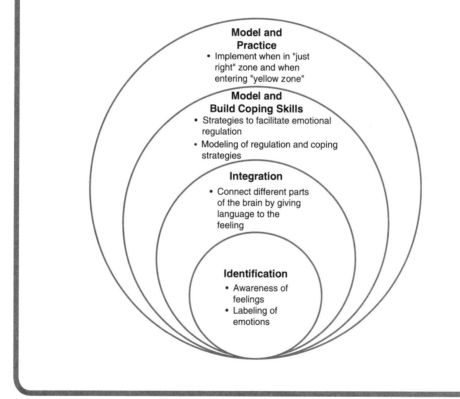

Model and Practice
- Implement when in "just right" zone and when entering "yellow zone"

Model and Build Coping Skills
- Strategies to facilitate emotional regulation
- Modeling of regulation and coping strategies

Integration
- Connect different parts of the brain by giving language to the feeling

Identification
- Awareness of feelings
- Labeling of emotions

self-regulation one day, and the next day they may have difficulty with the same activity or situation. This does not represent a failure. It only suggests that the brain is continuing to work toward integrating the new developmental skill.

Think of Jane's story above, for example. One day after working with her teacher on modeling appropriate expression of emotional identification and regulation, she was able to express herself when she became angry, saying, "This writing is too hard. I'm getting frustrated and I need help." Her teacher was proud and excited that Jane was able to communicate her emotional state and her needs at the same time. By Jane's communicating in this way, her teacher was able to provide her with the right support to get her back into a regulated state and to determine how to teach her the writing skill that the class was working on. The next day, however, when the class was asked to fill in words to complete certain sentences, Jane became overwhelmed, threw all of her pencils on the floor, and raised her fist in an attempt to hit her desk mate. Ms. Sperry felt discouraged and as though all of the work they had been doing together was not working. She wondered, "Why was Jane able to identify her emotions, express herself, and ask for help yesterday, and today she reverted back to her 'red zone' state of dysregulation?"

These setbacks can often feel disheartening and discouraging. It may seem as though all the work you are doing with the student is not working or may not even be worth it. *Know that this is a typical part of brain development. It takes time to grow new neural connections and even longer for those connections to solidify. As long as you are seeing progress, even if it is only tiny glimpses on certain days, then you know the connections are beginning to form.* While there are certain developmental expectations for students to achieve when it comes to regulation, it is up to us, as the adults in their lives, to create a safe, predictable, structured, and consistent environment. Your understanding of each student's individual needs will help them to reach an optimal state of regulation. This takes time, patience, and understanding.

DEVELOPMENTAL MILESTONES IN REGULATION

Our ability to regulate and calm ourselves *ideally* grows in capacity as we develop over time. As mentioned in the introduction, regulation is dependent on our relationships, brain and body functions, and mind processes. Some children and adults develop better regulation strategies than others, and some develop regulation strategies more quickly than others. With proper support, guidance, safe environments, and opportunities, students can thrive in their ability to regulate. When thinking about regulation, it is also important to think about how different cultures view the concept of regulation. Western cultures tend to emphasize the notion of "self-regulation," whereas other cultures often discuss the importance of being in community. With this in mind, it can be helpful to view regulation within the context of being in relationship with others. This is often called co-regulation, rather than self-regulation, which we defined in Chapter 1 and will expand on in Chapter 3. We will also explore how to integrate various cultural conceptions of regulation and utilize more "community-based" co-regulation constructs to help students build their regulation skills over time within the classroom community.

In *infancy*,[10-12] we often rely on sensorimotor strategies to soothe, such as swaddling, rocking, swinging, sucking on a pacifier, or listening to soothing music. Infants rely heavily on their caregivers to provide them with consistent, calming strategies to help with regulation. Infants who do not receive this attuned, responsive co-regulation tend to be more anxious and reactive. As infants grow, they begin to turn to familiar voices when they hear them, recognizing the sound of safe, consistent caregivers. They then begin to reach out to their caregivers for regulation: crying, raising their arms, communicating a desire to be held and soothed. Regulation happens through the combination of predictable and attuned caregiving that sends messages to the child that they are safe and can be soothed.

Early childhood[11,12] is a period of rapid brain growth and development that also serves as a foundation for emerging emotional regulation skills. When children develop language skills in preschool, they can better communicate their emotions, which helps them to adjust their arousal level and feel more regulated. Rather than cry or scream when they want something, like an infant, they can request something or express their opinion. However, even like adults, preschoolers have moments when they find themselves in a red or blue zone state and need help to get back to their "just right" zone again. Self-talk, or inner speech, also starts to blossom at this age, helping children form a running monologue of their emotions, build confidence, and ultimately, develop self-regulation.

Preschoolers[11,12] still need a large degree of co-regulation in order to help them work through their emotions, understand expectations, control their impulses, and develop empathy. They need someone to help put labels to their emotions and integrate those emotions with logic. Just as infants need consistent responses from caregivers, preschoolers need this as well. Providing children this age with an appropriate level of external structure helps them navigate their emotions without the added pressure of managing their routines. Preschoolers are adept at learning from the adults around them. They watch us as we regulate our own emotions and take note of those strategies. When preschools have positive role models who demonstrate healthy self-regulation, such as frustration tolerance, flexibility of thought, and controlled emotional expression, preschoolers too can learn how to better self-regulate.

By *kindergarten*,[11,12] many children have the capacity to identify different feeling states—sad, happy, or angry—and communicate them with feeling identification words. Many kindergarteners still need assistance in communicating these feelings "in the moment," particularly in challenging or frustrating situations. At this age, children gain more understanding of cultural expectations and social norms, have more ability to control their impulses, and typically realize that the world does not revolve around them. This allows them to follow along with classroom expectations that may conflict with their desires at times, although they may need reminders of those expectations.

As demands begin to increase in *first and second grade*,[11,12] children are better able to take on these challenges as they develop a sense of personal pride and a higher degree of social- and self-motivation. A higher level of integration is building within the brain, allowing students to better understand their internal emotional states, what may trigger a dysregulated state, and how to cope with these big emotions. Children of this age are beginning to expand their social world and experience a desire to have more independence. It is often around this time that a higher level of social-emotional connectedness and regulation becomes more relevant as children start to navigate more complex social situations. First and second graders need guidance in knowing what is best in certain social situations (particularly those that are unstructured like lunch and recess), how to flex their emotional tolerance muscles, and how to adapt to various social circumstances. In this way, social situations may become more triggering or overwhelming, which can impact self-esteem and a feeling of social connectedness. For example, Jane wanted to connect with peers but did not know how, which resulted in her disruptive and at times aggressive behaviors. One of the main skills we can teach during this time, which will be discussed further, is how to support students in developing an appropriate (or collaborative) way to communicate their emotional states and needs, so that they can adjust to varying social situations and learn how to navigate them without becoming dysregulated. This is a challenging social-emotional developmental task, one that many adults continue to struggle with—communicating in a way that is not too passive but also not too aggressive.

By the *third, fourth, and fifth grades,*[12,13] children can hold the duality of emotions that sometimes conflict. "I was happy I got first place in the spelling bee but sad that my best friend did not win." This stage marks the use of situational cues to determine someone else's feelings, even if the situation does not match the facial expression. When this first starts to occur, children can get confused about this mismatch and require guidance in interpreting what someone actually meant. Given the level of social-emotional growth that occurs at this stage, it is important for children to have adults with whom they can process conflicts of emotions, complex social-emotional experiences, and reconcile unjust social circumstances. At this age, children care more about the way they are perceived by peers, which results in a quick learning curve on regulating their emotions. Rather than cry in front of the class when reprimanded for not having their homework, they must fight back tears to save face with their group of friends. By fifth grade, most children have strategies to help with self-regulation, such as problem-solving, seeking advice from friends, internal reflection, and use of distractions (e.g., playing basketball, using the iPad or tablet, drawing). It is at this age that many children feel a sense of emotional self-efficacy—the ability to effectively manage their own emotions.

During these later childhood years, children are faced with more complex social situations and interactions. Effective ability to regulate their emotions and navigate social communication becomes even more important. Teaching third-, fourth-, and fifth-grade students about different types of communication and providing them with information about assertive and collaborative communication tools can protect students against bullying, prevent bullying all together, and support students in developing more rewarding, and long-lasting friendships.

As mentioned previously, with the right adult support, modeling, and teaching, children tend to progress through a certain set of steps to develop regulation skills. Adults often need support with emotional regulation as well; we can use the same steps with ourselves to practice and model appropriate emotional regulation and reach the next level of "emotional intelligence." Again, while these steps tend to progress in a linear fashion, development itself is not linear. We can see this in ourselves as adults: one day we express ourselves better than we do the next day. We need to offer the same grace and leniency with students

Supportive Diagram

Our ability to regulate and calm ourselves ideally grows in capacity as we develop over time; some students develop better regulation strategies than others. At different developmental levels, regulation will look different, but no matter what, regulation is in part dependent on our relationships.

Infancy
- Rely on sensorimotor strategies for regulation
- Rely on caregiver to provide consistent, attuned co-regulation

Early Childhood
- Emerging language skills allow for identification of wants, needs, and emotions
- Use self-talk to assist with regulation during new and challenging tasks
- Continue to rely on caregivers to provide consistent, attuned co-regulation

Preschool
- Rely on external structure and consistency to navigate their emotions
- Look to caregivers as models for regulation
- Continue to rely on caregivers to provide consistent, attuned co-regulation

Kindergarten
- More consistent identification and expression of emotions
- Improved awareness of cultural norms, impulse control, and awareness of others' needs allows for better regulation
- Continue to rely on caregivers to provide co-regulation, albeit less frequently

1st and 2nd Grade
- Self-motivation increases the capacity to take on more demands with less external structure
- Improved integration of the brain allows for better awareness of emotions and ability to implement coping strategies
- Rely on caregivers to navigate challenging and unstructured social settings that may cause dysregulation

3rd, 4th, and 5th Grade
- Use situational cues to infer what someone else may be feeling
- Increased ability to implement self-regulation strategies and feel emotional self-efficacy
- Rely on caregivers to process conflicts of emotions, complex social-emotional experiences, and reconcile unjust social circumstances

who are juggling a wide variety of internal and external demands. The best thing we can do for ourselves and for students is to be patient, knowing that with time, repetition, and practice, we will begin to see change.

There are many reasons why you may see children continuing to struggle with regulation throughout childhood. In Jane's case, for example, her early childhood attachment trauma and neglect impacted her brain's ability to develop a sense of safety, connection, predictability, and regulation. Other children may exhibit difficulty with regulation because they are not getting enough sleep or not eating enough before school starts in the morning. Others may have processing speed deficits, academic disabilities, sensory processing disorders, attention deficit hyperactivity disorder, or other attention deficits that make learning as well as academic environments overwhelming for them. This can impact their brains' ability to access appropriate regulation skills. As teachers, it is important to understand what is underlying the behavior, and how regulation impacts a student's ability to behave appropriately at school. If you can identify what might be impacting a student's regulation and help integrate different areas of his brain, you can then best support him moving forward. This starts with asking "why" a student might be acting a certain way.

Additionally, it is important to note that many students, particularly those who are identified as gifted, demonstrate **asynchronous development**.[14] While they may be advanced in certain academic or cognitive areas, their social and emotional development may be delayed. Asynchronous development can be confusing for teachers, parents, and students themselves. Often times when we see students excel in certain areas, we expect that they should excel in all areas.

> **Asynchronous development:** the idea that not all areas of development are progressing at the same rate, causing a gap in abilities.

Reflective Activity

Think about the students in your class in regard to their level of development of emotional regulation. Can you identify which stage of development they may be in (particularly those who may be struggling)? Take notes on how you can help support each student in their development of emotional regulation. What extra supports might he/she need?

(Continued)

(Continued)

Name of Student	Stage of Development	How Does This Impact Learning?	Extra Support Needed

PROMOTING REGULATION IN THE CLASSROOM

In this chapter, we will discuss three strategies that teachers can use in the moment when facing a red or blue zone state of regulation. Not only will these strategies help decrease the child's dysregulation in the moment, but they will also continue to build the protective relationship, support regulation, and begin to build and maintain the teacher-student dyad that we discuss in Chapter 3. By engaging in these strategies, regulation will be enhanced, which will ultimately improve learning for all students.

Before implementing these strategies, it is important that you consider the basic needs of your students, such as when they last ate, how much sleep they got, and if they need to use the bathroom. If a student does not have any of these needs met then it will be very difficult for them to remain emotionally regulated. Offer a snack, a drink of water, or a bathroom break; these simple acts may help your student get back to a state of regulation to better engage in learning. While you cannot necessarily influence how much sleep they received, it may help you better understand why a particular activity is challenging or why they may be demonstrating more challenging behaviors that day. Such basic needs target the lower part of the brain. As we've mentioned, if the lower part of the brain is not regulated, it will be very difficult for the student to access the higher-level thinking in the upper part of the brain that they need in order to learn.

As noted, modeling from adults is especially important for children to build emotional regulation skills. There are many different ways to engage in emotional regulation. Each person, and each student, is going to find different strategies that are regulating. Before you can help a student become regulated, you first need to start with yourself: what is something that you find calming, healing, regulating, or relaxing? For some, it could be going on a hike and getting back to nature. For others, it could be getting a massage, engaging in mindfulness activities, practicing deep breathing, going to the gym, eating healthy foods, taking a bath, reading a book, or listening to music. Again, think about strategies that target the lower part of the brain, that will be regulating to you. Such activities tend to include movement and sensory-based activities.

Popular culture in the United States often idealizes independence, being able to take care of yourself, and doing it on your own. Many other cultures prioritize the community, taking care of others, and working together to complete common goals. We hope to expand on the notion of self-care and self-regulation to *community care* and *community regulation* and discuss how that can be applied to a classroom setting. Within the classroom setting, this may look more like fostering an environment where students are able to take care of each other,

Reflective Activity

Modeling regulation is a critical part of helping your students emotionally regulate themselves. Your regulation is also critical for co-regulating with students who are easily dysregulated. Thus, finding ways you can engage in regulating activities, both in and out of the school environment, is important. Think about activities that are regulating to the lower part of your brain.

What is regulating to you?

- _____
- _____
- _____

What do you find healing, calming, or rejuvenating?

- _____
- _____
- _____

What activities do you already engage in that help with regulation?

- _____
- _____
- _____

What activities can you intentionally engage in to help with regulation?

- _____
- _____
- _____

support each other in developing a sense of safety and regulation, and be a "safe base" for each other as a classroom as a whole. In Chapter 3, we will be expanding more on these concepts and strategies and discuss how the principles of regulation can be applied on a more "classroom community" level.

As we will discuss in Chapters 4 and 5, it is also necessary to pay attention to sensory input and understand how overall sensory integration impacts regulation. There are many sensory experiences that can be regulating, including certain smells, tastes, and sounds. However, many sensory inputs can also be dysregulating. These regulating and dysregulating sensory inputs can vary greatly depending on the individual. Once you have an awareness of what activities and sensory inputs are regulating and dysregulating to you, you can then help the students you work with begin the process of regulation.

Strategy 1: Breathe, Body, Begin

There are many wonderful mindfulness resources available.[15,16] We have integrated a few in this chapter that we feel would be helpful for teachers. A basic set of steps helps children develop regulation and emotional expression skills. These steps include helping them stop, breathe, use their words to express how they are feeling, and figure out how to solve the problem. We call this the "Breathe, Body, Begin" cycle. You can do this at certain points in the day as a whole class, even when students may not seem dysregulated. Morning meeting and after lunch are two great times to have students engage in emotional regulation skill-building activities. Using this strategy one-on-one with a student "in the moment" will also be effective. Once you know your class better, you can get a better sense of when they might need this strategy throughout the day. The more practice children get with this, the more integrated their brain will be and the better they can access this coping strategy when needed.

Keep in mind that you, as a teacher, can also benefit from implementing this strategy yourself throughout the day. There may be times of the day when you feel yourself getting more dysregulated than others. Or there may be situations where you need to stop, engage in this strategy to get yourself more regulated, and then respond to the student. *Remember that your regulation is key to the regulation of your students.*

1.   Breathe: Begin by teaching your students the power of their breath. Children as young as 18 months to 3 years old can begin to learn how to take deep breaths. Teach your students to "breathe in through your nose as if you are smelling a rose" and "breathe out through your mouth as if you are blowing out a candle." You can practice breathing while blowing bubbles and experiment with long, slow breaths and short, fast breaths while watching the different types of bubbles that emerge. Make this a playful and fun way to explore different ways to breathe. As students are breathing in and out, have them place one hand over their heart and one hand on their stomach to feel the changes in their body. Explain that breathing is a superpower that

Supportive Diagram

The "Breathe, Body, Begin" cycle is a strategy you can use to help promote regulation in yourself and your students. Morning meeting and after lunch are two great times to have students engage in emotional regulation skill-building activities.

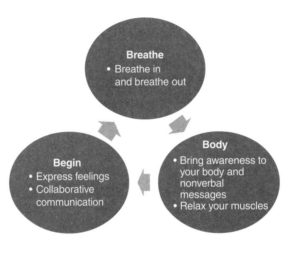

helps calm our heart rate and helps our brain be better able to solve problems.

2. Body: Next, help your students build an awareness of how our feelings impact our bodies. For example, when we are sad, mad, scared, or even overly excited, our muscles might get really tight, our heart might start beating quickly, or we might squeeze our fists. You can help students create a "body map" to identify where in their body they feel certain emotions, as well as what is triggering for them. Sometimes we might get stomachaches, headaches, or our breathing might speed up. You can also use "mindful moments"[17] to increase students' awareness of their bodies. For example, teach the students to relax their muscles, including the heart muscle, by engaging in an activity called progressive muscle relaxation. You can prompt them to squeeze all of their muscles from "your toes to your nose" as tight as they can, and then release, prompting them to relax their muscles. This helps students better learn what their bodies are communicating to them.

Supportive Diagram

Using the chart below, identify which activities you can use as "mindful moments" throughout the day to help increase students' awareness of their bodies. In the space provided, think about other "mindful moment" activities that may be specific to the needs of your students.

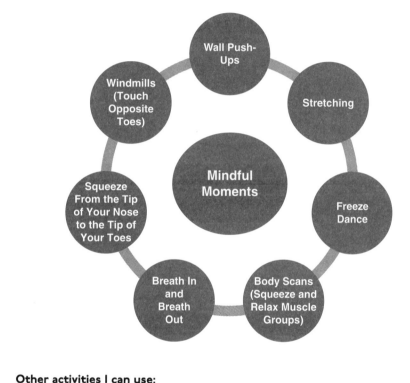

Other activities I can use:

_____   _____

_____   _____

_____   _____

3. <u>Begin</u>: Once the students have taken some deep breaths and relaxed their bodies, they will be more prepared physiologically to express how they are feeling and what they need. This tool is very important, not only in the

classroom, but also at recess or during more unstructured social activities that may be difficult to navigate. As mentioned above, as children get older, social situations become more complex, and striking the balance between passive and aggressive communication becomes more complex. As teachers, or as the adults in their lives, you can help your students by giving them the language they need to solve the problem. This is called "collaborative communication" and "collaborative problem-solving."

For example, when Jane was dancing or out of her seat, the teacher could lead the whole class in a "mindful moment" by dimming the lights, having them breathe together as a class, encouraging them to engage in a muscle relaxation activity, and asking them to stretch. Ms. Sperry could then have the students sit back down and comment on how she understands that sometimes sitting for long periods of time can be difficult, so taking time to breathe and move our bodies helps our brains get ready to learn. Introducing a "mindful moment" activity to the classroom every day can help foster emotional development and build positive self-regulation skills.

Then, later in the day at recess, Isabella became upset at Jane because Jane was standing too close, giving Isabella hugs and pulling on her shirt in an attempt to initiate play. Because knowing how to initiate social contact with peers was hard for Jane, she tended to engage in behaviors that were frustrating to other students. Not knowing how to handle the situation or what to say, Isabella kept running away from Jane. Jane and Isabella became upset with each other, and Jane ended up hitting Isabella. This can be viewed as a behavioral problem resulting in Jane receiving a consequence such as losing recess time, or it can be interpreted as an opportunity to provide both Jane and Isabella with the necessary skills to develop new neural connections in their brains by using the skills discussed in this chapter. After taking some deep breaths and relaxing their bodies, Ms. Sperry can use the "begin" step with Jane and Isabella to build skills around how to communicate with each other by stating how they *feel*, and what the *problem is*.[8] With the help of a teacher, Jane might say, "*I feel* sad because Isabella won't play with me. *The problem is* that I want to play with Isabella, but she keeps running away from me." The teacher or recess staff may then help Isabella say, "I *feel* frustrated because Jane is tugging on me and hugging me. The *problem is* that I want to swing, and I don't want to be hugged."

Once they are both in a more regulated state, they can access the prefrontal cortex part of their brain and be better able to engage in collaborative communication. The teacher can then reframe the situation and help them with collaborative problem-solving by presenting them with options, such as asking Jane to work on keeping her hands to herself while they swing together or take a break by finding another friend to play with.

Strategy 2: Check Your Nonverbals

Nonverbals are any form of communication not given through words. Children who have been in stressful or traumatic events or environments are often hypersensitive to nonverbal communication. When we are regulated, for example, our facial muscles relax, allowing us to smile. Our vocal cords relax, allowing us to have a calm voice. Our bodies relax, allowing us to have an open posture. We are fully invested in the relationship, not distracted by internal or external stressors. This type of nonverbal communication and body language presents as safe, calm, regulated, nontriggering, and approachable. However, when we are dysregulated, our facial muscles tighten, which communicates anger or frustration. Our vocal cords and jaws tighten, creating a stern voice. Our bodies tighten, creating a closed posture. We become distracted relationally by our internal cues of stress. This posture and nonverbal stance may often be interpreted as threatening and uninviting to others.

Children who endure stressful and traumatic events interpret nonverbal communication in different ways that may not always be accurate.[18] For example, Jane experienced attachment trauma at an early age, and her nervous system was always on edge, waiting for the next bad thing to happen. This often caused her to misinterpret facial expressions and social cues to be more threatening than they were intended. This ultimately caused her to react in a way that often seemed out of proportion to the trigger. This is because her brain was trying to keep her safe, based on her view of the world. Students who have not necessarily experienced significant stress or trauma, but who have slower processing speeds or learning and/or attention challenges, may also have difficulty understanding and interpreting nonverbal cues. This can impact their ability to build relationships, understand social situations, and feel safe and regulated at school when social cues are passed around a mile a minute.

When we encounter students who are exhibiting symptoms of dysregulation or fight, flight, or freeze nervous system responses, it is important to pay attention to the messages we send them with our nonverbal communication. We want to make sure that our nonverbal messages are demonstrating safety and are nonthreatening. If students interpret our nonverbal communication as threatening in any way, this will trigger their nervous system to fall further into a state of dysregulation.

Nonverbal messages can communicate to the lower part of the brain whether or not someone is safe. The lower part of the brain, and in particular the amygdala, houses the threat response. Teachers, you can use your nonverbal communication to decrease students' threat responses and increase an overall sense of safety and regulation in the classroom setting. Some nonverbal communication strategies you can both do "in the moment" and practice regularly to prevent dysregulation include:

- Approach the student in a nonthreatening way. Having a relaxed, open posture with your arms at your side communicates that you are willing to engage in a positive conversation. Crossing your arms, tensing your muscles, and closing your posture communicates that you are already upset and may throw the student into a more dysregulated state.
- Position yourself on the same level as the student ("get small"). To do this, you can kneel down or sit down at his or her level. This creates a feeling of trust, mutual attention, and equal footing in the conversation.
- Become aware of your eye contact. Eye contact is not always best; sometimes too much eye contact can be overwhelming or triggering for some students when they are dysregulated. When students are in a high-pressure situation, in an anxiety-producing situation, or in a situation that is challenging to them, eye contact should not be demanded. Once you help the student balance her nervous system in order to become more regulated, then she will be in a position to engage socially and feel equipped to make eye contact more consistently.
- Monitor your tone of voice. Slow down, speak clearly, use a soft voice, and be consistent with your cadence. All of these help to foster a sense of warmth, understanding, and regulation.
- Be mindful of your facial expressions. As our tone of voice changes so do our facial expressions. If you use a calm,

quiet voice, your face relaxes and communicates empathy to the student. If you use a loud, frustrated voice, your face tightens, your eyebrows furrow, and your lips become pursed—all of which communicate fear and nervousness to the student.

Supportive Diagram

Nonverbal communication and body language can help teachers present themselves as safe, calm, regulated, nontriggering, and approachable to their students. When students are exhibiting symptoms of dysregulation, or "fight, flight, or freeze" nervous system arousal, it is important to pay attention to the messages we send them with our nonverbal communication.

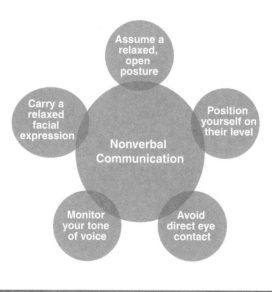

These are all different forms of communication that sometimes happen when you do not realize it, often in unconscious microsecond moments.[19] A student will pick up on these nonverbals and interpret them in different ways, which may also trigger the student to become more dysregulated. If you can monitor your nonverbal communication and adapt it to demonstrate a safe and unthreatening posture, you will create a safe environment for your students and will also help students who are in a dysregulated state to regulate faster. However, this can only happen if you are regulated and activating your social engagement system as well.[19]

Strategy 3: Attuned Listening

Active, **attuned listening** is a strategy that teachers can use "in the moment" to try to diffuse or de-escalate any situation and help a student get back to the "just right" zone for learning. Active listening is a communication skill that can build the protective relationship and continue to foster a positive teacher-student interaction. It includes not just hearing what the child is saying but also how it is being said, attending to body language, voice inflection, overall attitude, facial expressions, and the meaning of what children are saying so that they can be truly heard, understood, and validated. Professor of law and South African activist Thuli Madonsela said it best: "I need to listen well so that I hear what is not said." Active listening is a powerful tool that should be used and taught in all classroom settings and includes the nonverbal strategies we talked about above. Not only is it helpful for teachers to use with students, but it is also important for students to learn how to use these strategies with each other. In fact, teachers can even model attuned listening with each other. A classroom environment that fosters attuned listening will be an environment that encourages respect, connectedness, and acceptance.

Attuned listening includes re-framing back to the student what they have said, validating their internal emotional state, and helping them develop a resilient or adaptive outcome to the problem.[19] For example, when Jane became upset about completing the writing assignment and threatened to hit the student next to her, instead of moving Jane's behavior chart pin to the bottom, her teacher could say, "Jane, your body is telling me that you are feeling overwhelmed right now. I see that you are so upset that you feel like hitting someone. That must feel really scary or uncomfortable." While the teacher is kneeling down, checking her own nonverbals, and presenting herself in a nonthreatening way, she can continue to say, "I wonder if doing this writing assignment right now feels really hard? Maybe we can work together to figure out how to solve the problem?"

The success of attuned communication relies on our capacity to accurately sense someone else's state and communicate verbally, and most importantly nonverbally, our felt understanding of their emotional experience.[19] The goal with this type of "listening" is to help the child feel heard, understood, and validated, when she may not even understand herself what is going on inside of her brain and body. It is our job as adults and professionals in our students' lives to see each of these moments as an opportunity to grow their brain and provide them with an experience that is different from what they are used to,

Attuned listening: a communication skill that includes hearing not just what the person is saying, but also how it is being said; attending to body language, voice inflection, overall attitude, facial expressions, and the meaning of what the person is saying.

so that they can start making new neuronal connections. Over time, with consistent experiences such as these, the new neuronal connections in their brain will solidify, their sense of safety will increase, their behavior will improve, their associations with school and learning will change, and their brain's ability to learn will come online.

There are many instances when a student is frustrated, angry, or upset, and we do not yet know why. In a classroom setting, everything moves at a fast pace. Students are vying for the teacher's attention, and each student has his or her own individual social, emotional, behavioral, and learning needs. We imagine that as a teacher this can feel overwhelming at times. We also imagine that there are times when something happens, or a student responds a certain way, and you do not know what to do in that moment. Oftentimes not knowing what to do or how to handle a situation can be a trigger for us as adults and send us into a dysregulated

Reflective Activity

Active, attuned listening involves attending to the other person's body language, voice inflection, overall attitude, and facial expressions, in order to determine the actual meaning of what the person is saying. It is an important part of building a protective relationship and establishing co-regulation.

Think about a time when you were upset about something and talked with a friend, confidant, partner, spouse, or family member about the situation.		
What do you remember was helpful about how he/she responded to you?	What do you remember was *not* helpful about how he/she responded to you?	What ways did they use attuned listening in order to respond to what you were communicating?

state. ***It is okay to not know***—*we all find ourselves in that position.* Our brains are constantly working toward integration, and there is no shame in deficits in our knowledge. It is important to continue to ask "why," continuously exploring reasons for the student's dysregulation. It is possible to do this in a way that fosters a positive teacher-student relationship, rather than just wanting to know the answer.

One tool that one of the authors, Ashley, has found especially helpful, both at home with her kids as well as professionally is to describe. ***When in doubt, describe!*** When you do not know what to do, simply describe what you are seeing, thinking, feeling, or what you think others are seeing, thinking, and feeling. This is another way in which you are using attuned listening. For example, Jane's teacher might say, "Wow, Jane, I see that you are hiding under the table right now. I wonder if hiding under the table helps you feel safe? It does look cozy and safe down there. I feel curious to know what happened that made you feel unsafe."

Not only does describing help the other person better understand what is happening in the moment, but it also helps the student feel seen and heard. Not to mention, it buys you some time to figure out how to solve the problem by allowing your brain to get back into a regulated state before acting. Describing provides you some time to figure out what to do next. Describing techniques also help you connect with your students through integration of the brain. You connect language, logic, and more linear thinking as you describe the "felt sense" of the situation. When we think about the classroom community in the vignette, Ms. Sperry could go on to say,

> I think the other students are also curious as to why Jane is hiding under the table, and I wonder what we can all do to help her to feel safe and ready to come up and join us? Let's give her some more time to feel safe, and my guess is that she will come out when she is ready. If she doesn't, then I'll come back to check on her soon.

Here is a list of attuned listening phrases that use descriptive language you can begin to use with your students, and that your students can learn to use with each other. These phrases can help students better integrate the different areas of the brain in order to achieve regulation, as well as decrease the threat response in their lower brain so that they can access the higher-level problem-solving functions in their upper brain. It is important to use these techniques both during moments of regulation to *highlight positive interactions* in the classroom, as well as during moments of frustration or distress.

- It looks like you're frustrated and that probably feels uncomfortable. Let's figure out the first step together.
- I wonder if this assignment feels confusing; we can work together to figure out a different way.
- I can see your body is moving around a lot; I wonder if it would help to get up and stretch? Let's take a movement break.
- You got really sad when you needed to clean up. It's hard to do things we don't want to do. Is there something we can do differently when it's time to clean up again?
- I see that you're hiding under the table right now. I know you were just working on your math assignment. I'm curious to know what happened.
- Some students are talking in loud voices right now, so I'm having a hard time concentrating. Sometimes when things are loud, I have a hard time focusing.
- I see Jane and Tom are working hard to figure out the problem even though it's difficult! It makes me happy when I see teamwork.
- Everyone really cleaned up quickly; that was wonderful. Now we will have more time to focus on our art project.

Supportive Diagram

Sometimes it's helpful to have some "go-to" phrases in your back pocket to use with students who are dysregulated. This can help to provide them with a degree of co-regulation but also avoid triggering them from becoming more upset.

Try	Avoid
"It looks like this is hard. Let's figure it out together."	"You're giving me a hard time. You need to do what I tell you."
"I see this writing assignment is really overwhelming; let's take a quick break."	"You need to finish this before recess or you will have to stay in until it is done."
"It looks like James is bothering you because he is sitting so close to you. Do you want to tell him that you need some space right now?"	"James, stop moving around so much; you need to sit still and leave your friends alone."
"Go use the bathroom quickly and come back to finish your work. You will be able to concentrate better."	"You need to finish your work before you can use the bathroom."

Interactive Scenario

Read the short descriptions of behaviors displayed by students. Consider how you might use descriptive language in order to help the student better integrate the vertical and horizontal parts of the brain. Reflect on how this may be different than techniques you have used in the past.

Behavior
- Sanjay is sitting at his desk with his head down, seemingly not paying attention.

Maladaptive Response
- "Sanjay, now is not the time for a nap. Please sit up and pay attention."

Attuned Listening Response

Behavior
- Julia is dancing on the rug instead of lining up for recess.

Maladaptive Response
- "Class, it looks like Julia is the only one not ready for recess."

Attuned Listening Response

Behavior
- Jonathan throws his pencil and paper on the floor during Writer's Workshop.

Maladaptive Response
- "Jonathan, you need to pick that up and keep working. If you don't finish, you'll need to stay in at recess."

Attuned Listening Response

- For Jonathan, you might say: "Jonathan, oh, I see that you threw your pencil and paper on the floor. I wonder if you might be feeling frustrated. Sometimes writing can feel really hard. Let's take a break and see how we can solve this problem together."

- For Julia, you might say: "Class I can see that most of you lined up beautifully and are ready to go outside! It looks like a few of our friends are having a hard time calming their bodies enough to line up."

- For Sanjay, you might say: "Sanjay, your head is on the table, and you look tired. I'm curious as to why you have your head down. I wonder if there is something we can do to help you feel more alert?"

Now that you understand the importance of regulation as the foundation for learning and you better understand the early developmental stages of emotional regulation, you can be more aware of your own internal states of regulation and model the regulation process for students of all ages. In the next chapter, we will dive deeper into the importance of co-regulation and how the idea of the teacher-student dyad leads to increased regulation and ultimately improved learning for all students. We will also focus on cultural concepts of regulation and how to apply the idea of the classroom community to support connection, safety, regulation, and well-being for all students in the class.

CHAPTER 3

The Teacher-Student Dyad and Classroom Community

"One looks back with appreciation to the brilliant teachers, but with grati-
tude to those who touched our human feelings. The curriculum is so much
necessary raw material, but warmth is the vital element for the growing
plant and for the soul of the child."

—Carl Jung

Ben recently turned five and was about to start kindergarten. He was excited because he enjoyed preschool and was looking forward to getting back to school after a long summer break. However, when he realized he was going to a new school, with new teachers, all new kids, and a much larger campus to navigate, he became overwhelmed and very scared. He attended the orientation day with his mom and dad and had difficulty separating from them. He stuck close to his parents, often clinging to their legs or attempting to hide behind them. He did not respond when his teacher, Mr. Joe, excitedly approached him to welcome him to the classroom. Ben looked away and attempted to hide further, hoping to become invisible or disappear. His parents prompted him to look at Mr. Joe, make eye contact, and say hello. Ben did not; he only retreated further. His parents began to prompt him more urgently, attempting to pull him out from behind them again, telling him to introduce himself and act in a socially appropriate manner. However, this made Ben more uncomfortable, and he ran for the door. His parents shrugged, uncomfortably looking at Mr. Joe, nonverbally communicating that the level of anxiety, and nervous system arousal, among Ben *and* his parents was heightened. Mr. Joe did his best to soothe both Ben's and his parents' nerves—noting that it's normal for kids to need time to warm up—and welcomed them to class, allowing them to take their time and explore the room on their own.

What Mr. Joe, Ben, and Ben's parents may not have realized is that this interaction was the beginning of the formation of the teacher-student dyad, something we will explore in-depth in this chapter. This dyad serves as a protective relationship and primary means of regulation between a teacher and a student, ultimately serving to create a safe, trusting learning environment. In this chapter, we will consider how to use the strategies outlined in Chapter 2—Breathe, Body, Begin; Check your Nonverbals; and Attuned Listening—within the context of the teacher-student dyad. The ultimate goal will be for the teacher and the student to reach moments of co-regulation, which will then optimize the learning potential in the classroom.

UNDERSTANDING THE TEACHER-STUDENT DYAD AND REGULATION-RESPONSE CYCLE

A **protective relationship**[1] is defined as one that builds resiliency and protects students against developing negative symptoms from stress or traumatic life events. It helps students to develop a sense of relational safety, meaning the ability to be open, honest, and trusting with others. Protective relationships are the foundation for developing social, emotional, and physical health throughout their lives. Such relationships can be developed through building attunement and trust long enough to release oxytocin in the brain of both the student and teacher. Research shows that oxytocin is a chemical that, when released in the brain, helps to build a sense of connection, attunement, acceptance, and safety between those involved. This is the same chemical released in the brain of a mother and her baby at birth in order to establish a safe relationship.[2]

Protective relationship: a relationship that builds resiliency and protects students against developing negative symptoms from stress, or traumatic life events. It helps students to develop a sense of relational safety, meaning the ability to be open, honest, and trusting with others.

Highlighting the strengths of the student as well as using labeled praise are helpful ways to start building protective relationships with students. When you focus on what a student is doing well, this facilitates the release of oxytocin in the student and also in you, as the teacher. It is important not only for the student to feel connected to you but also for you to feel connected to the student. Once a positive connection is developed, students (and teachers) become motivated to maintain the positive relationship that they have built by continuing to engage in healthy relational experiences; this, in return, strengthens the connection and releases even more oxytocin in the brain. We will be discussing ways to find *shared joy* within the dyad later in this chapter. These mini-moments of shared joy act as a way to boost oxytocin levels in both the teacher and the student. They also provide a simple, easy, and fun way to maintain the healthy protective impacts of the **teacher-student dyad.**

Teacher-student dyad: a protective relationship between the teacher and the student that focuses on how the state of regulation of the teacher and student impact each other.

The first and most important way we can develop protective relationships and support our students in developing regulation and becoming active participants in learning is by focusing on the teacher-student dyad. This is achieved by creating a foundational sense of relational safety in the classroom and decreasing a sense of threat, danger, or fear that might occur. As we already explored, when the threat response is decreased, we are better able to access the parts of our brain that allow us to learn and problem solve. The idea of the teacher-student dyad is adapted from the research and clinical work that examines the parent-child dyad.[3–5] When looking at this unique dyad, we look at the state of regulation and the reactions of both the student and the teacher, as well as how their states of regulation impact each other. *A positive teacher-student*

Reflective Activity

Protective relationships are important for the development of social, emotional, and physical health, and are essential for learning. A protective relationship serves as the foundation for the teacher-student dyad. Take a moment to think back to when you were in elementary school:

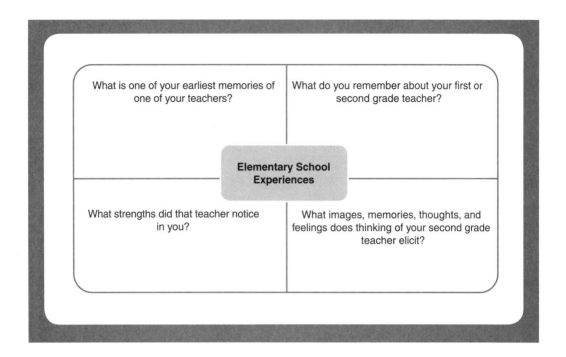

dyad ultimately uses the regulation and response pattern within the dyad to create co-regulation and connection between both the student and the teacher.

It is a challenging time for teachers and education in general. With low pay, limited classroom resources, and at times inadequate support, teachers may be feeling even more stressed. This additional systemic stress can trigger a threat response in the lower brain which can lead to a state of heightened nervous system arousal more readily. This ultimately impacts the relationship between teachers and students. *We want to focus on supporting the growth, well-being, regulation, and success of both the teacher and the student. If a teacher feels supported, regulated, safe, and self-assured then their students will feel the same.*

The teacher-student dyad regulation-response cycle is designed to help identify the state of regulation in both the student and the teacher. It helps to clarify their subsequent responses, and ultimately determines how each state of regulation and response impacts that of the other member of the dyad. The ultimate goal is to identify ways to change the regulation-response cycle to support the dyad in reaching a state of co-regulation that will lead to optimal learning.

Supportive Diagram

The teacher-student dyad regulation-response cycle can help inform the state of regulation in the teacher and the student in order to facilitate co-regulation.

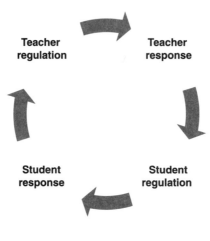

By using the diagram, you have the option to start with either the student's state of regulation or your own state of regulation. For our purposes throughout this chapter, we will start with the student's state of regulation. The following steps outline the process involved with the regulation-response cycle:

- **Step 1:** Identify the student's state of regulation. As discussed in Chapter 2, states of regulation include fight or flight (red zone), freeze (blue zone), and just right (green zone).

- **Step 2:** Identify the student's subsequent response that demonstrates how the student is behaving in response to their state of regulation. Examples for the fight responses in students may include hitting, punching, spitting, pinching, kicking, yelling, screaming, or other aggressive behaviors. It may also be more subtle such as crying, turning read, insulting others, eye rolls, and loud frustrated sighs. Examples of "flight" responses include running away, hiding under a table, not talking, or falling on the floor. "Freeze" responses may look like having tense muscles, or looking like a "deer in the headlights." They may also look like limited eye contact, putting your head on the desk, having glazed eyes, yawning, or even falling asleep. The "just right" zone typically looks like relaxed but alert stances, smiles, content faces, and appropriate participation.

- **Step 3:** Identify your (the teacher's) state of regulation in response to the student's regulation and behavior. Again, the options include fight, flight, freeze, or just right.
- **Step 4:** Identify your (the teacher's) response to your state of regulation. As adults, our fight nervous system response is hopefully less outwardly aggressive, but we still experience this nervous system response as heightened arousal. It might result in our muscles getting tight and our hearts racing, our voices becoming louder and firmer, and our faces turning red, or generally feeling hot. It also likely results in negative, "all or nothing" thoughts, or taking something personally. A freeze response may result in not knowing what to say or how to respond, we might feel cold, become stiff, have difficulty moving or articulating, and have difficulty forming cohesive thoughts. We may feel the urge to avoid the problem, put it off, or procrastinate.[6,7]

All of us, children and adults, move through various states of regulation and nervous system responses throughout the day. Some may feel more subtle while others more significant. While everyone experiences all states of regulation, we often have different behavioral responses to the state of regulation that we are in. What we know about the teacher-student dyad is that the state of regulation and subsequent response of one member of the dyad can impact that of the other.

In returning to our vignette, we recall that Ben was frightened about starting a new school and attempted to run out of the door during orientation night. After Mr. Joe went to introduce himself to another student, Ben's parents stopped him from running away and asked him what was wrong. Ben just responded, "I don't know." They attempted to help Ben feel more comfortable by commenting on the many nice things in the classroom. Ben looked around for a few minutes and told his parents he was ready to go home. He and his parents left without saying "goodbye" to Mr. Joe. Over the next few weeks, Ben did not want to return to school. He told his parents it was too noisy, too scary, and too big. He said he did not have any friends and that he was not going to go back. His parents persisted and took him to school every day despite Ben fighting them.

Ben cried about school at night before bed and yelled about school in the morning when he woke up. He screamed all the way in the car to the school and screamed when his parents carried him into the classroom, causing a scene in front of other children and parents. Mr. Joe remained attuned to himself throughout this process and noticed that his own nervous system response began to elevate when he heard Ben coming in the morning, screaming at drop off. He also began to notice that he was developing negative thoughts: maybe Ben didn't like him, and he was unsure of what he could do to help, as nothing he tried seemed to be working. Mr. Joe began to take Ben's response personally, and started to feel defeated and overwhelmed.

In this vignette, Ben is experiencing separation anxiety—excessive worry or fear about separating from a safe attachment figure. If we are looking at the challenge of separation anxiety through a relational lens and wondering how to use the power of the teacher-student dyad, we need to start with understanding "why" Ben is behaving this way. What is underneath this behavior? What is happening in his brain and nervous system? What is he trying to communicate to us, and how can we use the teacher-student dyad to help this situation?

While it may seem like Ben is being unreasonable or defiant or trying to "get out" of going to school, Ben is actually experiencing a threat response to his nervous system. He is interpreting the new, larger school environment and unfamiliar people as a threat to his health, safety, and well-being. Ben's amygdala—the threat response center in our lower brain—is in overdrive. There are times when we need our amygdala to respond in a way that signals a "life or death" situation, such as if we are being chased by a lion. Without this fight or flight response we would surely be eaten! Right now, Ben's nervous system (amygdala included) is responding the same way to the threat of a lion as it is to starting a new school. This seemingly maladaptive response is actually helping Ben to "stay alive" even though he is unable to function much beyond that. No wonder he can't form new friendships, participate in learning, or even step through the threshold of the classroom. As we get older, we are better able to regulate and modulate this response; however, right now Ben feels terrified,

Reflective Activity

Separation anxiety is not uncommon with students and can often be seen in classrooms of all grade levels. Students experiencing separation anxiety need a safe, trusting adult with whom they can co-regulate in order to achieve a "just right" level of nervous system arousal.

When have you experienced separation anxiety among your students?

_____

Why do you think this occurred?

_____

What were some strategies that helped?

_____   _____   _____

Was there anything that made it worse?

_____   _____   _____

frightened, alone, and as though his life were actually in danger. The threat response in his lower brain is so strong right now that he is unable to access the upper part of his brain that helps him to process, learn, and solve problems.

As Mr. Joe realized that Ben's brain-based response was protective and automatic, he was able to reframe Ben's behavior from being intentional to being something out of Ben's immediate control. Mr. Joe felt less defeated and overwhelmed about the situation and realized that Ben was genuinely feeling terrified. He knew that Ben was not yet feeling safe enough in his new environment to leave his parents, let alone engage with others or learn.

Interactive Scenario

Use the diagram below to visualize the regulation-response cycle within the teacher-student dyad of Ben and Mr. Joe. Options for regulation may include fight, flight, and freeze. The resulting responses could be behaviors (e.g., running away, yelling, hiding, crying, hitting), thoughts (e.g., "I hate school," "This is stupid," "I'm not good enough," "Why is this happening?"), or feelings (e.g., sadness, worry, anger, frustration). Notice how Ben and Mr. Joe are now in a cycle of co-dysregulation.

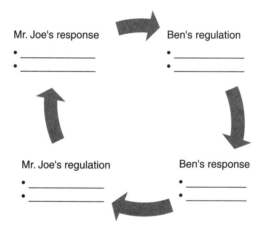

Mr. Joe's response
• _____
• _____

Ben's regulation
• _____
• _____

Mr. Joe's regulation
• _____
• _____

Ben's response
• _____
• _____

- Ben is in a *flight state of regulation* because he is feeling threatened by attending school in a new, bigger, noisier environment with unfamiliar people.

- Ben's nervous system *response is to flee—run away, hide, and try to escape.*

- Mr. Joe is also in a *flight state of regulation* when he hears Ben's screams and desire to leave. Ben's dysregulation is impacting Mr. Joe's state of regulation, and he also wants to avoid the situation.

- Mr. Joe's *response* is to feel as though there is nothing he can do to help Ben. He tries to pull Ben away from his parents and tries to distract him with other activities. When this doesn't work, he starts to focus on other children until Ben eventually quiets down on his own, entering a shutdown (freeze) nervous system response.

How can Mr. Joe use this information to build a positive teacher-student dyad that communicates safety, comfort, connection, and control? Can Mr. Joe bring awareness to how Ben's dysregulation is impacting his own state of regulation? Can Mr. Joe shift this cycle of co-dysregulation to a cycle of co-regulation with Ben to build safety and connection? Hold these questions in mind as we continue through this chapter.

When we are looking at the teacher-student dyad through the lens of IPNB and other brain-based relational models, it is helpful to better understand the processes occurring in the brain that impact the development of the dyad. Why is it so important to attend to our own states of regulation and that of our students? One reason is because of something in the brain called mirror neurons, and how those mirror neurons may impact regulation and learning.

THE POWER OF MIRROR NEURONS

As we continue to think about states of regulation in the classroom and how this impacts the teacher-student dyad, it is necessary to consider how different structures of the brain are involved.

Mirror neurons[8,9] are brain cells that are activated when a particular action is performed, and also when it is simply observed. So, in a way, when we observe something happening in our environment, our mirror neurons make the brain feel as though we are actually performing this activity ourselves.

While there is some controversy about mirror neurons in the scientific field,[9] many neuroscientists believe mirror neurons have wide implications for the development of empathy, theory of mind, learning, and even the development of language; research continues to emerge demonstrating this as well. Some individuals have mirror neurons that are more readily activated than others. For example, some research suggests that individuals with autism have mirror neurons that are less reactive than in others.[9] Mirror neurons have wide implications when considering how people learn to do things, respond to others, react to certain situations, and develop language skills. It also helps us to better understand and navigate the teacher-student dyad.

Mirror neurons: brain cells that are activated when a particular action is performed and also when it is simply observed.

Have you ever noticed how laughter and yawning can be contagious? Do you often cry when you watch sad movies or cringe when you see someone get hurt? Some neuroscientists believe this may be because the mirror neurons in your brain[9] are being activated. *Stress and dysregulation "rub off" on others and can negatively impact their state of regulation.* Let's say, for example, you've been driving in rush hour traffic for an hour and a half and get cut off. This results in you missing the next traffic light and being even more late for work. The person who cut you off yells and gives you the middle finger. Do you have the impulse to smile, wave, and apologize, or send an obscene gesture right back that mirrors their behavior? Or when flying on a plane and experiencing turbulence, the passenger next to you screams out in fear. His response would likely make others scream out, beginning to cause a state of panic within the plane. However, if the passenger next to you remains calm and says in a soothing voice, "It'll be over soon," this would likely have a different impact on the regulation of those nearby. The passenger's "green zone" regulation and messages of safety help you to also remain calm.

If we are calm and regulated, then the mirror neurons of those around us will be activated in a way that communicates safety. The same is true in the classroom. If there is a dysregulated student in your class, mirror neurons may cause your state of regulation to change as a teacher. If you are experiencing dysregulation (internal or external), then this will likely impact the regulation of your students. These dynamics heavily contribute to the teacher-student dyad.

In this book, we suggest that by understanding mirror neuron, teachers *can actually change* their students' state of regulation just by changing their own. Research has demonstrated that mirror neurons are connected to the limbic system, or the part of the brain connected with emotions.[9] Understanding that mirror neurons make emotions contagious can help when attending to and building the teacher-student dyad. This doesn't mean, however, that we should hide our emotions. It also doesn't mean that we can always change how we are feeling in the moment. As we have discussed, our bodies, brains, and nervous systems react in a certain way to keep ourselves safe, whether or not this response is adaptive or appropriate. We can, however, model appropriate identification of emotional and regulation states, and teach students how to respond to them in healthy and adaptive ways. *What is important to understand here is that how our state of regulation can impact that of others is actually based in the brain. If we bring awareness to it, and use the strategies outlined in this book, we can change our regulation-response patterns and create healthy teacher-student dyads that will ultimately improve learning and success for everyone.*

Supportive Diagram

Modeling appropriate identification of emotional and regulation states can help teach students to do the same. The same is true for modeling healthy and adaptive responses to our emotions and regulation states. Consider the following ways you can incorporate both into your classroom.

Ways to Model Identification of Emotions and Regulation States	Ways to Model Healthy and Adaptive Responses to Emotions and Regulation States
• "I'm feeling overwhelmed right now . . ."	• " . . . I need to take a deep breath."
• "This is getting very frustrating . . ."	• " . . . Let me take a break and come back to it."
• "This situation makes me anxious . . ."	• " . . . I'm going to relax my muscles."
• "The class is too loud for me . . ."	• " . . . I need to step out for a minute."

Understanding mirror neurons is one thing. However, changing their impact on our lives can be challenging, especially for those of us in caretaking and educational professions. Many of us come to such professions because we are highly empathetic and have a desire to support others, educate people, and help children to reach their full potential. Teachers in particular are loving, compassionate, eager, and dedicated to making a positive difference in their students' lives. This often means that you are highly empathetic, in-tune, and sensitive to those around you. Those of us in such professions are very susceptible to burnout, which means we have to take even more precaution to protect ourselves from others' emotional states and figure out how to harness the positive power of mirror neurons.

HARNESSING THE POSITIVE POWER OF MIRROR NEURONS

Being highly sensitive and empathetic in a caretaking profession can lead to higher rates of burnout, elevated levels of unhealthy stress, and secondary trauma. It can also impact our personal lives: people in such professions have been shown to have higher rates of divorce and overall emotional distress.[10,11] Because of this, it is of utmost importance to develop strategies that mitigate such harmful impacts so that we can protect our own health, well-being, efficacy of the work that we do, longevity of our careers, and healthy teacher-student dyads.

Early on in one of the authors, Ashley's, post-doctoral training, one of her professors discussed a strategy that has stuck with her. She said, "Be a mirror, not a sponge." When working with children and students who are impacted by learning challenges, trauma, or developmental delays, they may bring with them particular behavioral challenges, heartbreaking stories, and emotional distress. In part because of mirror neurons, these challenges, stories, and distresses can be absorbed by those around them and by those trying to teach them and help them to make positive changes in their lives. If we are not intentional about protecting ourselves from absorbing their stories and experiences, we can vicariously become impacted as well. By considering these common household items, we can practice being a mirror and avoid becoming a sponge.

Being a mirror means reflecting back the stories, experiences, states of regulation, and behavioral responses of the student as belonging to the student and not to you. You are mirroring back their emotional reaction, without any emotional reaction of your own. There is no need to agree or disagree with the student's behavioral reaction or emotional response; there is no obligation to "catch" or "match" the emotional response of the student. Simply mirror or reflect back what you are seeing. By using the "When in Doubt, Describe" technique in Chapter 2, for example, you are engaging in mirroring. Describing what you are seeing, similar to a sports announcer, allows you to put some space between yourself and your student's emotional response. This, in essence, creates a protective and reflective barrier between your own emotional response and that of your student.

We can attempt to prevent ourselves from being a sponge and absorbing the emotional states, experiences, and stories of students. "Sponging" is described as absorbing another person's negative emotions and responding to them with similar negative emotions.[12] If, for example, you are working with a student who becomes defiant and refuses to do anything you ask, you respond by absorbing their frustration and reacting to them in an increasingly defiant manner, resulting in a stand-off of wills or a struggle for power. We can help ourselves by noticing when we are being a sponge and engaging in strategies outlined in this book to regain a state of calm.

Here are some good questions to ask in order to determine if you are being a sponge or a mirror:

1. Does this feeling belong to me, someone else, or a mix of both?
2. Is this a typical response for me, or unique to this situation/student?
3. Am I carrying home emotions from work? Are they my emotions or the emotions of my students?
4. Is there something I would like to change about my response to a particular student?

This skill, like anything else new, takes practice and time to hone. Luckily, from what we know about how the brain develops, the more

Reflective Activity

Be a mirror, not a sponge; reflect, don't absorb. Write down examples of how to be a mirror and not a sponge, and/or write down examples of when you were a mirror and when you were a sponge.

Reflect on how differently it felt to be a mirror versus being a sponge:

_____

_____

_____

Image Source: Hunt Dougherty and pixabay.com/Clker-Free-Vector-Images.

you practice, the easier it gets; remember neurons that fire together, wire together.[13]

While we are now familiar with the potential negative impact of mirror neurons, it is important to think about how teachers and students can potentially benefit from harnessing the power of mirror neurons! *Put those mirror neurons to work and use them to their full potential. If we know that negative emotions are contagious, that means that positive emotions can be contagious as well.* How can you harness the power of positivity to make a brain-based difference in your life and that of your students? This has wide-ranging implications from developing both individual internal states of regulation, to impacting the dyad. If we take it even further, we can see how this concept can impact the development of empathy, to the classroom community as a whole, and be used to teach about diversity, cultural considerations, and acceptance of differences.

If we start with thinking about how we can use mirror neurons to help with our own regulation, consider ways that you can use the power of positivity to actually change your brain and overall nervous system responses. Surround yourself with people, places, and things that make you happy—these are the positive, regulating experiences we talk about in Chapter 1. Read a positive, supportive book, watch a feel-good movie, or grab lunch with friends who "get it." All of this is impacting you on a brain-based level.

In addition to using your mirror neurons to their full potential outside of the classroom, you can put them to work inside the classroom. Teaching your students about the power of mirror neurons can help to support their overall regulation, connection, and sense of safety as well. You can encourage your students to surround themselves with positivity, both inside and outside the classroom. Work with your students to develop stories of resilience, acceptance, compassion, safety, and connection. Help them begin to notice strengths in themselves and others. This is first modeled by you: take time to highlight your strengths, as well as the strength of *all* your students, and recognize the ways they are progressing throughout the school year.

We can subsequently think about how to expand this concept to the classroom community, as well as discuss meaningful cultural considerations. While you are building an awareness into how your students' reactions and behaviors impact you, it is also important to attend to societal and cultural biases that may be feeding into the work that you do. Understanding each other's backgrounds and

Supportive Diagram

Surrounding yourself and students with positivity can harness the power of mirror neurons to foster a regulated state. Consider the following ways you can routinely incorporate positivity and acceptance into your classroom community.

Incorporating Positivity

- Put pictures of family on the desks or walls
- Share or draw favorite memories from the school year
- Display uplifting and meaningful quotes
- Encourage students to give compliments to each other
- Have students highlight each other's strengths
- Do group projects that focus on gratitude (and not just in November!)
- Share stories of overcoming challenges

"ways of doing" can foster empathy. How can you create an environment of acceptance of differences, curiosity of others, and a love of learning? Thinking about ways to examine your own cultural background, values, and experiences can help you better understand how that may impact the lens through which you view the world. Your own cultural background may also impact how you interact with your students.

RUPTURE AND REPAIR

No one is perfect, and part of being human is knowing that mistakes happen—everyone makes mistakes. One of the authors, Jamie, always tells her clients that's why they put erasers on the end of pencils! It is impossible to be completely regulated at all times. Those mirror neurons are strong and can impact us without us even knowing or realizing it. That is ok! The good news is that we can fix these mistakes. Dr. Dan Siegel, the developer of the IPNB framework, calls these "**ruptures**" and "**repairs.**"[14]

"Ruptures" in the teacher-student dyad will happen; they happen in any relationship. An important piece of building a positive teacher-student dyad is noticing when ruptures occur. A rupture is when we make a mistake in how we respond to a student or when we are not able to stay in a regulated or co-regulated state with a student that we are working with. How we handle ruptures in the teacher-student dyad is by thinking about how to "repair" them. Many times the repair is an informative, healing, and meaningful moment for both the teacher and the student. When this is done correctly, the rupture and repair process can actually strengthen the teacher-student dyad.

Either member of the teacher-student dyad can make mistakes in the relationship that may cause a rupture. Model for students that everyone makes mistakes, and how to repair them is a valuable life lesson and skill. Ashley has worked in environments where teachers have been bitten, their hair has been pulled, and they have been spit on by their students. Other ruptures may not be so obvious: an eye roll, a loud sigh, a frustrated groan, a turning of the back, a passive comment. All such ruptures in the teacher-student dyad can be addressed!

While ruptures typically occur when one or both members of the teacher-student dyad are in a dysregulated state (fight/flight/freeze), repairs work best after everyone has returned to a "just right" zone. Waiting to move into the repair process after everyone has calmed down is most effective in teaching a new skill, encouraging problem-solving, and planning ahead for next time. This is because, from what we have discussed about the brain, when we are in a dysregulated state, we cannot access the part of our brain that allows for learning, problem-solving, and trying new skills.

Ruptures and repairs: mistakes that may happen within the teacher-student dyad that can be used to mend the relationship and make the dyad stronger than it was before.

The way to repair a rupture includes the following steps. Remember that your nonverbal communication and attuned listening skills will be an important part of this process.

1. Describe what occurred in an objective manner: This helps to clarify what happened and identify the facts of the situation, decreasing confusion regarding the situation.

2. Describe the emotional response of both the teacher and the student resulting from the rupture: This allows both the teacher and the student to understand the emotional response of the other person, allowing them to develop empathy for each other during a challenging moment. This step and the next step help the teacher and the student move toward a state of co-regulation.

3. Validate the emotions of each other: This step continues to provide support for the dyad in understanding each other's opinion and point of view.

4. Set limits around the behavioral response: This helps the dyad to understand the difference between emotions and behaviors. Clarify that all emotions are ok, but not all behaviors are ok. This helps to create a sense of appropriate boundaries and expectations, allowing each member of the dyad to take responsibility for a mistake that may have occurred.

5. Discuss an adaptive strategy for next time: This step helps the dyad identify how to do things differently next time. This allows the dyad to identify strengths of both members of the dyad and how they can use their strengths to approach such a situation differently next time. This will help them to create a plan in regard to how to move past the mistake, learn from it, and create the opportunity for growth so that a new outcome is possible next time around.

This process supports the development of new neuronal connections by allowing the teacher-student dyad to process and understand what went wrong (the rupture) within the context of a safe relationship. It fosters integration between the various brain regions by encouraging the use of logic, language, emotion, and empathy. This process is not shaming, blaming, or creating a situation where someone is getting "punished" for a moment of dysregulation. It supports acceptance and acknowledgment of both strengths and challenges, identifying ways to use the strengths of both the teacher and the student to support a more successful outcome next time around. If focuses on safety, connection, co-regulation, and skills building, all of which are necessary for growth and integration.

For example, let's say there is a teacher who works at a day treatment program for severely traumatized children. The children often become physically aggressive when they are triggered. All the teaching and administrative staff are trained in how to safely restrain children

Supportive Diagram

Ruptures occur in every relationship—that's ok! However, it is important to repair a rupture when it occurs in order to restore the teacher-student dyad. The result will be a strengthened relationship that encourages problem-solving and brain-based integration. The process of repairing a rupture will be most effective when everyone is calm and regulated. When a rupture occurs you can follow these steps in order to repair the teacher-student dyad:

RUPTURE

1. Describe what occurred
2. Describe the emotional response of each person
3. Validate the emotions of each other and identify strengths
4. Set limits around the behavioral response
5. Discuss an adaptive strategy for next time

when needed. However, there are still occasions when students will bite their teachers or pull their hair. Let's say a student, Cecilia, bit her teacher because she became upset when it was time to transition inside after recess. Her teacher attempted to hold Cecilia by the hand and lead her into the classroom when she was bitten. Once the incident has passed, and everyone has returned to a somewhat regulated state, the teacher can use the steps described above to repair the rupture, set limits, and plan for next time:

1. Describe what occurred: "Cecilia, you bit my arm when it was time to return to class after recess."
2. Describe the emotional response of each person: "I know you were really mad about recess ending. I know how much you love recess and wish we could spend more time playing outside. I love being outside with you and wish we could stay outside more too!"
3. Validate the emotions of each person: "I got really scared though, when you bit me. It really hurt my arm right here. See?"

4. Set limits around behavioral responses: "While it is ok to be mad about recess ending, it is never ok to bite or hurt other people. Not only does it hurt my arm, but it makes it harder for me to trust you. I love spending time with you, you are so fun and creative, and I really want to be able to trust you when we spend time together."

5. Discuss an adaptive strategy for next time: "Our relationship is really important to me, and I want for us to be able to enjoy spending time together in the future. How can we make sure something like this doesn't happen again? Let's think together about some ways that we can be mad in a safe way."

You can then use this time to brainstorm ideas together about how to handle things differently next time. It may be that Cecilia asks the teacher not to hold her hand when it is time to transition. It may be that the teacher gives Cecilia a longer prep time for the transitions or gives her a few extra minutes to move into the classroom on her own. If we are not mindful and intentional about how ruptures impact relationships between students and teachers, mirror neurons (in part) will continue to negatively impact the relational dynamics and make it harder to break the cycle.

Interactive Scenario

The chart below includes ruptures that may occur within a dyad. Fill in the language a teacher can use to repair the rupture, with the ultimate goal of coming up with a plan for the teacher-student dyad to do things differently the next time around. We have provided an example for you to follow.

Rupture	Repair	Plan for Next Time
1. The student becomes frustrated at the teacher and yells.	*I saw that you became really frustrated when we were working together and started raising your voice. It is ok to be mad and frustrated but it is not ok to yell because that was scary to me and the other students.*	*Let's think about how we can do things differently next time. How about, when you start to feel frustrated, give me a thumbs down and we will take a break.*

(Continued)

(Continued)

2. The student throws a pencil when it is time to clean up.		
3. The student won't come in from recess even though you've asked several times.		
4. The teacher yells when the class won't quiet down.		

2. A possible repair for #2 (above) might be "I wonder if you got upset when I said it was time to clean up. I know you weren't finished with your assignment yet. That must feel frustrating." A possible plan for next time might be "It is ok to be frustrated, but it is not safe to throw pencils. That makes me worried that someone might get hurt. How about next time you can ask me for a few more minutes to finish your paper?"

3. A possible repair for #3 might be "I know it is so hard to stop playing when you are having so much fun outside!" A possible plan for next time might be "How about next time you can be my special helper/line leader? That is a very important job, and we can work together so that we don't miss the activities we are planning to do after recess."

4. A possible repair for #4 might be "Class, I am sorry I yelled. I became very frustrated that you all were not listening. It was taking time out of our day and we have a lot of fun things to talk about." A possible plan for next time might be "Next time I will take a deep breath and stop myself from yelling, but I really need your help too so that you can quiet down when it is time to do so."

FACILITATING THE CONTINUED DEVELOPMENT OF A TEACHER-STUDENT DYAD

Throughout this chapter, we have discussed many things that help to build protective relationships, ways to harness the power of mirror neurons, and how to participate in the rupture and repair process.

The following strategies create a way to review certain concepts and facilitate attunement and awareness of the mirror neuron activity that are necessary for developing the teacher-student dyad. As we've discussed, relationships, regulation, and learning are all very interconnected. Continue to hold these concepts in mind as we discuss and review the following strategies.

Strategy I: Authenticity, Awareness, & Attunement

In order to fully develop protective relationships as part of the teacher-student dyad, we first need to ensure we have developed strategies to protect ourselves. *If our mirror neurons are left to run freely absorbing negativity, there will be nothing left for us to remain regulated enough to develop positive protective relationships.* We now know that regulation goes both ways. Students can often tell how teachers are feeling, even if teachers try to hide it. As we discussed in Chapter 2, they are picking up on your nonverbals and are often attempting to interpret (most likely unconsciously) what you are thinking, feeling, and in what state of regulation you are in.

1. *Be your authentic self* in a developmentally and professionally appropriate way. If you like to use humor, use humor. Jokes and humor are great ways to break a state of dysregulation, if done in the right way. If the noise in your classroom is overwhelming you, let them know. It is ok to say something along the lines of "I'm beginning to feel overwhelmed because the classroom is so noisy right now. I need a quiet break." If you see something that makes you excited, proud, joyful, or happy, let them know. Just as you absorb your student's state of regulation, they absorb yours. When you are able to name how you are feeling and model how to feel better, you demonstrate a healthy adaptive tool to improve the overall state of regulation in the classroom as a whole.

2. *Continue developing self-awareness* by noticing your state of regulation and how this might be impacting that of your students. Notice your students' state of regulation and how that might be impacting yours. It is the interaction of both teacher and student states of regulation that create the dynamics of the dyad, with the ultimate goal of finding a state of regulation—or shared joy/enjoyment—together (i.e. co-regulation). Notice your strengths and the strengths

of your student; how can you use your strengths to find moments of shared joy?

3. *Attunement to yourself* is another way you can facilitate a positive teacher-student dyad. Supporting teachers in first learning how to pay attention to their own cues and listen to what their "inner voice" is telling them about themselves can ultimately help to build attunement toward their students. We've discussed how to practice attuned listening to your students in Chapter 2; now we want to encourage you to practice attuned listening to yourself:

   - What is your body telling you?
   - What is the sensory environment telling you?
   - Did you get enough sleep last night or the night before last?
   - When is the last time you ate something?
   - Are there specific patterns or triggers that you notice?
   - What state of regulation are you in?
   - Did something happen outside of work that you are carrying with you?
   - What do you need right now to take care of yourself?
   - How can you return to a state of regulation that will best help to regulate your students?
   - How can you alter the classroom environment to help you and your students return to a better state of regulation?

In our example earlier in the chapter, it is evident that Ben's dysregulation and response are impacting the regulation and response of Mr. Joe. Mr. Joe is effectively picking up on Ben's nonverbal cues of dysregulation and recognizes that his own nonverbal cues might be communicating anxiety. Mr. Joe practices self-awareness and notices that he begins to feel dysregulated when he hears Ben screaming as he arrives in the morning. He notices this tends to send him into a flight or freeze zone, as he often feels as though he wants to avoid the situation or not deal with it at all. When he attunes to himself, Mr. Joe notices that negative thoughts are developing: he thinks there is nothing he can do to help Ben. Mr. Joe realizes he needs to do something to help himself regulate—get back to the "just right" zone—before figuring out how to solve the problem.

He allows himself to take a moment to practice the "Breathe, Body, Begin" strategy described in Chapter 2. He then feels more regulated and ready to approach Ben in a calm way. As Mr. Joe begins to feel

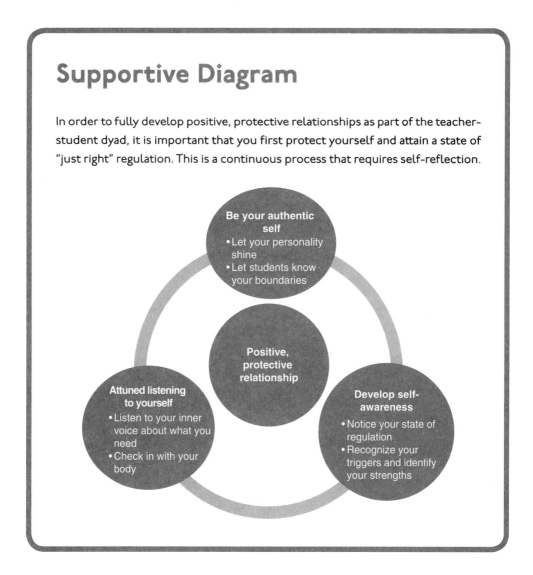

Supportive Diagram

In order to fully develop positive, protective relationships as part of the teacher-student dyad, it is important that you first protect yourself and attain a state of "just right" regulation. This is a continuous process that requires self-reflection.

Be your authentic self
- Let your personality shine
- Let students know your boundaries

Positive, protective relationship

Attuned listening to yourself
- Listen to your inner voice about what you need
- Check in with your body

Develop self-awareness
- Notice your state of regulation
- Recognize your triggers and identify your strengths

more regulated, he is then able to brainstorm and problem-solve new ways to respond to this challenge. He suggests that both Ben and his mom come a bit early to school, before the day starts, so that they can spend 10 minutes all playing together. This will allow Mr. Joe to explore being his authentic self around Ben. Over the course of the next few days, Ben, Mr. Joe, and Ben's mom spent about 10 minutes playing together before school started. This leads us into the next strategy.

Strategy 2: Mini Moments of Shared Joy

We understand that the thought of a teacher-student dyad in a class full of students who constantly need your attention may feel overwhelming, maybe even impossible, or completely implausible. In reality, most children in a general education classroom environment, and who are coming from relatively stable home environments, do not actually need a great deal of regulated and individualized "teacher-student dyad time" in order to feel safe, in control, and connected to the classroom community. In fact, research on how parents can build "secure attachments" with their children suggests that parents only need to be in tune and co-regulated with their children for 30 percent of the time.[15-17]

Other research on parenting suggests that it is not the quantity (or amount) of time you have with each child, but the quality of the time spent together.[18] *If we think about applying this to the classroom environment, two minutes of truly co-regulated shared joy will do a lot more in the long run than 10 minutes of frustrated work together. Most children only need "mini-moments" of regulated, shared joy to foster positive co-regulation within the teacher-student dyad.* This will help support a level of "just right" regulation enough to learn, participate, and engage in the classroom activities.

As we continue with our example, in the 10-minute morning play period, Mr. Joe uses nonverbal cues of safety, like getting on Ben's level, using a calm voice, and relaxing his face, when interacting. Ben starts to feel safer with Mr. Joe. Mr. Joe is able to be his authentic self and use his sense of humor to connect with Ben; they are able to begin to build a relationship together. They find shared joy in playing with cars and talking about the different features of cars. He uses attuned listening and re-framing, as described in Chapter 2, to help Ben make sense of his emotional experience. After the third day, Ben is no longer screaming when he comes to school in the morning even though the separation from his parents is still challenging. Ben and Mr. Joe have a special handshake they share every morning that fosters shared joy. Starting the next week, Ben tells his mom and dad that he is actually excited to play with Mr. Joe. After a few more days, Ben is able to go to school, wave bye to mom and dad, and be on his way. Ben has now developed a positive association with his new school. His school no longer triggers a threat response in Ben because he now feels a sense of safety and connection.

What do those "just right" shared-joy, mini moments look like in your classroom? Some examples may include:

- Laughing together over a funny joke
- Patting your student's shoulder or back

- Smiling from across the room
- Having a special or "secret" gesture that is meaningful to you both (thumbs up or "ok" sign)
- Labeled (very specific) praise (this will be discussed in more depth in Chapter 9)
- Bringing over a cup of water
- Student writing you a card of gratitude
- Teacher leaving a student a little note of gratitude
- Talking about a funny TV show or game that the student likes
- Joining with the student on a preferred activity
- Spending a few minutes at recess joining with the student while she is playing in the sandbox
- Singing a few verses of a song you both know
- Asking the child about their favorite sport/game/TV show/movie
- Showing interest in their interests by temporarily following the lead of the student
- Reflecting back to the student what you see them doing—"I see you are building a cool tower. I want to build one too."
- Identify and comment on strengths

These are all examples of how you can use the teacher-student dyad as a way to build positive, protective, supportive, and long-lasting, meaningful relationships with your students. These are the mini-moments that make all the difference, both for you and for the student! Can you think of things that get in the way of having mini-moments of shared joy? And ways you can increase them throughout your day?

Reflective Activity

The quality of the time that you spend with your students is an important part of establishing co-regulation. Finding *shared joy* is, therefore, another way to think about facilitating the teacher-student dyad.

(Continued)

(Continued)

Take a moment to think back to when you decided you wanted to be a teacher. What brought you to this field? What were your dreams, ideas, thoughts, hopes, and goals for educating others?

- _____
- _____
- _____
- _____

Now think of a recent day at work, and list below mini moments of shared joy that you had with your students.

- _____
- _____
- _____
- _____

Strategy 3: Ask for Help When Needed!

Remember, you are not alone. While working with children can be profoundly rewarding, it can also be exhausting, frustrating, and draining. Being aware of when you need help is an important step in this process. Identifying who is on your team, and who you can go to when you need a break, a shoulder to cry on, or someone to ask a question is a necessary step in maintaining healthy teacher-student dyads. You must take care of yourself in order to take care of others.

When thinking about Mr. Joe and Ben, let's say, for example, that resources or time did not permit Mr. Joe to spend 10 minutes with Ben and his mom before school started. What are some other options, additional solutions, or ways that Mr. Joe could ask for help in this situation?

Some additional solutions could include the following:

- Identify a safe person and safe place in the front office, someone who Ben and his mom could meet with prior to entering class in the morning. Ben and his mom can spend time there together, allowing Ben to feel safe.

Reflective Activity

Take a moment to think about who is in your corner. No one can do this work by themselves. Whether there is a school psychologist, support team on staff, another teacher or teacher's aide, someone at home, a spouse, partner, friend, or family member, take a moment to identify a few people you can go to both in the moment when you need support while on the job, and later when you need to debrief and/or vent.

In-the-Moment Support Person	Type of Support He/She Can Provide	Outside-of Work-Support Person	Type of Support He/She Can Provide

- Consider sensory input that may be regulating to Ben; explore noise cancelling headphones as Ben continues to comment on how noisy the new school is.
- Allow Ben and his parents to spend some time walking around the campus and meeting new people so that Ben can begin to feel more comfortable in the new setting.

The idea is that when we are in a dysregulated state, it is easy to fall into negative regulation-response cycles, and it may be hard to remember that there are actually other solutions. Once we take a moment to change our state of regulation, we can move toward co-regulation, access the part of our brain that helps to brainstorm, problem-solve, ask for help, and come up with new solutions!

CHAPTER 4

Foundations of Sensory Processing for Regulated Learning

"Most sensorimotor experiences occur within the context of a relationship and give them additional relevance through emotional connection."
—Jeanetta Burpee, M.Ed., OTR/L

Every day, Catalina, who just turned 5 years old, entered her Pre-K class with a different "treasure" that she had found the previous day. She cradled that treasure in her arms or grasped it tightly in her hand throughout most of the morning. Sometimes it was a leaf, a flower, or a rock; sometimes a stuffed animal, favorite toy, or Lego block; sometimes a bracelet, hair tie, or refrigerator magnet. No matter what her teacher did, Mr. Jones could never get her to let it go before lunchtime. However, this often became a distraction to the other students who wanted to touch or explore the new treasure that Catalina had brought. Mr. Jones did not want to make Catalina upset, but he also did not want to disrupt his classroom.

After a couple weeks of observation, Mr. Jones noticed a pattern: Catalina intensely fidgeted with the treasure when first entering the classroom, rubbed it calmly in her lap during circle time, set it next to herself at snack time, and rubbed it calmly in her lap again at story time. Upon returning from lunch recess, she never picked up the treasure for the rest of the day. She was clearly using it as a means of regulation until she felt safe and comfortable enough in the classroom to leave it behind. "Maybe," thought Mr. Jones, "I can provide her with a classroom treasure that can help her stay regulated but find something that does not distract other students."

One day when Catalina entered the classroom, Mr. Jones had decorated a small treasure chest with "Student Treasures from Home" written across the top. Next to it was a bin of classroom treasures that Mr. Jones felt were appropriate: a Tangle Jr. fidget, a cord bracelet, a soft piece of fabric, and a stress ball, to name a few. He told her,

> I notice that you always bring a treasure to the classroom. I brought some treasures for the class today, too. You can pick one of the classroom treasures and use it for as long as you need to throughout the day. Other classmates can pick a treasure if they need one, too. I also made a treasure box where all the students can put their treasures, so they don't get lost. Why don't you put your treasure into your box and pick one of my treasures for the day?

Sure enough, it worked!

Mr. Jones was supporting Catalina's need for tactile input in order to keep her regulated during the morning. This type of sensory input was calming for Catalina and facilitated her learning and engagement. *Rather than combat this natural tendency of Catalina's, Mr. Jones leaned into it, joining with her to better understand the underlying sensory need impacting her behavior, and saw positive results.* In this chapter, we will explore why sensory input is important and how sensory processing is relevant to a school setting. We will also explore ways that teachers can help facilitate sensory integration in the classroom, so that students can maximize their learning potential.

FOUNDATIONS OF SENSORY PROCESSING IN THE CLASSROOM

Sensory processing: the ability to receive, manage, and interpret messages from each sensory system.

Sensory processing impacts every area of learning, attention, and regulation. It is how we make sense of the world and interact with the world around us. *Sensory processing* is defined as the ability to receive, manage, and interpret messages from each sensory system.

Sensory input helps us move our bodies, learn new skills, and participate in activities throughout the day. We have eight different sensory systems that our brain must integrate in order to interact appropriately with our environment. These sensory systems include proprioception (body awareness), vestibular (orientation in space), tactile (touch), auditory (sound), visual (sight), gustatory (taste), olfactory (smell), and interoception (awareness of internal organs). **Sensory integration** is our brain's ability to orchestrate all of those sensations into meaningful behavioral and motor responses without becoming too overwhelmed, distracted, or disengaged. We will explore each of these sensory systems and their impact on learning later in the chapter.

The way we process, understand, and experience emotions is intrinsically intertwined with how we process sensory information around us. This is because the emotional center of our brain—the amygdala—detects threat and safety based on the sensory information it is receiving. If we hear a loud, jarring sound like a fire alarm, our amygdala is triggered to detect the possible threat of a fire. We become dysregulated and are on "high alert." If we smell the baking of an apple pie, our amygdala is triggered to detect the safety of our grandma's home. We feel calm and comforted, and we're better able to interact with those around us. The amygdala also integrates emotional memories from past sensory experiences, triggering an anxiety or fear-based response when a prior experience was negative, and excited or anticipatory response when a prior experience was positive. Thus, the sensory experiences we have throughout our lives can shape our emotions, regulation, and responses around future sensory experiences.

At the same time, our state of regulation also influences the way we perceive sensory information. You may have noticed that you have a varying tolerance for certain types of sensory input based on your emotional state. One of the authors, Jamie, for example, can generally tolerate a fair amount of auditory input—listening to music softly while having a conversation with someone with the refrigerator humming in the background. However, after a long day interacting with and regulating her toddler, Jamie's tolerance for auditory input tends to plummet. Music in the background becomes agitating, and the refrigerator humming seems like an airplane flying overhead. This is because when we are under stress, and thus have more adrenaline and cortisol pumping, the ability of the amygdala to accurately assess fear and safety is impaired. Our senses are also heightened in order to engage in a fight or flight response and keep us more aware of our environment.

Sensory integration: the brain's ability to orchestrate all sensations into meaningful behavioral and motor responses.

In times of actual life-threatening stress, such as a burglar in our home, it is important and necessary for our senses to be heightened so that we can hear light footsteps, see in the dark, and be more aware of where our body is moving in space. However, as seen in Chapter 3 with the example of Ben's response to separating from his parents when attending a new school, during times of non-life-threatening stress, this heightened nervous system response can be a barrier to how we engage with those around us, how well we are able to adapt to our surroundings, and our ability to become regulated enough to learn.

Our brains must attend to sensory input to determine if it is threatening, worth more attention, intriguing, or able to be ignored. Usually when we are first exposed to a form of sensory input, our brains pay close attention, but after time, if our brains are functioning well, we are able to habituate to that input, get used to it, and filter it out. Think about a dog barking behind you when you're reading at a coffee shop. Likely the first time you hear it bark, your brain will alert you to turn around to see the size of the dog, if the dog is on a leash, and what the dog is barking at. After you determine the situation is safe, the next time you hear the dog bark, you are likely better able to tune out the noise and continue reading. This is because the parasympathetic nervous system kicked in to calm your sympathetic nervous system in order to bring the autonomic nervous system back into balance for a regulated state of arousal (see Chapters 1 and 2 for a refresher on that terminology). If your parasympathetic nervous system did not kick in, maybe due to a recent negative experience with a dog, you would find it difficult to stay focused on a cognitive task like reading because your brain would be experiencing a heightened form of stress.

In this way, the sensory environment impacts a student's state of regulation and arousal. *Sensory input is often what we use to help get us back to a balanced nervous system.* Many of the ways children do this are functional and integrated into their everyday lives without second thought. For example, a student who is losing focus might rock back and forth slightly to help pay attention better, which engages the vestibular sensory system. A student who is nervous might calm herself by putting her fingers in her mouth, which engages the oral sensory system. A student like Catalina who is seeking comfort might hold onto something, which engages the tactile sensory system. Chuck E Cheese is a cautionary example of how an environment full of sensory stimulation can impact a child's regulation. All of the fluorescent lights, loud noises, and unstructured movement tend to amp up kids, making them more vulnerable to meltdowns. On the other hand, consider the calming effect of lavender oil, classical music, and ambient lighting after bath time, which helps prepare a child for sleep. Sensory input truly does have a powerful impact on our state of regulation.

Sensory input also informs our movements and behaviors: we physically respond to sensory information. We might lean in closer when we hear something interesting. We might curl up when we see something frightening. We might retract our hand when we feel something mushy. If our sensory systems were not communicating this information to our brain, then our muscles would never receive a signal from the brain to relax or contract. This is also how we learn to coordinate our own body movements. For children who are curious explorers of the sensory environment, this means more movement and more responses. As adults who have learned to habituate to certain sensory inputs or have learned to control impulses around certain sensory experiences, it can sometimes be difficult to understand why a child

Supportive Diagram

The way we respond to various sensory inputs in the environment influences our emotions, which in turn impacts our state of regulation and the behaviors that we exhibit. Let's look at how this cycle may look for Catalina in the opening vignette, as seen in the parentheses ( ).

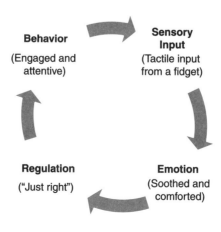

Behavior
(Engaged and attentive)

Sensory Input
(Tactile input from a fidget)

Emotion
(Soothed and comforted)

Regulation
("Just right")

cannot do the same. But this is why play, and particularly sensory-rich outdoor play, is so critical to a child's development.[1] A child can use those sensory experiences to control his movements, understand his behavioral responses, control his impulses, and learn about the way things work—over the course of many years. This, of course, has many implications for academic environments. *Every student processes sensory input differently, requiring different amounts of sensory input to respond to the demands of the school environment in order to maintain an appropriate level of engagement, perform classroom activities effectively, and remain regulated. As teachers, you have a unique role in fostering the sensorimotor development of your students, which we will explore next.*

TEACHER-STUDENT DYAD AND SENSORY PROCESSING

As outlined in Chapter 2, the formation of a teacher-student dyad has a powerful impact on how a student regulates and engages in learning. The same is true for how we process sensory information. From infancy, our experiences with sensory input and motor output are often paired with a positive or negative emotion that can have a lasting impact on the nervous system. The brain remembers these experiences and draws on those memories when we face similar experiences in the future. This is how the brain learns to wire itself in a certain way, and why we feel certain emotions with different sensory input or motor output. If we have repeated positive sensory experiences, then positive emotions will be paired with it, such as the yummy smell of grandma's cookies, the comforting sound of a mother singing a lullaby, the joyous thrill of a rollercoaster, or the soothing touch of a favorite stuffed animal. If we have repeated negative sensory experiences, then negative emotions will be paired with it, such as the noise of screeching chalk on a chalkboard, the sulfuric smell of hard-boiled eggs, the uncertain void of being in the dark, or the gag-inducing texture of eggplant.

An important consideration here is that what is regulating to one person may be overwhelming to another. While one person may gag while eating eggplant, another may really enjoy it. Similarly, with rollercoasters, while one child may love them, another may be terrified—developing negative associations with amusement parks for the rest of their lives. These individual differences are an important consideration when working with students and searching for the "why" underlying their behaviors.

However, *being in safe, attuned, co-regulatory relationships increases the capacity of the neurological system to explore sensory experiences in any environment.* It can turn negative sensory experiences into something more manageable, creating less stress on the brain and allowing for more exploration and more learning. A child may accept watching fireworks in the lap of a beloved caregiver when she can barely tolerate them sitting by herself. A child may delight in sharing stories in the dark with a trusted adult when he would not dare to enter that space by himself. A child may cling to a best friend while touching a manta ray for the first time when she would never attempt this if she were

Reflective Activity

Being in a safe, co-regulatory relationship can actually decrease the amount of stress we feel during certain sensory experiences. This helps to foster an increased sense of safety, which allows us to better explore the environment, engage in a situation, and/or attend to information. Contrarily, being in an unattuned, poorly regulated relationship can increase the amount of stress in certain sensory environments. This can create more dysregulation and sense of fear, negatively impacting the ability to explore, engage, or attend.

Think back to your sensory experiences in childhood (e.g., riding a rollercoaster for the first time, eating a new food, holding a snake for the first time, watching fireworks for the first time).		
What emotions do you remember feeling?	Who was there with you?	How did the presence of that person change your experience?

alone. The reverse is also true; if a child is not co-regulated with the adult in their life, the dysregulated behavior will escalate: the Fourth of July will evoke anxiety, entering a dark room will induce fear, and trips to the aquarium will turn into nightmares of meltdowns.

We know through research that repeated explorations of sensory information are what helps shape our world, as well as our movements and responses within that world.[2] This starts in infancy with the caregiver-infant dyad, whereby safe, reciprocal interactions allow the infant to feel comfortable looking at, touching, and hearing new sights, textures, and sounds. For an infant who spends extended time in the neonatal intensive care unit, the perception of a comfortable sensory environment is negatively impacted not only by the adverse sensory experiences of needles, tubes, and beeping machines but also by the inherent limitations of establishing a caregiver-infant dyad. The interrupted establishment of the caregiver-infant dyad results in the infant's being limited in his ability to find a calm, alert state in his sensory environment. This will impact the sensory preferences of that child, which will later be reflected in how he interacts with his sensory environment at school. We will explore this further in the next chapter.

In schools and classrooms where sensory input abounds, forming a positive teacher-student dyad is critical in helping students feel safe exploring their sensory environment and meeting the intense sensory demands of the environment. *When students feel threatened, unsafe, or uncertain in the classroom, they become either (1) more aware of the sights, sounds, smells, and tactile experiences through a heightened level of arousal or (2) less engaged with sights, sounds, smells, and tactile experiences by "zoning out" or "shutting down."* Learning requires students to see the information being taught, hear the instructions from the teacher, and interact tactilely with materials. All of these sensory inputs are critical to the learning environment.

As a teacher, you play a vital role in how a student navigates the sensory input in a classroom through use of co-regulation in order to increase a student's capacity to learn. Remember that the language and nonverbal cues that you use make a difference. In the example with Catalina, Mr. Jones could have approached her and said, "You're always touching things you're not supposed to. Maybe this will help you keep your hands to yourself?" He could have said this with a loud sigh, an air of frustration, avoiding eye contact, and had a loose body posture—all communicating that while he was "sort of" willing to help, he was not really engaging in a positive teacher-student dyad, and was more annoyed than anything else. But Mr. Jones instead used positive, supportive language and nonverbal communication that conveyed he was on Catalina's team; he was willing to do this through a co-regulatory relationship. In the next section, we will explore how each sensory system can impact learning, helping to establish a better understanding of how teachers can influence each student's regulation.

SENSORY SYSTEMS AND THEIR IMPACT ON LEARNING

If you recall the diagram of the vertical brain from Chapter 1, properly processing and integrating sensory information is one of the foundations of a child's participation in the learning process. In fact, research from sensory-deprived orphanages illustrates the negative impact this can have on cognitive, motor, and psychological development.[3] On the flip side, research shows that sensory over-stimulation, particularly in low-income areas where there are higher levels of noise, environmental smells, and denser populations, also negatively impacts the social-emotional development of a child and inherently impacts learning as well.[4] While being in positive relationships can sometimes mitigate the effects of too much or so little sensory input, in general, the sensory needs of the child must first be met. This is because the child may be so understimulated or overstimulated that he does not have the capacity to connect with someone else. *Therefore, it is important to have a balance of sensory stimulation and recognize that certain sensory inputs are important in different situations.* This is where a teacher's attunement to students' sensory preferences comes into play. Children tell us through their behaviors which sensory inputs are regulating and dysregulating to them. As adults, we need to be attuned enough to watch for and listen to what they are communicating. Always remember to ask "why?"

Visual

Visual input is what we see, such as lights in the gymnasium, colors in art class, facial expressions of peers, recognizing letters, orienting numbers correctly, copying shapes, completing worksheets, and following the teacher at the front of the classroom. School provides a huge amount of visual input throughout the day. One example is

Supportive Diagram

As you read through this section, you can refer back to this diagram to gain a better understanding of where each of the senses is located on the body.

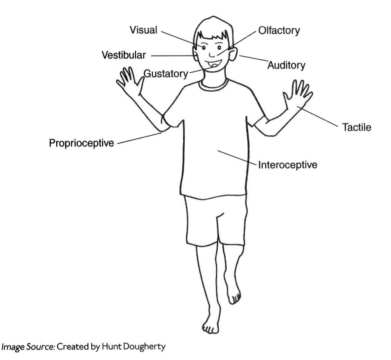

Image Source: Created by Hunt Dougherty

fluorescent lighting, which is typically what illuminates school classrooms and hallways, yet research suggests this type of lighting is overstimulating to many children, particularly those with attention deficit hyperactivity disorder, autism spectrum disorder, and sensory processing disorder—to the point of impacting attention and learning.[5] Another example is the amount of artwork, posters, charts, and signs on the walls of classrooms. Research suggests that children actually learn better in environments with minimal visual distractions on the walls.[6]

Visual input is primarily processed in the occipital lobe of the brain, located at the back part of the cerebrum. Bright colors, sunlight, crowded worksheets, and fast-moving objects (like many cartoons) can all be stimulating to the visual system. Pastel colors, dim lighting,

Visual input: what we see.

simple pictures, and slow-moving objects (like fish in an aquarium) tend to be more calming. *When the visual system receives too much input, it can result in headaches, rapid blinking, shielding the eyes, avoidance of eye contact, or inability to focus. When the visual system does not receive enough information, it can result in boredom, tiredness, or losing one's place when looking at something.* The visual system often works in conjunction with the auditory and language systems to help with reading, writing, and math. The visual system and motor system also work together to help with eye-hand coordination activities, such as writing, tying a shoe, catching a ball, cutting with scissors, and stringing beads.

When a child has difficulty processing visual input, it can be a sign of a visual perceptual deficit. While the eyes take in visual information to inform us of what we see, *visual perception* refers to higher-level cognitive skills for how we utilize the visual input received by the brain. It is what we do with the information that we see. Visual perceptual skills include visual attention, visual memory, visual sequential memory, visual form, and visual-spatial skills. Students use visual perceptual skills to copy information from the board, write on the lines, remain focused when reading, and find a certain object in a pencil box.

It is also important to differentiate between visual processing and oculomotor difficulties. *Oculomotor skills* refer to the functions that occur when the muscles of the eyes work in an appropriate manner. This includes acuity (how near/far the eyes can see), convergence (both eyes working together), tracking (following an object using only the eyes), and saccadic movement (rapid back-and-forth movement of the eyes). Difficulty with these skills is usually indicative of how the eyes are functioning and not how the brain is processing visual information. While a child can certainly fall into both categories, many children have one without the other.

Auditory

Auditory input is what we hear, such as instructions from the teacher, announcements over the loudspeaker, the hum of the air conditioner, conversations with peers, echoes in the gymnasium, a cacophony of instruments in music class, or hearing your name being called. Most of the classroom instruction provided at school comes in the form of auditory input.

Auditory input: what we hear.

Auditory input is primarily processed in the temporal lobes of the brain—one on each side, just above the ears. *In general, lower frequencies and volumes are calming, while higher frequencies and volumes are energizing.* As different frequencies and volumes are detected, muscles in the ear expand or contract to allow those frequencies to pass through. If these muscles are weak, then too much noise can pass through, particularly low frequencies. Thus, filtering out noises in the environment—the air conditioner, a fish tank, fluorescent lights buzzing—is difficult because those noises tend to be at lower frequencies. In particular, hearing your name called, listening to directions, and understanding what is being communicated can be challenging because human speech is at a higher frequency and must "compete" with the unfiltered low frequencies.

Auditory input also helps establish our spatial awareness through sonar tracking. Sonar tracking is what we use to determine how near or far something is in relation to us. Usually we attribute this skill to animals like bats and dolphins, but it is something that we do unconsciously as humans every day. Think about when you're driving in your car and you hear an ambulance—before you even see it, you can determine the general direction it is coming from and when it is getting closer. This skill is also used when finding our way in the dark. Often the auditory system works in conjunction with the vestibular system to maintain our balance because both are processed in the ear.

While the ears take in auditory input to inform us of what we hear, auditory processing skills, like visual perceptual skills, are the more complex, higher-level cognitive skills that rely on the integration of auditory input and language skills. Auditory processing skills consist of discrimination, figure-ground, memory, and sequencing. In school, students use auditory process to filter out what the teacher is saying amid other sounds, remember a series of instructions, and hear the subtle differences between similar-sounding words.

Tactile

Tactile input: what we feel when we touch something.

Tactile input is what we feel when we touch, such as a teacher's hand on a student's shoulder, a hug from a peer, holding a pencil to write, playing in the sand box at recess, molding clay in art class, the texture of the rug during circle time, or how our clothes feel against our skin.

Tactile input is processed in the sensorimotor area of the brain, located in the parietal lobe, right behind the frontal lobe. Touch is one of the primary ways we detect safety and comfort from people and objects around us—just as Catalina was doing in the opening vignette. There is a considerable amount of emotion attached to touch, and touch is critical in the development of the brain. Our experiences of touch in early infancy are foundational to how our brains respond to touch later in life. Preemies who are poked and prodded with life-saving devices generally have negative associations to touch that can last for many years.[7] Children in orphanages who are rarely held can develop delays in sensory processing, cognition, motor function, and growth.[3,8,9] We need positive touch not only to survive but also to thrive, although keep in mind that each student's perception of positive touch will vary. For example, one student may see a hug as regulating and comforting while another student may shy away when asked to give a hug.

There are different types of tactile input. While there are individual sensory preferences and needs, there are also generalized ways touch can be regulating and dysregulating. *Light touch is tactile input that brushes against the skin. This type of input provides a large amount of stimulation and is often dysregulating.* Think about a spider web on your arm, a tag against your neck, or being tickled. Deep pressure touch is tactile input that provides information about the muscles, joints, and tendons, and helps ground you and establish body awareness, such as a massage or a hug. Tactile input can be passive, meaning it is imposed, or active, meaning it is self-initiated. *Passive input is often more stimulating and dysregulating than active input.* The phrase "you can't tickle yourself" is actually true and highlights the different way our brain responds to passive versus active tactile input. For example, a student might turn quickly when she feels someone brush up against her back when standing in line. That same student might not react at all when she sits right next to a peer at a crowded school assembly.

Tactile discrimination helps us to determine what we are touching without being able to see—called stereognosis—such as digging through the bottom of a backpack to find a pencil rather than a highlighter, chapstick, or a stick. Tactile discrimination also helps us perceive letters, numbers, and figures drawn on our skin without our looking—called graphesthesia. Children who do not discriminate tactile input will have a difficult time differentiating their fingers and what they hold in their fingers, almost as if they are wearing rubber gloves. As you can imagine, writing is particularly challenging for children with poor tactile discrimination.

Proprioceptive

Proprioceptive input: information from our muscles and joints about our body position.

Proprioceptive input is the feedback we gain from our muscles and joints about our position in space. Essentially, it is our awareness of our body, such as navigating the classroom, running across the playground, crossing the monkey bars at recess, sitting next to other peers during circle time, using appropriate pressure when writing, or imitating dance moves in physical education (PE) class.

Proprioceptive input is processed in many areas of the brain, including the sensorimotor area in the frontal lobe and parietal lobes, and the cerebellum. Proprioceptive information from specialized receptors help detect force and vibration, as well as create a body map. The proprioceptive system is what allows us to adjust our force when lifting, pushing, pulling, or throwing objects—something many of us do so naturally. Proprioceptive awareness also helps us determine the texture of the surface through a tool, such as what type of paper we are writing on. For example, we can *feel* that using a pencil on sandpaper is different than using a pencil on construction paper. Input from the kinesthetic system also determines how much we should move a certain body part and where that body part is located in relationship to other body parts.

Proprioceptive input also provides calming sensation to the brain and body. During deep pressure input or "heavy work" activities, the parasympathetic nervous system is activated, which brings our brain and body back into a regulated state when overstimulation occurs. Heavy work activities might include pushing, pulling, or squeezing something. *Use of proprioceptive input is one of the most powerful ways a child can calm down when she is dysregulated. Utilization of proprioceptive activities throughout the day can also help prevent meltdowns—one of the reasons why recess can be so critical to learning!*

Vestibular

Vestibular input: how we detect movement, understand our relationship to gravity, and regulate our attention.

Vestibular input is how we detect movement, understand our relationship to gravity, and regulate our attention level, such as sitting upright in a chair, regaining balance when accidentally bumped by a peer, rock climbing in PE class, or staying in one place during circle time.

Vestibular input is processed in the cerebellum and the sensorimotor area of the frontal lobe but has connections in over 90% of the cerebral cortex, which means that vestibular input is critical to our higher-level thinking. Input from the vestibular system is initially processed in the inner ear via structures called the semi-circular canals, the utricle, and the saccule. The semi-circular canals have fluid that moves as your head moves in various positions or spins in a circle, helping us stay balanced. The utricle and saccule are sensitive to linear movement and our relationship to gravity. The cerebellum (located in the back of the brain) uses vestibular input to help with balance, muscle tone, and motor control. The sensorimotor area of the brain uses information from the vestibular system to help with motor coordination, posture, and position in space.

The vestibular system also helps regulate our attention and arousal level by way of the reticular activating system (RAS) in the brain stem. We activate this system all the time without realizing it. For example, when you are bored in a meeting and start to doze off, swiveling in your chair or bouncing your knee helps you to regain focus and wake up your brain. Both of these actions involve the vestibular system.

Oral

Oral input is what we taste and smell, such as a teacher's perfume or lotion, body odor from other peers, the woody taste of a recorder in music class, a peer's pickle sandwich at lunch, rubber balls in PE class, a mealy apple, or an air freshener in the bathroom.

Olfactory input, or what we smell, is processed in the frontal lobe. **Gustatory input,** or what we taste, is processed in the parietal lobe near the sensorimotor area. Both of these systems are incredibly stimulating, which is why eating is one of the most complex and intense sensory experiences—and we do it at least three times per day!

Olfactory input: what we smell.

In addition to taste and smell, there is a large amount of proprioceptive input that is involved in putting something into our mouth. Research has shown that chewing gum *prior to* taking a test can briefly enhance performance in certain cognitive areas by raising cortisol levels to counteract stress. However, chewing gum *during* a test can actually distract the brain from the task at hand.[10] Have you ever seen athletes chewing aggressively on their mouth guards? That, too, is to help maintain an appropriate level of arousal.

Gustatory input: what we taste.

Interoception

Interoception is our ability to detect our internal needs, such as going to the bathroom, identifying hunger, knowing when to put on a sweater for recess, or taking a break in PE when overheated.

Interoception is often called the "hidden sense." This includes recognizing signals for breathing, heart rate, hunger, thirst, temperature changes, tiredness, and the need to urinate or have a bowel movement. *Interoception allows us to detect that something is off and then address that need in the near future. It is something we often take for granted and often overlook in students who struggle with this.* For example, students may be unnecessarily chastised for not going to the bathroom before class starts, not being able to "hold it," complaining of being too hot when the room seems comfortable, demanding water because they are "so, so thirsty" even though they just came back from the drinking fountain, or not eating anything all day long.

Many of our interoceptive cues are communicated to the brain via the vagus nerve. When we have physiological needs that must be met, the vagus nerve sends signals to help those needs get met in order to keep the autonomic nervous system in balance. Thus, when we are regulated and attending to our bodies, we can adequately respond to our internal signals. When we are anxious, overworked, or depressed, our brain shifts focus from meeting the needs of our interoceptive system in order to regulate our arousal. Think about a time you were nervous before a big presentation: after you finished, you were famished from not eating all afternoon but didn't realize it until that moment. However, if we are in a constant state of distress, as are some students, interoceptive signals are altered, which can result in physical symptoms, such as stomach aches, diarrhea, constipation, headaches, rapid heartbeat, or daytime wetting.[11]

Research continues to emerge on the strong connection between our emotions and physiological responses, which is why sometimes we can confuse our emotions with interoceptive needs.[12] "Hangry" (hungry + angry) is a great example of this. When our blood sugar drops as a result of not meeting our need to eat, we can become easily irritated. We may appear to be angry when we're actually just hungry. *Making sure students have all their interoceptive needs met is therefore very important for the process of learning and regulation.* They are not something that should be dismissed, put on hold, or used as an incentive ("if you do this, then you can have a snack, use the bathroom, or get a glass of water").

Interoceptive input: what our internal organs are feeling.

Reflective Activity

Think back to your preschool, elementary, or junior high classroom and recall the sensory environment. Was there a class pet that brought a strong odor to the room? Did the teacher like to play music in the background? Were the chairs hard and uncomfortable?

Now think about your current classroom as a teacher. What artwork and posters are on the walls? Is there natural light from the windows? How often do students get up to move around? Are there sensory experiences that students often complain about?

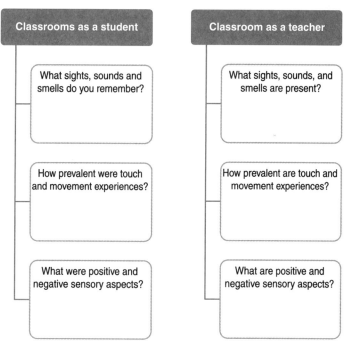

Classrooms as a student	Classroom as a teacher
What sights, sounds and smells do you remember?	What sights, sounds, and smells are present?
How prevalent were touch and movement experiences?	How prevalent are touch and movement experiences?
What were positive and negative sensory aspects?	What are positive and negative sensory aspects?

FACILITATING SENSORY INTEGRATION FOR MORE ENGAGED LEARNING

Now that we've navigated all the sensory systems, how they present in classroom situations, and their importance in a learning environment, it is important to consider how you can facilitate sensory integration

Reflective Activity

Not all activities in your classroom will be relaxing for your students. However, it's important to have a balance between tasks that may be more stimulating and stressful, and activities that may be less stimulating and calming. Use this chart to think about activities you do that are stressful and relaxing. Think about how to achieve a better balance, considering the strategies listed below.

Stressful Sensory Activities

_____
_____
_____

_____
_____
_____

Relaxing Sensory Activities

 Available for download at **resources.corwin.com/ClassroomBehaviors**

in your classroom. While each of the sensory systems has a unique and "differentiated" role, it is critical for all the systems to be integrated and "linked," just as the interpersonal neurobiology framework suggests. When a student has strong sensory integration that produces efficient motor movements, engaged social interaction, and effective regulation, learning can then be maximized. Here are a few strategies you, as teachers, can incorporate into your classrooms in order to promote sensory integration. Remember that these strategies must be embedded within a positive relationship that incorporates supportive language, attunement to each student's individual needs, and understanding of nonverbal cues. They also demand that you are in tune with the nonverbal cues and behaviors of your students—something that you may do naturally without even realizing it.

Strategy 1: Celebrate Movement

It seems that students these days are so wiggly! This can be attributed to an amalgamation of less outdoor play time, more screen time, more structured activities, and longer school days.[1] We imagine that it's exhausting for teachers to remind students to sit down, sit correctly, and keep hands to themselves repeatedly. Rather than constantly combating a student's need for movement, try leaning into this need instead—just as Mr. Jones did with Catalina's need to touch something.

A. Jean Ayers, PhD, known as the mother of sensory integration, targeted the vestibular, tactile, and proprioceptive systems in her study and research of sensory processing starting in the 1970s. She recognized these systems as the main senses that inform us about our body and set the foundation for development, learning, and regulation. In fact, Dr. Ayers felt that the vestibular system supported and informed all other sensory systems.[13] When a child's movement is restricted, this also restricts the activation of the vestibular sense, resulting in fidgeting, inattention, low arousal, poor motivation, and dysregulation. By allowing students the opportunity to move around the classroom and explore things hands-on, you are not only helping students learn more about themselves and the environment but also helping them better integrate the information learned during the lesson plan.

Brain breaks and movement activities are a highly effective way to integrate movement and touch into the classroom on a regular basis. With the number of recesses and frequency of PE dwindling in schools, it is even more important that students have the means and opportunity to move around in the classroom. In fact, research shows that in schools where students were given more opportunities to play at recess, in-class attention increased, overall behavior improved, and stress was reduced.[1] When movement-based activities are integrated into lesson plans, students show better attention during the lesson and better academic outcomes.[14] Movement also helps increase blood flow to the brain, which in turn increases the capacity of the brain to learn. While many teachers are willing to integrate movement-based activities into their classrooms, they often feel ill-equipped and would like additional training on how to do this effectively.[15] Here are some ideas to get you started. Try just one or two per day to start with, and slowly work up to integrating three to five movement opportunities per day outside of recess and PE.

Supportive Diagram

It is important to know the age-appropriate sustained attention spans for your students so that your expectations match developmental expectations. Knowing developmentally appropriate attention spans may help reduce your frustration and enhance your understanding of your students' needs, ultimately helping you to be more regulated as well. Inserting a movement-based activity in between periods of attending can help to "reset" your students' brains and bodies for improved learning.

4-year-olds = 8 to 12 minutes	6-year-olds = 12 to 18 minutes	8-year-olds = 16-24 minutes	10-year-olds = 20 to 30 minutes	12-year-olds = 24 to 36 minutes

NOTE: Active-Play, Active-Learning, a program funded by the Michael & Susan Dell Center for Healthy Living, also has physically active, fun strategies for brain breaks that can be integrated into various aspects of learning.[16]

When are good times for movement?

- At the beginning of the day
- Before starting any new demanding, or academically challenging activity
- After a long period (more than 20–30 minutes) of seated learning
- Before transitioning to a new classroom or new subject
- While waiting in line
- When you notice your students need a break

What are good movement activities?
Short duration (less than 2 minutes)

- Chair push-ups
- Wall push-ups
- Jumping jacks
- Windmills

- Stretches—hands, fingers, arms, legs, back, neck
- "Head, Shoulders, Knees, and Toes" song
- Deep breathing while placing your hand on different body parts
- Body squeezes
- "Tense and Release"

Medium duration (2–5 minutes)

- Yoga
- "Shake Your Sillies Out"
- "GoNoodle" songs
- Dance break
- Freeze dance
- Pass a ball around the class (while standing at their chairs or in a circle)
- March around the class
- "Simon Says"

Long duration (more than 5 minutes)

- Yoga
- Make a "rain storm" (using your hands and feet)
- "Pass the beat" (e.g., clap, clap, stomp, stomp) around the class
- Human knot challenge
- Classroom scavenger hunt

In addition to these more structured activities, set up guidelines for other student-led, movement-based options in the classroom. This can not only empower the students but also give them more independence and bolster your trust in them.

- Let students sit where they choose for silent reading.
- Allow students to make choices about flexible seating.
- Assign student responsibilities each day: taking attendance, passing out papers, collecting papers, getting out classroom-based journals or notebooks, picking up scraps, setting the activity timer, and erasing the board.
- Give students the option to stand if needed after a certain period of time (e.g., 20 minutes).
- Provide a bin of appropriate fidgets that students can access.

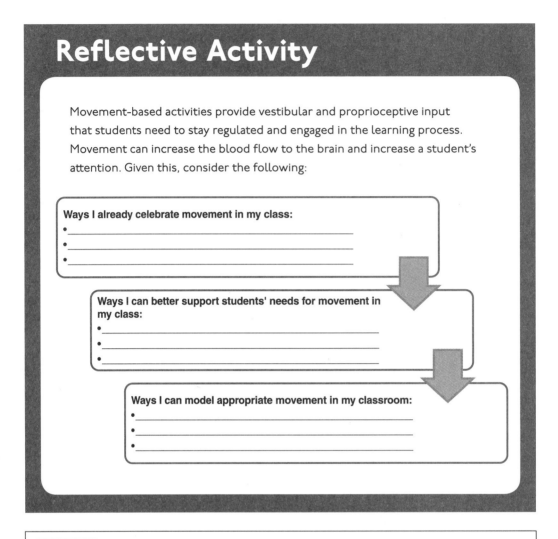

Reflective Activity

Movement-based activities provide vestibular and proprioceptive input that students need to stay regulated and engaged in the learning process. Movement can increase the blood flow to the brain and increase a student's attention. Given this, consider the following:

Ways I already celebrate movement in my class:
- _____
- _____
- _____

Ways I can better support students' needs for movement in my class:
- _____
- _____
- _____

Ways I can model appropriate movement in my classroom:
- _____
- _____
- _____

online resources Available for download at **resources.corwin.com/ClassroomBehaviors**

Strategy 2: Create a Sensory Nook

Sometimes we all need a break or an escape—a chance to step away for a bit before diving back into a demanding task. By creating a safe place in your classroom where students can go when they feel dysregulated, they will not only feel supported but also learn ways to use sensory input in order to re-regulate. This space must not be used in a punitive way or as a reward, as we mentioned in Chapter 3. A sensory nook, or cozy corner, is a tool to help students get their autonomic nervous system into balance, so they can better participate in the learning experience. In the opening vignette, Mr. Jones could have easily used a sensory nook with Catalina to help her transition into the classroom in the morning or to help her regulate after challenging activities. At first, students may need to spend more time here or access the sensory nook more frequently. Over time, as they feel safe and have been given appropriate challenges, they won't require spending as much time here. As noted in Chapter 1, learning cannot occur when a child is dysregulated or disengaged, so spending more time at his desk will not be beneficial until he is regulated.

Here are some things every sensory nook should include:

- Comfortable seating, such as large pillows, bean bag chairs, or a padded rocking chair
- A canopy, or tent, to minimize the amount of fluorescent light in the area (or you can simply remove the fluorescent light tube from above the sensory nook)
- Opportunities to engage the proprioceptive system, such as stress balls, squishy pillows, geoboard with rubber bands, chalkboards with chalk, and/or a donut therapy ball
- Noise-cancelling headphones to filter out auditory input
- Calming visual opportunities like picture books, a glitter jar, night light projector, and/or a fish tank (real or LED-based)
- A visual cue, with corresponding instructions as needed, such as a poster to prompt students in taking three deep breaths
- A visual schedule and an image of the "zones of regulation" to help facilitate communication with the student and an understanding of the student's state of arousal

Signs that students may need to access the sensory nook:

- A change in affect, attention, or arousal level that is negatively impacting the learning experience (for either that student or the students around him)
- When transitioning into the classroom or between activities in the classroom is challenging
- The student is displaying behaviors that are atypical, suggesting increased dysregulation for any number of reasons (e.g., not enough sleep, did not eat breakfast, dad left on a business trip, mom just had a baby, etc.)
- Emotional dysregulation in the form of crying, early signs of frustration, worry, making comments such as "I'm not good enough," or "I'm never going to get it." Saying mean things, or threatening to throw things or to hit/kick others

Supportive Diagram

A sensory nook is a safe space where students can go in order to calm down before engaging in the learning process. When a student is more regulated, she will be better able to take in information and access higher cognitive skills. It is important to include calming activities for a variety of the sensory systems, such as pillows, stress balls, noise-cancelling headphones, and picture books.

Image Source: Created by Hunt Dougherty

- When a student becomes withdrawn, has difficulty communicating, puts her head down on the desk, or begins to isolate herself
- The student specifically requests to use the space

Strategy 3: Use Multisensory Learning Experiences

By bringing different sensory elements into everyday classroom lessons and activities, you can not only enhance your students' integration of sensory input but also enhance your students' learning experiences. All students learn differently, and we need to embrace that fact. *Classroom instruction tends to favor auditory and visual inputs, yet tactile, vestibular, and proprioceptive inputs are just as important for making new neurological connections*. These multisensory learning experiences will also help with the "top-to-bottom" or vertical integration of the brain that we discussed in the Chapter 1. This vertical integration allows our emotions, sensory experiences, motor actions, and cognitive functions to all work together, strengthening each area and allowing for more complex thinking. You can get creative in how you weave sensory activities into your classroom curriculum, and you may be using many of these currently. Here are a few examples to get you started or to help you build on what you're already doing:

Math:

- Play hopscotch when adding, subtracting, multiplying, or dividing numbers and have students record their answers on a sheet of paper.
- Roll dice to do multiplication tables, squares, greater than/ less than, adding numbers, subtracting numbers.
- Use dominoes to do greater than/less than, adding numbers, subtracting numbers, multiplying numbers, and dividing numbers.
- In pairs, roll a ball back and forth or use a zoom ball to complete multiplication tables.
- Use fun tactile manipulatives as counters, such as mini porcupine balls, cotton balls, pasta shapes, or stickers.
- Use dot art markers for counting, adding, subtracting, multiplying, or dividing.
- Create "math facts" songs or poems—you can do this individually as a teacher, in small groups, or as a whole classroom.
- Do math facts while playing clapping games.
- Put math flashcards in a bin of rice, sand, beans, or dried pasta, and then have each student draw out a flashcard and give the answer (you can do this as a whole classroom or in small groups with different tactile bins and have students rotate).
- Trace math facts "in the air" with your finger.
- In small groups, have students complete math facts with their bodies (e.g., one student makes his body into the number 1, one student makes her body into a plus sign, one student makes her body into the number 2, one student makes his body into an equal sign, and one student makes his body into the number 3).

- Explore the classroom to find different shapes and/or examples of symmetry.
- Play math bowling: put a number on the bottom of each bowling pin and have students roll a ball to knock down the pins. The small group can work together to solve the math problem (e.g., add all the numbers, subtract all the numbers).

Reading:

- Listen to an audiobook while following along in a written book.
- Have the student stand up when reading aloud in class.
- Have the student hold something tactile (stuffed animal, stress ball, fidget toy) when it is his turn to read.
- Sit or stand in different places in the room during silent reading.
- Play classical music in the background during silent reading.
- Stomp, clap, or tap along to word syllables.
- Pair each sight word with a movement.
- Play reading bowling: put a sight word or vocabulary word on the bottom of each bowling pin and have students roll a ball to knock down the pins. The small group can work together to read the words and/or define the words..

Spelling and Writing:

- Sit or stand in different places in the room.
- Draw a picture to go along with what you wrote.
- Use thought bubbles, idea charts, and graphic organizers.
- Break up into groups and act out journal responses, essay outlines, and narrative ideas.
- Use different pencil colors for different drafts of writings or different writing assignments.
- Use individual dry erase boards with dry erase crayons (or individual chalkboards with chalk).
- Trace letters or spell out words "in the air" using a finger.
- Do "yoga writing" by making different letters with your body.
- Do spelling activities with magnetic letters.
- Find and cut out spelling words from magazines—then glue them onto paper to make them into a sentence.

- In pairs, roll a ball back and forth or use a zoom ball to spell out different words.

NOTE: The Learning Without Tears[17] curriculum has a variety of multisensory activities that can be integrated into writing and spelling activities.

Social Studies and History:

- Create maps and map keys using different craft materials, such as yarn, tissue paper, glitter (every teacher's favorite!), sequins, and pom poms.
- Bring in compasses and have groups of students follow a set of compass directions to reach an end goal/prize.
- Encourage students to reference a globe when talking about geography.
- Show pictures and play sounds from different geographic regions.
- Have each student cut out an individual state and work as a class to create a map of the United States.
- Use "dress up" as a way to have students emulate famous people in history.
- Act out important stories in history after reading about them.
- Put important dates or events on flashcards and have students place them in order or match them up.

These are just a few strategies to get you thinking about using sensory input in your classrooms. The activities above are ways to enhance learning experiences and facilitate a more integrated, regulated brain for all of your students. Including just one multisensory learning opportunity per class period will do wonders for your students! In the next chapter, we will explore sensory preferences and sensory processing differences in more depth, as well as provide you with more specific classroom sensory accommodations.

Interactive Scenario

Read each scenario and consider the behavior each student is demonstrating. Based on the strategies listed above, think about how to support the student's sensory need within the classroom in order to facilitate more regulated, engaged learning.

(Continued)

(Continued)

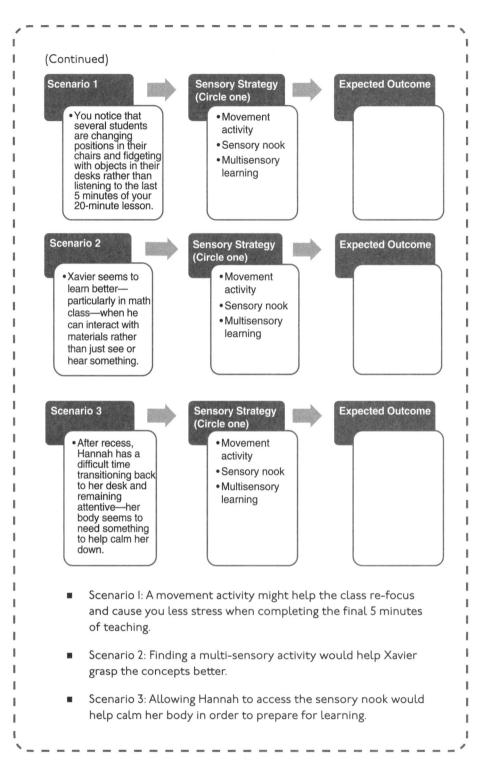

Scenario 1	Sensory Strategy (Circle one)	Expected Outcome
• You notice that several students are changing positions in their chairs and fidgeting with objects in their desks rather than listening to the last 5 minutes of your 20-minute lesson.	• Movement activity • Sensory nook • Multisensory learning	

Scenario 2	Sensory Strategy (Circle one)	Expected Outcome
• Xavier seems to learn better—particularly in math class—when he can interact with materials rather than just see or hear something.	• Movement activity • Sensory nook • Multisensory learning	

Scenario 3	Sensory Strategy (Circle one)	Expected Outcome
• After recess, Hannah has a difficult time transitioning back to her desk and remaining attentive—her body seems to need something to help calm her down.	• Movement activity • Sensory nook • Multisensory learning	

- Scenario 1: A movement activity might help the class re-focus and cause you less stress when completing the final 5 minutes of teaching.

- Scenario 2: Finding a multi-sensory activity would help Xavier grasp the concepts better.

- Scenario 3: Allowing Hannah to access the sensory nook would help calm her body in order to prepare for learning.

CHAPTER 5

Building a Sensory Smart Classroom

"He [the child] brings into this room the impact of all the shapes and sounds and colors and movements, and rebuilds his world, reduced to a size he can handle."
—Virginia M. Axline in *Dibs: In Search of Self*

Evan was a curious learner who enjoyed going to school to be with his friends and participate in math class. His parents would often boast about his math abilities, more so in amazement because both of them had masters degrees in fine arts and disliked math in school. It therefore came as a surprise when Evan's second grade teacher told his parents that he was struggling to complete his work on time, particularly in math class. "He seems to just stare off into space and needs constant verbal redirection to keep working," said Ms. Prescott. "I don't know if he's bored or has attention difficulties or just doesn't feel like doing the work." That was even more intriguing to Evan's parents because often he would independently complete his math homework first without any signs of distraction. Being a curious learner herself, Ms. Prescott thought it appropriate to further investigate this situation after feedback from the parents.

After considering Evan's math abilities, which were slightly above average for his age, and his eager engagement in group instruction, she started to think more about the environment. At home, come to find out, Evan completed his homework at the formal dining room table sitting in a chair that faced a wall with only two simple paintings: an apple next to a bell and a wine bottle next to a clock. However, Ms. Prescott, being the exuberant teacher that she is, decorated her room with multiplication tables, geometric shapes, top math students of the week, clocks from the different time zones, and various projects students had completed throughout the year on the walls. Hanging from the ceiling, to make learning more exciting, were all the math operations. Maybe Evan wasn't bored or disengaged after all—maybe he was just distracted by all the visual input in the room?

Ms. Prescott decided to do an experiment. She had also recently run across a research article in the doctor's office that suggested students may learn better with less visual stimulation on the walls.[1] Sure enough, when she removed some of the artwork from the walls, left up only the most recent student projects, and took down the hanging objects, not only Evan but also all the other students seemed more engaged and focused when doing independent work. The visual sensory input was too difficult for most students to filter out, and in particular was difficult for Evan. Had Ms. Prescott not examined "why" Evan was having difficulty in math class, she would have continued to think Evan had behavioral issues.

This is just one example of how sensory input impacts learning. There are many different sensory systems in addition to the visual system that can influence how a student takes in information about the world. *Sometimes one sensory input can positively impact learning through providing a means of regulation while another sensory input can negatively impact learning through causing dysregulation. And all students respond differently to different types of sensory inputs.* So how do you, as a teacher, recognize and balance the sensory needs of every student in the classroom?

SENSORY PREFERENCES AND SENSORY PROCESSING DISORDER— WHAT'S THE DIFFERENCE?

We all have preferences for different sensory inputs—these preferences can help to regulate us or can cause us to become dysregulated. However, with a sensory preference, the response is typically adaptive and does not result in a fight, flight, or freeze moment. Your sensory preferences impact how you take in information, whether you tend to be more extroverted or introverted, your learning style, and the activities in which you engage. We tend to shy away from sensory input that is more challenging for us to process and lean into sensory input that we process more readily. For example, a child who prefers auditory input might enjoy engaging in conversation, have an interest for music, and like audio books. A student like Evan who can get overwhelmed with a large amount of visual input might prefer to wear sunglasses inside, read books with a bookmark to follow along, and like to sit in the front of the classroom.

Sensory preferences may impact your arousal level differently at different points in the day, even if it's the same activity. One of the authors, Jamie, has a preference for vestibular input and likes to be moving throughout the day. She sometimes goes for a run in the morning to increase her arousal level before starting the day. At other times she goes for a run in the afternoon to relieve stress, which ultimately decreases her arousal level. While Jamie likes to be active, this preference for vestibular input never impacted her ability to focus in the classroom or attend to homework assignments. On the flip side, Jamie does not prefer auditory input. After a long day at work, she likes to have 10 to 15 minutes of quiet time to decompress—no TV, no radio, no music. She does not like loud environments such as concerts or Times Square. She enjoys reading a book over listening to a podcast and finds loud trucks outside to be jarring. Yet she can participate in all these activities without becoming dysregulated or stressed.

It is important to consider how your sensory preferences as a teacher may impact your students' regulation. Does your preference for visual input—bright colors and fun designs—cause a student to become easily distracted, like Evan? Does your preference for low amounts of auditory input cause a deafening silence that actually makes it hard for students to focus? Do you get easily agitated when students crowd around you at circle time because the tactile input is too much?

The way you manipulate the sensory environment can influence your students' state of regulation and engagement. This might look different at different times of the day. Low lights, calm music, and yoga might be a good choice after transitioning into the classroom from lunch and

Sensory preference: sensory input(s) that you tend to rely on more heavily when interacting with the environment, processing information, and learning.

Reflective Activity

Look at the chart below to determine your sensory preferences. Reflect on how these preferences may enhance or inhibit the learning environment. Consider how these preferences impact certain students in your classroom who have specific sensory needs.

Tactile	Visual	Auditory	Vestibular/ Proprioceptive	Gustatory/ Olfactory
• Fidget with something • Twist your hair • Tap on the table with a pen or fingers • Rub on your arms • Rub your hands together • Integrate hands-on activities into the classroom	• Keep the blinds open • Turn all the lights on all day • Hang bright artwork and posters on the wall • Use multicolor pens or markers when writing • Don't mind clutter on the desk • Integrate videos into the classroom	• Play music in the background when working • Keep the window open • Talk loudly and with enthusiasm • Integrate audio books or video clips into teaching material	• Move around the classroom during instruction periods • Doodle on papers or on the board • Shift positions in your chair • Integrate movement-based activities into the classroom	• Wear perfume or cologne • Bite on nails • Eat snacks in the classroom • Drink coffee, tea, or water in the classroom • Chew on your pen when writing

recess. Lights on, upbeat music, and short movement bursts might be a good choice before the final class of the day. As you get to know your students and classroom dynamics better, you will likely find some patterns of what sensory input is necessary at certain times during the day.

Supportive Diagram

Recognizing the difference between calming and alerting sensory inputs is the first step in understanding how you can help manage the regulation in your students simply by changing their environment. Look at the lists below and consider which sensory inputs would be beneficial at certain points in the school day.

Calming Sensory Inputs	Alerting Sensory Inputs
• Quiet, instrumental music	• Loud, fast-paced music
• Lavender, chamomile, eucalyptus, and jasmine essential oils	• Mint, orange, and cinnamon essential oils
• Deep pressure inputs (hugs, body squeezes, weighted objects)	• Light touch (tickling, brushing against the skin, scratchy textures)
• Rubbing a soft object	• Sour and spicy foods like pickles, lemonade, sour candy, flaming Cheetos, Takis, and red hots
• Chewy foods like gum, fruit leather, dried fruit, beef jerky, and granola bars	• Spinning in a circle or going upside-down
• Rocking back and forth	• Flourescent lights and direct sunlight
• Low lighting and natural sunlight	• Fast, ever-changing visual stimulation (TV, videos, people moving around)
• Slow, repeated visual stimulation (lava lamp, fish tank, starry globe)	
• Warm room temperature	• Cold room temperature

In contrast, children and adults with **sensory processing disorder** (SPD) process sensory input in ways that are not adaptive, meaning the sensory input interferes with their daily activities, causing a functional level of impairment.[2] With some children, SPD causes a fight, flight, or freeze response almost every time, sending out a signal of distress that communicates, "I can't do this!" or "This is not safe!" This is more than just a preference—the neurological system is not appropriately processing sensory information to the degree of dysregulation. For example, a child who seeks proprioceptive input may hug peers too hard without realizing it, resulting in loss of friendships; a child who is sensitive to tactile input may be constantly distracted by how her shoes feel on her feet to the point of removing them,

Sensory processing disorder: neurological difference in the way that the brain takes in, responds to, and uses sensory information that results in an inappropriate response.

resulting in having to stay inside for recess; a child with auditory sensitivity might cover his ears and hide under his desk when the loudspeaker comes on, resulting in missing out on part of the lesson plan. An estimated 5 percent to 16 percent of children have SPD, with boys at a higher prevalence than girls.[3] Because of research done at University of California San Francisco (UCSF), we now have tangible evidence of differences in how neurotypical children process sensory input versus children with SPD.[4,5] Researchers at UCSF found differences in white matter connectivity, which is responsible for relaying sensory messages in the brain, for children with SPD compared with children without SPD.[5] In addition, we know that some children with SPD have higher sympathetic response (fight or flight) and lower parasympathetic response (calming)—this means they more readily perceive sensory stimuli as threatening and require a longer period of time to regulate afterward. Also, children with SPD may habituate too slowly or too quickly to sensory stimuli, meaning that they require more exposure than others to "get used to" certain sensory inputs and respond appropriately.[6,7]

Children who are hypersensitive to sensory input, for example, take longer than their neurotypical peers to habituate to the same stimuli over time, so their threat response systems get activated each time they're back in that situation. After several exposures to those negative situations, the brain begins to anticipate the threat, thereby heightening the stress response even more. Sometimes this means the child will run away from a situation, avoid a sensory experience, or become easily distracted. This is a similar pattern that happens when a child experiences trauma. They cannot be "talked through" the situation or "reasoned with" because access to the higher-level thinking (cognitive cortex) has been blocked by the stress response. *This is not behavioral—the behaviors are an outpouring of an attempt to do whatever necessary to get back to a regulated state. These children often experience a stress response on a more frequent and more intense basis, and they can remain in elevated states of stress for longer periods of time than neurotypical children. Co-regulation in the form of the teacher-student dyad is therefore extremely important for children with SPD, as is removal of the child from the environment that is causing dysregulation.*

Typically, when people think about sensory processing, they think about kids who get overstimulated to the point where they exhibit severe anxiety, avoidance behaviors, and attention issues. But what about the children who are understimulated? Or the children who

Supportive Diagram

Often, sensory-related dysregulation results in physiological changes—changes to the body and its functions—or behavioral changes. These anomalous changes are often reflected in signs and symptoms that can be seen by other people, not just internal changes in the person who is dysregulated. Recognizing these distress signs is a critical piece in helping a student with SPD get back to a regulated state, as facilitated by the co-regulation between you and the student.

Signs and Symptoms of Sensory-Related Distress:	
• Hands over ears	• Sweating
• Rubbing eyes	• Heavy breathing
• Tuning out	• Wide eyes
• Refusal to separate from caregiver	• Disorganized behavior
• Irritability	• Aggressive behavior
• Avoidance of social interactions	• Poor frustration tolerance
• Rigid behaviors	• Stubbornness
• Uncontrollable meltdowns	• Physical withdrawal
• Anxiety	• Increased or anxious talking
	• Yawning

cannot differentiate between inputs? Or the children who just seem uncoordinated? In 2007, a new model for sensory processing was developed in order to better categorize SPD.[3] From this model, we see that sensory processing can be broken down into three categories: sensory modulation, sensory discrimination, and Sensory-based motor disorder. Generally, sensory processing concerns do not occur in isolation: if there's an issue in one sensory pattern or subset, there's likely another that is out of balance.[3]

Sensory modulation is the brain's ability to adjust the response to incoming sensory input in order to maintain an appropriate arousal level. With sensory modulation disorder, the brain has a difficult time with sensing, regulating, and/or habituating to sensory input, which results in an atypical physiological response.

Supportive Diagram

Sensory Processing Disorder (SPD) can be broken down into distinct categories that help to better understand how a student might be responding to sensory input. Understanding these categories is an important first step in helping to support a student's sensory needs within the classroom.

```
                    ┌─────────────┐
                    │   Sensory   │
                    │ Processing  │
                    │  Disorder   │
                    └─────────────┘
        ┌──────────────────┼──────────────────┐
┌─────────────┐    ┌─────────────┐    ┌─────────────┐
│   Sensory   │    │   Sensory   │    │Sensory-Based│
│ Modulation  │    │Discrimination│   │Motor Disorder│
│  Disorder   │    │  Disorder   │    │             │
└─────────────┘    └─────────────┘    └─────────────┘
      │                                      │
   ┌──────────────┐                   ┌─────────────┐
   │   Sensory    │                   │  Postural   │
   │Hyposensitivity│                  │ Instability │
   └──────────────┘                   └─────────────┘
      │                                      │
   ┌──────────────┐                   ┌─────────────┐
   │   Sensory    │                   │  Dyspraxia  │
   │Hypersensitivity│                 │             │
   └──────────────┘                   └─────────────┘
      │
   ┌──────────────┐
   │Sensory Craving│
   └──────────────┘
```

Adapted from Miller et al. (2007). [3]

- Children who are *hyposensitive (i.e., underresponsive)* require *more* of a certain stimulus in order for their brains to detect that something changed in their environment. They are less sensitive, have a high tolerance, and habituate quickly to sensory input. A child who takes multiple prompts to respond to his name, for example, may be hyposensitive to auditory input. A child who does not realize she is bleeding after falling at recess may be hyposensitive to tactile input. A child who slouches in his chair and has a low arousal level may be hyposensitive to vestibular input.

- Children who are *hypersensitive (i.e., overresponsive)* to sensory input require *less* of a certain stimulus in order for their brains to detect that something changed in their environment. They are more sensitive, have a low tolerance, and habituate slowly to sensory input. A child who must wash her hands immediately after touching glue, or otherwise a meltdown will ensue, may be hypersensitive to tactile input. A child who covers his ears at an assembly or starts running around the classroom when it is loud may be hypersensitive to auditory input. A child who refuses to try any of the school lunches may be hypersensitive to oral input.

- *Sensory craving* is reflected in children who seek sensory input in a way that causes more dysregulation. They are not necessarily more or less sensitive or have difficulty with habituation; they just have an insatiable need for sensory input. A child who runs his hands through the sand over and over again at recess to the point of getting excited may crave tactile input. A child who constantly changes positions in his chair without ever being able to focus may crave vestibular input. A child who makes noises to herself constantly throughout the day may crave auditory input.

Sensory discrimination is the brain's ability to differentiate one sensory input from another sensory input and interpret the meaning of that sensory input. Children with sensory discrimination disorder have difficulty telling the difference between sensory stimuli or using the information from stimuli in a functional manner. For example, telling the difference between a pencil and a marker by only using the sense of touch (i.e., not looking) requires tactile discrimination. If a child does not have proper tactile discrimination, she may want to empty the entire contents of her backpack to find a pencil on the bottom because she cannot adequately do this by just using her sense of touch. Usually, but not always, sensory discrimination disorder co-occurs with sensory modulation disorder because the child is either not detecting enough of that input in order to differentiate it (hyposensitive) or responding to an input in such a heightened way that they cannot differentiate it (hypersensitive).

Sensory-based motor skills—praxis and postural stability—require the integration of our tactile, proprioceptive, and vestibular systems in order to perform various actions with our body and manipulate other objects. If any one of these systems is out of balance, there is a good likelihood that some form of praxis or postural stability will be challenging.

- Postural stability serves as our foundation of support. We must have adequate proximal (i.e., close to the body) stability in order to manipulate objects away from our body. For example, a child might have poor handwriting because maintaining a stable position in the chair is taking up so much energy or focus (more about this in Chapter 7). Or he may flop all over the rug during circle time because he cannot support himself to sit in an upright position. Or she may avoid the swings for fear she will fall off from not having good enough postural support.

- Praxis is the ability to come up with an idea, plan out a motor sequence for that idea, and execute that motor plan to achieve a goal. Children who have dyspraxia require more time and energy to carry out tasks that seem routine. They might not "catch on" as quickly or might do things "awkwardly." For example, when putting on socks, they must think about how wide they need to open the sock, how much force is required, how they need to balance their body to bring their foot up to put on the sock, which way the sock needs to be oriented in relationship to the toes, etc. This takes a lot of work—and that's just one small part of their day! Frequently children with praxis difficulties are reported to be "uncoordinated," "lazy," taught basic things that seem to come naturally to others, take a long time to make decisions ("he can never decide what he wants"), perform tasks inconsistently ("she *can* do it but most of the time she wants me to do it"), and/or throw tantrums or get frustrated easily. Because children with dyspraxia often experience failure with motor-based activities, they can become avoidant, perfectionists, anxious, or controlling, all in an attempt to protect themselves from getting dysregulated.

As you can see, the processing of sensory input is critical to how we respond, interact, move, and regulate. Everybody needs a different amount of sensory input to elicit the optimal arousal level and be able to perform tasks. Too much sensory input can make us over-aroused (red zone), and too little sensory input can make us under-aroused (blue zone). Staying regulated occurs when we achieve an optimal, "just right" arousal level and can effectively handle the demands

Supportive Diagram

Recognizing the difference between sensory preferences and sensory processing disorder (SPD) can help you identify the ways the sensory environment of the classroom impacts certain students, and to what degree those students may need support. Monitoring both sensory preferences and SPD in your classroom will help your students to achieve "just right" nervous system arousal for improved attention and learning.

Sensory Preference
- Adaptive response to sensory input
- Sensory input you rely on in order to take in information and learn
- Impacts arousal level but does not elicit fight, flight, or freeze response

Sensory Processing Disorder
- Maladaptive processing of sensory input
- Impairs function and participation, including classroom learning
- Often causes "fight, fight, or freeze" response

placed on us while a variety of sensory inputs are present. This is only possible when the brain effectively organizes incoming sensory input. We will explore how this applies to each of the sensory systems later in the chapter.

RECOGNIZING DIFFERENT SCHOOL-BASED SENSORY NEEDS

Schools and classrooms are the ultimate environments for sensory input. Not to mention every classroom has its unique sensory experiences. Adapting to all these sensory experiences throughout the day can be challenging for many students, especially on top of the learning and social demands of each day. As teachers, you can help to lessen the stress and dysregulation that students experience in response to sensory inputs by making alterations to your classroom setup and providing access to certain accommodations.

Typically, an SPD does not emerge spontaneously—there is a history since infancy or toddlerhood. However, stress, added demands, and life transitions can all contribute to an increase in various sensory-related behaviors. This is because when the neurological system is already under duress from trying to process different sensory input, the window of tolerance is already quite narrow. The child may be able to curb some of this duress at times, but when additional stress is added to the nervous system, this becomes increasingly challenging, and sensory input becomes that much more dysregulating. Not surprisingly, school is one of the places where children experience additional stress and added demands, so behaviors related to sensory processing differences are not uncommon.

As a reminder, an estimated 5 percent to 16 percent of children have sensory processing differences; in a class of 30 students that means between one and four students may have an SPD. Not to mention nearly 90 percent of children with Autism also have some form of SPD, and between 40 percent and 60 percent of children with attention deficit hyperactivity disorder have SPD.[5,8] Research also suggests that children who are gifted tend to be more sensitive to the sensory environment, making them more vulnerable to a stress response.[9] This means it is highly likely that at least a handful of students will benefit from sensory-based accommodations. As we mentioned before, even children without a diagnosis of SPD will have sensory preferences that impact their learning, just like all adults do as well!

It is important to recognize that children with an SPD often try to impose more control in many areas of life because their bodies and the environment feel so out of control to them. This need for control and rigidity is their way of establishing a safe, predictable world that they can trust. Patience, understanding, and flexibility on your part, as a teacher, are therefore very important. As mentioned in Chapter 4, a positive teacher-student dyad can impact the way a student responds to his sensory environment. For students with SPDs, the effect of a stable, trusting relationship is heightened when the sensory environment feels safe and predictable. Even if your personal perceptions do not match their sensory experiences, it is important to listen, acknowledge their feelings, engage in shared attention, and then problem solve what to do next. The following are strategies that you can use in your classroom to identify, understand, and respond to different sensory preferences and SPDs.

Strategy 1: Check the A's

Just as it is important for you to monitor your nonverbals in order to promote regulation, as we outlined in Chapter 2, it is important for you to monitor the nonverbal cues from your students. As noted, this attunement to students' nonverbal cues helps you to better understand what each student is attempting to communicate. It allows you to search for the "why" and begin to explore what might be underneath each student's behavior. Students who are more susceptible to changes in sensory input typically respond by changing their *atten*-tion, *a*ffect, or *a*rousal level. By asking questions about each "A," you can check-in with students' sensory preferences and sensory processing differences.

- **Change in attention:** this is the level of interest or engagement the student displays.
  - Is the student checking out of or not focused on the situation? This could be a sign that the student is overstimulated (yellow zone or red zone) and looking for a way out or could be a sign that the student is understimulated and needing more input to engage (blue zone).
  - Is the student looking around the room, daydreaming, or seemingly inattentive? This could be a sign that the student is understimulated and needing more input to engage (blue zone) or could be a sign that the student is distracted by other sensory input in the room (yellow zone or red zone) like Evan in Ms. Prescott's room).
  - Is the student hyperattentive? This could be a sign that the student is overstimulated and on high alert (yellow zone or red zone).
  - Is the student more engaged? This could be a sign that the sensory input provided is meeting his/her needs to facilitate better learning (just right zone).
- **Change in affect:** this is the emotion or feeling the student displays.
  - Is the student wide-eyed? This could be a sign that the student is overstimulated and on high alert (yellow zone or red zone).
  - Is the student tense or rigid in movements? This could be a sign that the student is overstimulated and is uncomfortable with the situation (yellow zone or red zone).

- ○ Is the student floppy or clumsy in movements? This could be a sign that the student is understimulated and is not engaged in the situation (blue zone).
- ○ Is the student more relaxed? This could be a sign that the sensory input provided is meeting his/her needs to facilitate better learning (just right zone).
- ○ Is the student smiling and laughing? This could be a sign that the sensory input provided is meeting his/her needs to facilitate better learning (just right zone).
- **Change in arousal level**: this is the level of alertness the student displays.
  - ○ Is the student fleeing from the situation? This could be a sign that the student is overstimulated and needs to escape the situation (yellow zone or red zone).
  - ○ Is the student pushing away from the situation? This could be a sign that the student is overstimulated and does not want to participate because it's too overwhelming (yellow zone or red zone).
  - ○ Is the student getting overly excited or frustrated? This could be a sign that the student is overstimulated and cannot effectively manage his/her emotions (yellow zone or red zone).
  - ○ Is the student becoming more appropriately alert? This could be a sign that the sensory input provided is meeting his/her needs to facilitate better learning (just right zone).
  - ○ Is the student dropping into the blue zone? This could be a sign that the student is overstimulated or understimulated and cannot effectively manage his/her emotions.

Interactive Scenario

Students who are more susceptible to changes in sensory input typically respond by changing their attention, affect, or arousal level. By asking questions about each "A," you can check in with students' sensory preferences and sensory processing differences. Read the short scenarios below and determine which "A" is being impacted by sensory input in the classroom. Remember to keep in mind if the change is positive or negative.

- Beth entered the kindergarten classroom in a happy, relaxed mood after her Mom dropped her off.
- When singing songs during morning circle time, Beth kept looking around the room at other students and often turned to look at the door to the hallway.

- Paulo expressed that he was eager for lunch and recess, and this was clear in the way that he was fidgeting in his chair and talking out of turn.
- When Paulo returned from recess, he put his lunchbox in his cubby, sat in his chair, and waited for the teacher's instructions.

- Nathaniel walked quietly in line to the third grade assembly and found his seat appropriately in the bleachers.
- Once the lights turned off, music started, and the magic show began, Nathaniel started clapping loudly, cheering raucously, and jumping up and down in the bleachers.

- Bella shared her "Me Museum" project in front of the class with good eye contact to the audience, a relaxed posture, and a bubbly voice.
- After returning to the carpet to sit between two other classmates, Bella seemed rigid and uncomfortable.

- Beth is displaying a negative change in attention, likely due to the auditory input from singing.

- Paulo is displaying a positive change in attention, likely due to receiving the vestibular and proprioceptive input he needed from eating lunch and playing at recess.

- Nathaniel is displaying a negative change in arousal level, likely due to the visual and auditory input present at the assembly.

- Bella is displaying a negative change in affect, likely due to the tactile input from sitting next to peers.

Strategy 2: Recognize and Relate

Once you are in a regulated state, a huge step in recognizing sensory stimulation in the classroom is being aware of the different sensory systems outlined in Chapter 4. With this foundational knowledge, you can explore your own classroom to identify what may be facilitating or hindering the learning of your students. It is important that you are in a regulated state before you engage in this process. *When considering different sensory needs, it is important to look for patterns—when do you see the behavior, how often do you see the behavior, how long does the behavior last, and does the behavior happen in other environments? It is also important to consider when the behavior started and if the behavior has happened in the past.* For some students, on certain days it may be easier to manage the sensory input than on others. You can use the charts below to determine how certain students may be responding to sensory input and if they may need additional support regulating themselves around these inputs.

Visual

Hyposensitivity	Hypersensitivity	Discrimination (visual perception)
• Visual posturing • Complains eyes are tired when looking at a book • Difficulty focusing on a still image; prefers moving images	• Avoids being in a room with bright lights • Squints or rubs eyes when coming in from recess • Difficulty focusing on a detailed picture • Skips math problems • Complains of headaches	• Has trouble differing between letters and/or numbers • Difficulty finding a specified object in a busy/complex picture • Copying from the board is challenging • Poor ability to categorize/sort

Auditory

Hyposensitivity	Hypersensitivity	Discrimination (auditory processing)
• No response to name being called • Must use touch to get child's attention • Makes noises in quiet environments • Seems to "zone out" • Asks for music to be turned on or turned up	• Covers ears • Easily upset in loud environments • Makes noises to drown out other sounds	• Confuses words easily (when speaking or listening) • Poor ability to adjust volume of voice • Difficult time learning new songs • Multi-step directions are challenging

Tactile

Hyposensitivity	Hypersensitivity	Discrimination
• Seeks touching things • Poor personal space • Holds objects in hands • Fidgets with objects • Loves touching shaving cream, sand, paint, glue	• Bothered by messy textures (wants to wash hands) • Anxious when near others • Prefers the back or front of the line • Shies away from social touch	• Must touch everything • Constantly runs hands through same texture • Unable to find something in bottom of backpack without looking • Poor fine motor skills

Proprioceptive

Hyposensitivity	Hypersensitivity	Discrimination
• Slouches when sitting in a chair or on the floor • Seems to always be jumping or bouncing • Love crashing into people or objects • Seeks hugs or squishes • Writes hard • Fatigues easily	• Avoids jumping activities • Pushes away from hugs • Writes very lightly	• Falls out of chair because does not adjust posture • Falls or bumps into objects • Does not use the right amount of force to push/pull/grasp • Delayed right/left awareness

Vestibular

Hyposensitivity	Hypersensitivity	Discrimination
• Changes positions constantly in chair and on rug • Does not seem to get dizzy • Poor safety awareness • Decreased balance, seems clumsy • Low muscle tone ("floppy body")	• Prefers sedentary activities • Gets upset when someone bumps from behind • Refuses to climb the play structure • Clings to people/objects • Avoids sitting on unstable surfaces	• Falls out of chair • Trips when walking up the stairs or falls when climbing • Poor balance especially with eyes closed • Unable to communicate head orientation with eyes closed

Oral

Hyposensitivity	Hypersensitivity	Discrimination
• Loves spicy, sour, flavorful food • Makes noises constantly with mouth • Requests gum or chews on straws • Smells objects frequently	• Limited food variety • Refuses to eat around strong food smells • Sensitive gag reflex • Comments about the smell of body odor or people's breath	• Bites tongue or cheek when chewing • Difficulty moving tongue • Overstuffs mouth • Poor ability to describe feel of food in mouth • Difficulty telling if something smells good or bad

Interoceptive

Hyposensitivity	Hypersensitivity	Discrimination
• Needs to pee "right now!" • Isn't hungry until "starving" • Body temperature runs hot • Doesn't stop until exhausted	• Feels heartbeat pounding • Urinates frequently throughout the day • Dislikes having a bowel movement • Poor tolerance for any sign of hunger	• Difficulty knowing when to use the restroom • Needs reminders to eat or drink throughout the day • Confuses emotions with internal needs

Sensory-Based Motor Difference

Postural Disorder	Dyspraxia
• Difficulty sitting up in a chair or during circle time • Fatigues easily • Slumps, slouches, or hunches over work when sitting • "W" sits	• Seems unsure about how to perform a task • Prefers to do the same activities over and over • Avoids learning new activities, particularly those requiring coordination • Appears clumsy and uncoordinated • Performs activities and movements in an inefficient manner • Has a difficult time navigating the classroom

After you review these charts and identify a sensory preference or possible SPD, it is important to relate to that student. Let him know, by using supportive and understanding language, that you recognize his sensory needs and are there to support him. Acknowledge that things may be more challenging for her, and problem-solve a solution together. This will not only continue to strengthen the teacher-student dyad and build trust but also create a safe environment that might allow the student to expand his "just right" zone for certain sensory inputs.

In Evan's case, Ms. Prescott might approach Evan individually and say,

> I see that you are looking around the room a lot and wonder if the posters on the wall are making it harder for you to get your work done? Sometimes they are distracting to me too, because there is just so much to look at! I wonder if maybe I just have too many things hanging on the walls? Let's do an experiment to see if taking down some of the posters will help.

Ms. Prescott is coming alongside Evan, relating to him, and helping to address his sensory preferences—in this case an aversion to too much visual input. It is important to note that students with SPDs may be even more susceptible to critique, misunderstanding, and blame—all of which ultimately lead to dysregulation—so establishing a safe relationship that focuses on addressing the underlying challenge rather than the surface behavior is that much more important.

Strategy 3: Accommodate to Regulate

It is nearly impossible to accommodate all the varying sensory needs in a classroom of 20-plus students. However, there are some fairly common sensory accommodations that every teacher can consider in his/her classroom. It is important that these strategies be implemented alongside a co-regulatory relationship, like a positive teacher-student dyad. The positive teacher-student dyad will help to foster more regulation while these strategies are in use. Remember that children with an SPD already have varying states of arousal and are experiencing a stress response. It is important that they understand you are doing these strategies "with them" rather than "to them." It is important that they know these strategies are not a means to "call them out" but rather a means to "call them back" to learning. As always, your tone of voice, nonverbal cues, and attuned listening skills are integral to the success of implementation of these strategies.

Remember that these strategies should not serve as a replacement for additional therapy, if that is warranted (see Chapter 10 on when to refer to an occupational therapist). *Students will need time—allow for 1 to 2 weeks—to adjust to these strategies, not only because the novelty must "wear off" but also because their nervous system needs time to respond and make new neuronal connections. Sometimes this means a trial-and-error process over the course of several weeks. This also means celebrating the small wins while still working toward the end goal.* For example, Ms. Prescott might have an end goal of having Evan focus on his work for 12 minutes without needing redirection rather than the 3 to 4 minutes he focuses before looking around the room. After removing a handful of posters that seem to be the most distracting, Evan is now sitting for 7 to 8 minutes before he needs verbal reminders from Ms. Prescott—that's twice the amount of time as before! While it's not quite where she wants him to be, as his nervous system continues to make positive connections and is not as stimulated with visual input, his capacity for maintaining attention will continue to grow.

Note that strategies that are listed "in general" are likely things that could benefit every student in order to foster a positive sensory environment. Other strategies are more specific to the sensory patterns of certain students.

Visual

In general . . .

- Remove unnecessary visual input from the classroom walls, including: old artwork, posters not relevant to current lesson plans, items hanging from the ceiling, bright designs. Keep the essentials, such as: a clock, daily schedule, homework agenda, posters relevant to the current lesson plan, and signs that serve as directives.
- Make a visual schedule for the day using pictures. The visual schedule should represent each activity, and be split up into a morning and afternoon schedule.
- Balance the amount and type of colors used in the room. Pastel colors are generally more calming than bold, bright colors.
- Use a visual timer, such as one with a red indicator, to help students visualize the amount of time remaining for certain tasks.

Hyposensitivity	Hypersensitivity	Discrimination
• Use paper with red and blue lines to provide contrast to help with orientation to the line. • Highlight important areas on worksheets to facilitate attention. • Have the student use different colors of pencils when writing. • Face the desk toward a window. • Encourage the student to sit in the front of the classroom.	• Turn off the fluorescent lights. Use natural sunlight as much as possible and place floor lamps around the room. • Use reading and writing corrals during independent work. Binders and heavy-duty folders are good economical ways to create visual barriers. • Fold worksheets into quarters and have the student complete one quarter at a time to prevent overstimulation. • Allow the student to wear sunglasses in the classroom.	• Highlight important areas on worksheets to facilitate attention. • Make a number and letter desk "cheat sheet" with commonly forgotten or reversed symbols. • Use a slantboard or three-inch binder to promote better visual attention and convergence. • Remove extraneous information from around the dry erase board or assignment board. • Make the font size larger on worksheets.

Auditory

In general . . .

- Be conscientious of your own volume level and cadence when talking. There may be times of day when a louder volume or softer volume is better for your students.
- When giving instructions, talk slowly, pause before repeating them, and repeat the instructions the same way. This will help all students better process the input.
- Try to minimize environmental sounds within the classroom. Think about the type of pencil sharpener you have available. Think about where desks are situated in relationship to the air conditioner. Think about times of the day when it's better to have the windows closed. Think about the sound of your shoes on the floor.

Hyposensitivity	Hypersensitivity	Discrimination
• Allow the student to listen to music through headphones during independent work time. • Play classical music during independent work time to help filter out the low frequency environmental din.	• Have several pairs of noise-cancelling headphones for students to access whenever needed. • Play classical music during independent work time to help filter out the low frequency environmental din. • Consider starting a "lunch club" for students who get overstimulated with the noise in the cafeteria. This can be a small group of students who gather in a teacher's office or classroom in order to eat and socialize in an environment with low auditory stimulation. • Place rugs, carpets, or drapes in rooms with high ceilings to decrease the echoing sound.	• Encourage the student to sit in the front of the classroom to facilitate lip reading (something we all do naturally!). • Group with students who are less talkative.

Tactile

In general . . .

- Let students approach you rather than you approaching them, particularly in the first several weeks of school. This will help you gauge students who like tactile input versus students who are less comfortable with tactile input.
- Ask permission before touching a student on the shoulder, hands, or back—this form of light touch can be stimulating and potentially dysregulating.

- Use a high-pile rug with extra padding during carpet time to provide more comfort.

Hyposensitivity	Hypersensitivity	Discrimination
• Allow students to use fidget toys in the classroom. Note that not all fidget toys are beneficial or help facilitate improved attention, especially those that light up or make noise. Jamie's favorites include: textured Tangle Jr., flippy chain, Wacky Tracks, and Whatz It fidget. • Put Velcro under the desk for the student to rub. • Rub feet on a textured piece of material placed under the desk. • Use a vibrating pen or pencil.	• Provide cushions or core discs (the "squellet" is Jamie's favorite) to decrease the tactile input from hard chairs. • Stand in the front of the line or back of the line. • Use a basic, soft pencil grip to minimize tactile input from the hard pencil.	• Provide Jumbo Grip pencils and/or pencil grips (Grotto grip and Crossover grip are Jamie's favorite) for more tactile feedback when writing. • Use a vibrating pen or pencil. • Encourage the student to describe the texture of different materials used in the classroom. • Have the student use a transparent pencil box and backpack.

Proprioceptive

In general . . .

- Use this type of sensory input when a child becomes overstimulated, as it tends to be the most calming. This might include: squeezing a stress ball, body squeezes, helping to carry something heavy, erasing the chalkboard or dry erase board, wall pushes, or jumping in place.
- Teach students ways to give themselves calming, regulating proprioceptive input such as joint compressions, bear hugs, chair push-ups.
- Have bean bag chairs or stadium seats available for students to use during carpet time, particularly for children who have difficulty sitting upright.

Hyposensitivity	Hypersensitivity	Discrimination
• Sit in a chair with arms for more support and structure. • Loop TheraBand (red or green resistance is best) around the front two legs of chairs for students to put their feet in and stretch. • Allow the student to carry around or wear a backpack filled with books (keep to 7 to 10 percent of the student's body weight). • Used a weighted blanket (keep at 7 to 10 percent of the student's body weight) or a core disc placed on the student's lap during circle time. • Ask the student to help with "heavy work" activities in the classroom: wiping down boards, taking down chairs, carrying books, pushing the lunch basket. • Have the student wear a compression shirt and/or shorts.	• NOTE: typically students do not respond in this way to proprioceptive input.	• For students who press hard when writing, place a binder, folder, or other semi-squishy surface under the paper to provide additional feedback. • Use sand paper, chalkboards, tissue paper, and magnetic boards to practice writing on different surfaces. • Allow the student to carry around or wear a backpack filled with books (keep to 7 to 10 percent of the student's body weight). • Ask the student to help with "heavy work" activities in the classroom: wiping down boards, taking down chairs, carrying books, pushing the lunch basket.

Vestibular

In general . . .

- Integrate body breaks and movement activities into your schedule and curriculum. Stretching, yoga poses, jumping jacks, shaking "sillies" out, and walking around the classroom are all great!
- Teach your students small movements they can do in their chairs when they start to notice their body getting restless

or their attention waning. Ideas include: crossing then uncrossing your legs, moving your head in a circle, small wiggles back and forth on your butt cheeks, nodding your head up and down several times.

- Provide alternative seating options for your students. Ball chairs, wobble stools, standing desks, and rocking chairs can all be helpful for particular students.
- Make sure the chair height and desk height are appropriate for your students. Students should have chairs that allow their feet to be flat on the floor with hips and knees at 90 degrees (an "L" shape). The table or desk height should allow for the elbows to rest comfortably at a 90-degree angle (an "L" shape).
- Monitor the amount of homework you are giving in order to allow for students to have adequate outdoor play time after school. Regulation through vestibular-based activities outside of school also impacts regulation during the school day.
- Advocate for intermittent recesses throughout the school day and the need for regular physical education classes.

Hyposensitivity	Hypersensitivity	Discrimination
• Encourage intermittent standing, even when doing desk work.	• Allow to stand at the back of the line.	• Have the student use an alternative seating option.
• Use a vibrating pen or pencil.	• Avoid approaching or touching from behind because the student may be fearful of becoming unbalanced.	• Provide more support when sitting on a rug, such as a stadium seat, bean bag chair, or wall to lean against.
• Have the student use an alternative seating option (wobble stool or ball chair).	• Make sure the student's feet can be firmly planted on the ground when sitting in a chair; if not, provide a stool or phone book for the student to place his feet on top.	• Allow the student to sit or lay on the ground when completing independent work.
• Use a core disc (a.k.a. wobble cushion) on the chair or on the floor.		
• Allow the student to spin, seated on the teacher's chair, ten times in each direction.	• Allow the student to sit in a rocking chair during silent reading.	• Let the student stand near a wall or stabilizing surface when doing balancing activities.
• Engage the student in chair stretches.	• Encourage swinging and sliding at recess.	
• Allow the student to take extra movement breaks, as needed.		

Oral

In general . . .

- Remove air fresheners, and refrain from using spray air fresheners—the synthetic chemicals in these are not beneficial for anyone.
- When using essential oils in the class, remember that scents like lavender, rose, chamomile, eucalyptus, and jasmine are calming. Cinnamon, orange, peppermint, and rosemary tend to be more alerting and energizing.
- Allow students to access water bottles and snacks throughout the day, particularly during independent work time. Many children and adults find that chewing on something or sucking something through a straw is helpful to maintain focus.

Hyposensitivity	Hypersensitivity	Discrimination
• ARK therapeutics makes a wide variety of "chewlery" and pencil toppers that students can use for oral input. • Crunchy snacks provide tactile and proprioceptive input to the mouth, which can be alerting, especially during independent work time. I typically recommend: trail mix, popcorn, pretzels, carrots, celery, or apples. • Mints and cinnamon candies are very alerting, which can help students better focus. • Allow the student to use scented markers or crayons. • Allow the student to have a cold water bottle with a straw at his desk.	• Chewy snacks (including gum) provide proprioceptive input to the mouth, which can be calming, especially during independent work time. I typically recommend: fruit leather, dried fruit, beef jerky, or bagels. • Dry erase markers have strong odors, whereas chalk, dry erase crayons, and SMART Boards are low odor. • Be conscientious of the amount of hairspray, perfume, cologne, or lotion that you wear.	• ARK therapeutics makes a wide variety of "chewlery" and pencil toppers that students can use for oral input.

Interoceptive

In general . . .

- Do not dismiss when a student is communicating a bodily need, even if you feel she is using it as "an escape." Many of our emotions can cause physiological reactions—such as needing to urinate when nervous—so it is important to explore "why" a student is repeatedly requesting a bodily need to be met.
- Talk about different signals that our bodies might give to let us know when we are thirsty (dry mouth, sore throat, headache, sweating), hungry (stomach pain, grumbling sound), tired (sweating, body slouching, heart beating fast or slow, eyes drooping), or need to use the bathroom (bladder pain, leg shaking).
- Integrate yoga into the class with a focus on deep breathing, feeling changes in heart rate, and checking in with the body. Yoga can help students slow down and attend to the needs of their body.

Hyposensitivity	Hypersensitivity	Discrimination
• Encourage the student to wear a vibrating watch that notifies when to urinate, drink water, and/or have a snack.	• Have the student take three deep breaths with his hand placed over his heart when feeling overwhelmed with a body signal.	• Have the student take three deep breaths before determining if something is an internal body signal versus an emotion.
• Have the student take breaks every hour to check in with her body regarding internal cues.	• Allow the student access to water and snacks throughout the day.	• Provide a visual representation of different emotions and how those may be reflected in body signals.
• Allow frequent movement breaks to encourage a change in position.	• Grant access to the bathroom no matter how frequently it is requested.	

Sensory-Based Motor Difference

Postural Disorder	Dyspraxia
• Provide more supportive seating options for desk work and circle time. • Allow frequent movement breaks. • Have the student lay on the ground on his stomach with a three-inch binder when doing independent work.	• Provide a visual schedule for each activity. • Break down activities into their component parts. • Make a map or drawing of a plan before executing. • Model what you want done in addition to providing verbal cues. • Be patient and understanding!

In the example with Evan, Ms. Prescott identified that it was possibly the amount of visual input on her walls that was causing him to become distracted at times. To accommodate his sensory preference, she could also suggest that he use a privacy board or corral in order to filter out some of the visual input on her walls. Ms. Prescott may find that some days Evan does not need these accommodations, while other days he does. She may notice that when Evan is engaged in more challenging math activities, he becomes more easily distracted with the visual input. The idea is that he has options available to help him regulate and stay focused when needed.

As you can imagine, recognizing and accommodating sensory needs within a classroom take practice, experience, and patience. In Chapter 10, we will explore more about the resources available to help support students with more intense sensory needs. Having a foundational understanding of SPD will help you discern when a student may need a referral to an occupational therapist. Keep in mind that students who experience "blue zone" dysregulation in response to sensory input—like freezing up, acting rigid, seeming disinterested ("checking out"), and appearing internally anxious—are often overlooked. While students with sensory-based dysregulation who are being disruptive to the class because they are in the "red zone" typically gain more attention, it is important to recognize that "blue zone" dysregulation will equally impact the student's ability to engage in education-based activities. In the next chapter, we will explore other learning disabilities that often overlap with SPD and pose unique challenges within the learning environment.

Interactive Scenario

Complete the chart below to gain a better understanding of how you might differentiate and support the sensory needs of students within your classroom.

Student behavior	Sensory preference or SPD?	Which sensory system is most involved?	Supports that may be beneficial
Trevor pushes anyone who stands too close to him in line. He absolutely refuses to touch the class pet. He frequently washes his hands throughout the day.			
Will comes in from recess dripping in sweat and needs you to remind him to drink water. At snack time he doesn't eat much but 15 minutes later says that he's "starving" and cannot wait until lunch to eat.			
Patricia will sometimes ask the students around her to be quiet when working. She participates well in group activities but seems to prefer more independent work.			

(Continued)

(Continued)

Mateo likes to lean up against the bookcase during circle time. He bounces his feet up and down when sitting in his chair.			
Alexa needs constant reminders to sit in her chair and can sometimes be seen wandering around the room. At recess she can't seem to get enough spinning on the tire swing.			

- Trevor likely has an SPD that can be categorized as hypersensitivity to tactile input. He would benefit from having a place at the front or back of the line. He might accept touching various textures if he is wearing gloves.

- Will likely has an SPD that can be categorized as hyposensitivity to interoceptive input. He would benefit from having a water break integrated into his recess time, as well as keeping an extra snack at his desk for when he gets hungry after snack.

- Patricia likely has a sensory preference whereby auditory input can sometimes be too much. She could benefit from sitting near peers who are quieter. She needs a balance between time by herself and time with other people.

- Mateo likely has a sensory preference whereby proprioceptive input is calming and regulating. He could benefit from putting a red TheraBand on the front legs of his chair. He might also do well holding a stress ball in circle time if you don't want him leaning up against something.

- Alexa likely has an SPD that can be categorized as hyposensitivity to vestibular input. She would benefit from using alternative seating, such as a ball chair or wobble stool. She would also benefit from movement breaks throughout the day.

CHAPTER 6

Developing an Awareness of Individual Differences and Promoting Integration

"All students can learn and succeed, but not in the same way and not in the same day."

—William G. Spady

Mrs. Walters was a fourth-grade teacher in a large, busy, and active classroom environment. The halls and the classroom were often echoing and loud. You could hear, for example, people's voices and feet walking from way down the hall. This often impacted the noise level inside the classroom. Mrs. Walters had a loud voice but found her instructions to be drowned out by the noise in the environment. This was frustrating to her and her students. The students in the class were noisy as well, needing repeated prompts to remain quiet and listen. She found herself talking for most of the day, requesting over and over that her students quiet down and listen, which was exhausting. Not to mention that Mrs. Walters was already sensitive to auditory input herself, so she frequently went home feeling very depleted.

Mrs. Walters noticed that a quieter student in her class, Pablo, often looked around the room, seemingly not paying attention. When she called on him to answer a question, he responded by asking, "What?" as though he wasn't listening. He usually sat with his head down on the desk, looking up at the ceiling, or doodling on his paper. His arousal level usually did not match that of the other rambunctious students in her classroom. Mrs. Walters noticed when she spent time with him at his desk to see if he was grasping the concepts, he misunderstood what she was saying. When she asked him to repeat her instructions, he would repeat them incorrectly, or mispronounce a word she had just said. It was evident that Pablo was having difficulty understanding, processing, and keeping up with language-based components and auditory information in the classroom.

In an environment where most of the information is presented in an auditory format (as most schools are), it can be challenging for students who struggle with processing auditory information to keep up with the curriculum. This is also true for students who have difficulty with processing speed, phonetic awareness, and attention, to name a few. In this chapter, we will explore some common learning-based challenges that impact students and the implications on their regulation and participation in classroom activities. We hope to celebrate the individual differences that each student brings while also providing teachers with strategies to support those differences in a way that facilitates learning success.

RECOGNIZING INDIVIDUAL DIFFERENCES

One of the most amazing, awe-inspiring, and exciting considerations regarding the brain is that while all our brains are made up of the same structures, features, anatomy, and basic functions, we are all born with our own unique temperaments, personalities, strengths, preferences, and vulnerabilities. We saw this already in Chapters 4 and 5 regarding how we process sensory input and use it for motor output. This is something Ashley has noticed throughout her work with children, but most strikingly, and personally, when she experienced the difference between the births of her two boys. One came into the world kicking and screaming, while the other was quieter, more observant, taking in the world around him with a curious, wide-eyed sense of wonder. One demonstrated the strength of his lung capacity for an hour, while the other calmed down more quickly. From birth, they demonstrated very different temperaments, sensory preferences, and personality traits. Their differences hold true to this day; one is sensory seeking while the other leans toward being more sensory avoidant. One prefers to sit, draw, and read, while the other is always on the move—climbing, running, and jumping. One is more extroverted and social, while the other prefers to be with just one or two people. One likes being at home and is slower to warm up, while the other is always ready for the next big adventure. They navigate the world in a different way; they process, learn, and take in information in very different ways—and they have since birth. Genetics are an amazing thing, and it is so exciting to see, on a personal level, how two boys from the same parents, living in the same environment, are so incredibly different!

This, we believe, is a very important concept to keep in mind when we work with children: no two children, despite their similarities, are going to be alike. No two children, who, for example, both have the same diagnosis of attention deficit hyperactivity disorder (ADHD), dyslexia, or autism spectrum disorder (ASD), are going to present with the same temperaments, personality styles, sensory preferences, or interests. While of course there will be some patterns and similarities between them, we have to treat each child as their own unique individual, taking time to get to know them, so that we can best understand how to educate them.

What initial, quick, basic, and easy questions can we ask to begin to get a better understanding of each student's individual differences? We can break the questions up into four different categories including sensory preferences, temperament, flexibility, and interests.

Questions we can ask to better understand each student's individual differences:

- *Sensory preferences:*
    - Is the student sensory seeking (do they like the stimulation that the sensory environment brings: getting dirty, doing lots of activities, fast movements, and singing out loud)? Or,
    - Is the student more sensory avoidant (does sensory input overwhelm them: they prefer sedentary activities, are hesitant to touch new things, like the quiet)?

- *Temperament:*
    - Is the student slow to warm up; does he or she take time to get comfortable in new situations? Are new things harder to get used to? Are they more introverted? Or,

- - Is the student more outgoing and eager to interact? Enjoys being social and interacting with others? Does he or she initiate play with others frequently?
- *Flexibility:*
  - Does the student transition easily from one task to the next? Would you describe him or her as "go with the flow?" Or,

Reflective Activity

Teachers, you can use these questions at the beginning of each school year as a way to get to know your students better. You can also use them to think about yourself, your preferences, temperament, personality, and style.

Take a moment to answer the questions above about yourself:

Sensory Preferences	• _____ • _____
Temperament	• _____ • _____
Flexibility	• _____ • _____
Interests	• _____ • _____

Now take a moment and answer them about a student in your classroom:

Sensory Preferences	• _____ • _____
Temperament	• _____ • _____
Flexibility	• _____ • _____
Interests	• _____ • _____

- Does the student take time to adjust to new tasks and take longer to transition? Would you describe him or her as more controlling?

- *Interests:*
  - What activities does the student gravitate toward (more hands-on activities, drawing, paper/pencil, drama, building, reading, etc.)? And,
  - Which activities does the student seem to dislike or avoid?

The answers to the questions above will tell you quite a bit about each student you are working with. More than you think. These questions will help you better connect with each student on an individual level and strengthen your relationship with him or her. The answers will inform you of how a student might learn best and why she might be responding a certain way in any given situation. While you cannot cater to all the individual needs of students at all times, you can adjust your classroom environment, type of activity, and the way you interact with a student when you see her struggling. You can also better understand the ways you might need to facilitate a more integrated approach to learning.

MOVING TOWARD INTEGRATED LEARNING

Historically, educators, scientists, and researchers have discussed the concept of teaching to each individual's learning style. This concept has been widely discussed, and more recently, this way of thinking has taken a turn. We agree that based on the highly connected nature of the brain, it is actually better to lean toward integrated teaching, which will then support students in integrated learning and overall brain-based integration.[1] This also supports the idea in Chapter 1 of "linkage" and "differentiation": while each student will have individual learning differences, it is also important for each student to have an integrated approach to learning. What do we mean by *integrated teaching*, *integrated learning*, and *overall integration*? By **integration,** we mean our brain's ability to cohesively combine the information from a variety of sources and parts of the brain in order to use that information to achieve a goal. We are working from an integrated state when we are able to access and utilize the different areas of our brain easily, and when they work together in harmony.[2]

> **Integration:** the ability to combine the information from a variety of sources and parts of the brain in order to use that information cohesively to achieve a goal.

This is easier said than done, as we have various strengths and challenges when it comes to learning. Our brains all have "preferences"— tasks or activities that come naturally, and tasks that are more difficult. Of course, we all tend to gravitate toward tasks and activities that are easier for us and avoid or neglect activities that are more challenging. As we will explore in this chapter, this is why it is important to move away from teaching toward strengths and move toward integrated learning. This suggests that we can focus on ways to support students in developing skills that may be challenging within the context of their strengths, and with a level of support and collaboration. As we discuss throughout this book, and particularly in this chapter, we hope to highlight ways to identify both the strengths and vulnerabilities of students and teachers, and ways to use strengths as a means to bolster areas of vulnerability.

What scientists are learning more and more about is the interconnectedness of the different regions of the brain and how integrated all the processes need to be in order to function successfully.[1,2] It is vital for the various brain regions to work together in order to function successfully. *Typically, when we see dysregulation, academic challenges, or what looks like disruptive, defiant, "lazy," or "manipulative" behavior, it likely means that an area of functioning in the brain hasn't yet fully integrated.* Integration, therefore, is the overall goal. Students should therefore be allowed the opportunity to have access to many different ways of learning in order to reach their full potential.

In our vignette above, for example, Pablo is having difficulty accessing, fully utilizing, and accurately processing auditory information. This suggests that his brain was not yet fully integrating auditory information in order to process language; there was a breakdown somewhere along the auditory pathways that was resulting in inefficient and ineffective processing.[3] If Mrs. Walters only focused on Pablo's visual strengths for learning, then he would be missing out on a wide variety of other learning experiences, the auditory pathways in his brain would not have the opportunity to develop as strongly, and brain-based integration would be even more difficult for him to achieve. It will therefore be important for Mrs. Walters to support Pablo by allowing him to rely on his visual strengths while giving him auditory input *at the same time.* For example, he can read a book while also listening to the audiobook at the same time. Thus, in using his visual strength, he can improve the areas that are more challenging for him, leading toward more integration.

As scientists have discovered, the more you use a certain part of the brain, the stronger that part of the brain will get—"neurons that fire together, wire together." The less we use a certain area of the brain, that part of the brain will get "pruned" away—this is called "use it or lose it." Just like a gardener trims trees, if there are neuronal connections that we are not using, they will also get trimmed away, and it will be harder and harder for us to use that part of the brain and ultimately that skill. **Pruning** is a vital process to our brain's overall health. Through trimming away unused neuronal connections, the brain makes more space for the frequently used neuronal connections to be accessed more efficiently,[4] thus promoting more integration in different areas of the brain. While this is a necessary process, it is also one reason why we do not want to only teach to a student's strengths. If we exclusively teach to each student's strengths, then they won't have the opportunity to practice the activities that are more difficult for them, and those neuro- nal connections will get pruned away, causing their weaknesses to get weaker. Again, it is important to think about ways we can use a child's strengths to build up their areas of vulnerability within the context of a regulated and protective teacher-student dyad.

Pruning: the process of removing neuronal connections in the brain that are damaged, degraded, or unused.

Supportive Diagram

Teaching in a more integrated manner—that incorporates both horizontal and vertical processes—can facilitate cohesive learning and understanding. When the brain is not adequately integrated, then students can experience difficulty grasping concepts, engaging in active learning, or performing activities in the classroom, which will ultimately lead to dysregulation.

| Adequate integration | Age-appropriate processing and learning | Regulation in the classroom |

| Over-pruning and incomplete integration | Inefficient or ineffective processing and learning | Dysregulation in the classroom |

This is a tricky balance, however, because as we know, if something is harder for us, we tend to avoid it, not want to do it, or become more easily frustrated when expected to engage in such tasks. A student who has dysgraphia, for example, has difficulty with handwriting skills. This makes handwriting very difficult for them. The skills they need to practice are therefore often the source of dysregulation. How, then, do we support them in developing this skill without causing them heightened amounts of stress? We can do so by incorporating the ideas of co-regulation (which we've discussed in detail throughout this book), integrated learning, universal learning,[5] and utilizing a multi-modal sensory approach. We can also do this by identifying and utilizing a student's strengths and allowing them to utilize their strengths as a way of bolstering functioning in areas that are more challenging for them.

- *Integrated learning* is provided by allowing students access to more of a holistic learning process.[6] This means creating activities that integrate different areas of the brain, while also integrating the curriculum across disciplines, like learning math through dancing and singing, for example.
- *Multimodal sensory learning* allows for the opportunity to learn through various sensory inputs to help solidify knowledge. Reading a book while also listening to the audiobook, for example, can help students with reading because they are able to see it and hear it at the same time. Writing with the paper over sandpaper, finger painting, writing letters in shaving cream, and using manipulatives in math are all examples of ways to integrate sensory input into learning.

Here are some other ways you can consider applying integrated learning to your classroom setting:

- Add cross-body movement before or during a lesson plan (examples include: touch right elbow to left knee then left elbow to right knee, draw a large infinity sign in the air, rotate at the waist with arms out to the side like a helicopter).
- Encourage students to think about different ways to solve a problem or come up with the same answer.

- Play music in the classroom or allow students to doodle when completing independent work in order to bring out their creative energy.
- Help students, both individually and as a class, to name their emotions after completing a challenging activity, taking a test, or preparing for an aptitude test.
- Read a passage in a story and have students act out the passage with a partner.
- Encourage students to draw a picture scenario that complements the story they have just written (or heard).
- Think about how a particular fiction book intersects with what has been taught in history.
- Split up the class into groups and arrange learning centers that apply certain concepts in several different ways.
- Allow time at the end of class for students to share what they learned.
- Allow time at the end of class for students to reflect on how they can apply the concepts in real life.
- Ask students what they want to learn about at the beginning of each unit, and have them explore those concepts further, either individually or in groups.
- Use interactive floor mats to facilitate the learning of math concepts through movement.
- Preview new lessons with students the day before, and encourage them to think about questions they can ask when they discuss the topic the next day.

Here are some ways you can consider applying multimodal sensory learning to your classroom. Chapter 4 has many more ideas on how to use multimodal sensory learning concepts, particularly Strategy 3.

- Write down a journal entry, and then read it to a partner.
- Create a diorama after reading a book.
- Make a visual map of an essay outline.
- Use songs and rhyming to remember grammar or math concepts.
- Include short answer, fill-in-the-blank, and multiple choice questions on tests.
- Design your own book jacket that highlights the main plot of the book.

Reflective Activity

Incorporating integrated and multimodal sensory learning strategies into your classroom will benefit all your students by supporting their individual differences. Consider ways you already incorporate these strategies and/or ways you could incorporate these strategies even more.

Integrated activities	Multimodal sensory activities
• _____	• _____
• _____	• _____
• _____	• _____
• _____	• _____

Which integrated or multimodal sensory learning strategies would benefit you most when learning something new? How do these use your strengths to support your vulnerabilities?

_____

_____

_____

 Available for download at **resources.corwin.com/ClassroomBehaviors**

TEACHING STUDENTS TO SEARCH FOR THE WHY

Just as teachers can use the concepts outlined in this book to better understand students' behaviors and support integration in their learning, students can learn the same concepts and become active participants in their own learning process. Teachers, you can teach your students to search for the "why." This will provide students with the opportunity to develop a curious outlook on learning, an acceptance of mistakes, and an eagerness to ask questions. This will also continue to support students in building and developing overall brain-based integration and regulation. By starting the school year off introducing this framework, you can help students to foster an outlook on learning that creates curiosity, acceptance, and awareness. It will provide students with an opportunity to gain insights into their own strengths and vulnerabilities. Exploring reasons why certain activities may be more difficult than others, or why certain tasks come more easily than others, can help them learn about their brains, hypothesize about their learning styles, and ask questions to get to know themselves better. Not only can they learn strategies to advocate for themselves, but they can also feel more motivated to build skills to better navigate frustration, social situations, and academics.

How can you go about teaching students to search for the "why"? Incorporate the following three ideas at the beginning of the school year. You can get creative with how to implement these ideas in your specific classrooms based on information and strategies we've provided throughout this book.

Setting the tone for the school year:

1. *Knowledge is an endless journey*: Start the year off introducing the concept of searching for the "why" and the magic of asking questions by emphasizing that knowledge is an endless journey. It is impossible to know everything, and that is ok. The key is to be curious because this is what helps build understanding and self-awareness.

2. *Teach students about the brain*: Let them experience how amazing the brain is and how it is ever-changing and growing. *The Whole Brain Child*[7] has many resources for teaching kids about key concepts of the brain. Create "zones of regulation" charts to put in the room so they can reference them as they move through different states of regulation. Explain to them why integrated learning and multimodal sensory learning are so important.

3. *Ask and answer questions*: Provide them with opportunities to answer the questions listed at the beginning of this chapter regarding sensory preferences, temperament, flexibility, and interests. They have been adapted below

so that students can ask them about themselves and gain a better awareness of their learning needs. They can also take time to ask them about a friend so that they can get to know one another better—continuing to build an integrated classroom community:

- Sensory preferences: Do you like getting dirty, playing with shaving cream, laying in the grass, eating with your hands, OR do you prefer staying clean, washing your hands often, using utensils? Do you like hanging on the monkey bars, going on rollercoasters, swinging, and playing sports, OR do you prefer reading a book, sitting and observing, doing craft activities, playing an instrument? Do you like singing aloud, telling your thoughts to others, listening to loud music/TV shows, going to large social events, OR do you prefer singing in your head, writing down your thoughts, playing/sitting in silence, being in smaller groups of people?

- Temperament: Do you like trying new things and meeting new people? Do you prefer to observe others and interact with people you know? Do you like going out and doing things, or are you more of a home-body?

- Flexibility: How do you feel when you have to go somewhere new or different? How do you feel when something in your bedroom, backpack, or classroom is different from the way you left it? How do you feel when someone asks you to do something different from the way you want to do it? Is it easy for you to "let go," or do you like to be in control?

- Interests: List three of your favorite activities. Why do you like them? (Only one of them can be screen-based!) List three of your least favorite activities. Why don't you like them?

While incorporating the three steps above sets the tone for the school year, the additional ideas below can be used throughout the year to reinforce and emphasize the importance of individual differences.

Ideas to use throughout the school year:

- *Teach students about the power of praise:* help them to learn how they can praise themselves when their inner voice is

Supportive Diagram

Teaching your students to search for the "why" will provide them with the opportunity to develop a curious outlook on learning, an acceptance of mistakes, and an eagerness to ask questions. This will also continue to support students in building and developing overall brain-based integration and regulation as well as creating an integrated classroom community that values and respects individual differences.

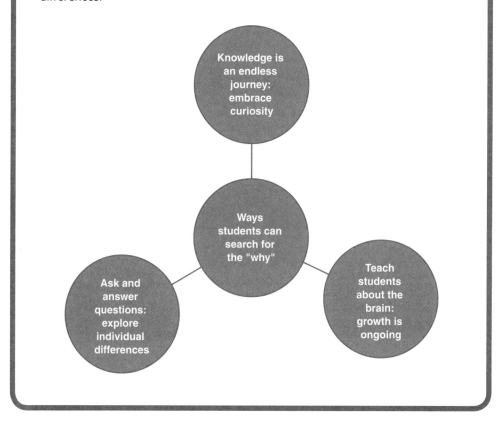

being critical. Give them lists of praise statements they can practice saying *to themselves*; some ideas include:

- o   I am brave.
- o   I am strong.
- o   This hard, but I can do this.
- o   I can figure out this tough problem.
- o   I can take it one step at a time if I need to.
- o   I can ask for help and that is ok.

- o   Making mistakes means I'm learning.
- o   Taking a break can be a good thing.
- Encourage praise statements that students can give *to peers* to foster a safe, collaborative, and integrated classroom community:
  - o   That's a creative idea. I never thought of that!
  - o   I have fun playing with you.
  - o   Your story is really unique and imaginative.
  - o   You are really good at math; it's a tricky subject for me.
  - o   You are a talented artist.
  - o   Wow, that was hard, and you made it look easy!
  - o   Great job working through that problem. I know it wasn't easy for you.
- Explain what *reflecting* means, and allow opportunities for reflection in your classroom. For example, put a "reflection box" in your classroom with slips of paper that have different prompts that students can answer. Some examples include:
  - o   What is harder for my brain to learn?
  - o   What comes easily to my brain?
  - o   What can I do to challenge myself?
  - o   What can I do to help myself?
  - o   Who can I ask for help?
  - o   Do loud noises stress me out?
  - o   Do I prefer writing a story or drawing a picture?
  - o   What would I like to work on this year?
  - o   What can I do to learn something new?
  - o   How do I know when I need a brain break?
  - o   What can I do during a brain break?
  - o   What makes me feel happy (or angry, or sad, or frustrated)?

The suggestions above are helpful for all students in order to help them build an awareness of their unique learning styles, strengths, and vulnerabilities. This allows them to take an active role in their learning, which in turn encourages integration. It also facilitates the building of a classroom community in which students can support each other in their vulnerabilities by tapping into their strengths. Some students will have additional needs. Strategies to support such students, who, for example, may have a learning disability, will be discussed below.

LANGUAGE-BASED LEARNING DISABILITIES

Using an integrated approach to teaching can benefit all students in your classroom. While we all have strengths and challenges in the ways our brains learn and function, some students have impairments that meet the criteria for language-based learning disabilities such as dyslexia, dysgraphia, and dyscalculia, which we will take a few moments to discuss below. These diagnoses are based on patterns of processing information resulting from different areas of the brain having difficulty working together. These students, in particular, will benefit from a more integrated approach to learning and will also likely need more extensive, structured, and intensive support inside and outside the classroom.

The topic of language-based learning disabilities is expansive, and vital when you work in education. There are many wonderful books and researchers who have written on this topic such as Maryanne Wolf,[8] and Daniel Franklin,[9] among others. You have likely, hopefully, also gained experience regarding learning disabilities in your training. We will therefore not spend too much time on them here but will highlight some important facts, features, misconceptions, and warning signs, while providing you with references if you'd like to learn more. Again, while there are common patterns, signs, and symptoms of learning disabilities, each child is different. These diagnoses serve as a starting point to understanding the individual differences of the student. *It is also of utmost importance to remember and understand the power of early intervention. Your professional observations and insights are critical to getting students the support they need, particularly given the amount of time you spend with students on a regular basis.* We will explore the ways you can do this in Chapter 10.

Supportive Diagram

Language-based learning disabilities reflect individual differences in the way students process language, such as learning vocabulary, expressing themselves on paper, memorizing math facts, and reading.

(Continued)

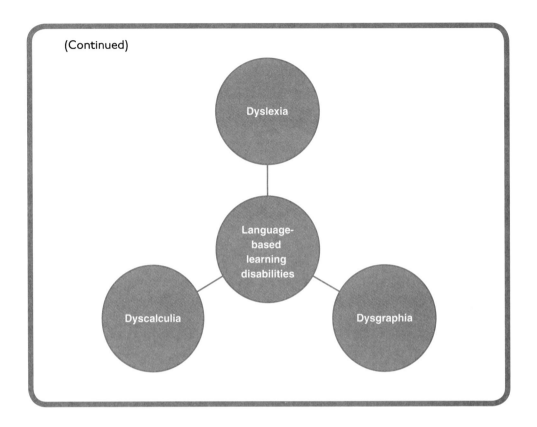

(Continued)

Language-based learning disabilities including dyslexia, dysgraphia, and dyscalculia cause language-based learning to be more challenging for such students. They may have greater difficulty with vocabulary, reading, writing, getting their thoughts down on paper, expressing themselves, memorizing language-based information, and utilizing rote memorization. They may have greater difficulty with fluency in reading, writing, and math, remembering math facts quickly and accurately and processing more subtle sounds. Often kids with language-based learning disabilities have difficulty with phonetic decoding and phonological processing. They may struggle with retention and often times teachers may feel as though their student's learning isn't "sticking." This is because they may have difficulty with retention, recognition, and retrieval skills making new learning more challenging for them.

The Diagnostic and Statistical Manual of Mental Disorders, the fifth edition of the classification by the American Psychiatric Association[10] and an important diagnostic tool, estimates the prevalence of all learning disorders (including impairment in writing as well as in reading and/or mathematics) to be about 5 percent to 15 percent worldwide. This percentage is similar to the incidence of developmental dyslexia, which is about 17 percent.[11]

- *Dyslexia* is a learning disability characterized by a difficulty with reading. People with dyslexia often have difficulty reading at a good pace without making mistakes. This may also impact reading comprehension, spelling, and writing. Children with dyslexia often have difficulty with phonetic (i.e., sound) awareness, or matching letter sounds to their written form. They have difficulty with decoding and sounding out words which typically results in poor spelling ability. If this is not addressed very early on, it can have a negative impact on the child's learning and academic success. It can also impact self-esteem, a sense of self-worth, and a positive overall sense of self.[12]

- *Dysgraphia* is described as a language-based learning disability where a student has a specific set of writing challenges. Children with dysgraphia often have difficulty with handwriting, typing, and spelling. One of the main signs of dysgraphia is messy handwriting or difficulty with graphomotor functioning. Most students with dysgraphia have incredible ideas of things they want to write but have difficulty getting their thoughts down on paper. Again, there is a mismatch between the intellectual reasoning and their output, or their ability to demonstrate the amazing things that are going on in their brain.[10-13]

- *Dyscalculia* is a learning disability that centers around math, including an individual's ability to understand numbers and learn math facts, the prevalence among school-aged children ranges between 3 percent and 6 percent. Students with dyscalculia may have difficulty learning how to count, have trouble with telling time, and struggle when completing arithmetic problems.[14]

Common warning signs associated with language-based learning disabilities include[10-14]:

- *Dyslexia*
  - Slow, limited vocabulary
  - Difficulty rhyming

- ○ Trouble associating the sounds of letters to their corresponding shapes
- ○ Difficulty with rapid naming tasks, such as "tell me all the sea animals you can think of"
- ○ Challenges in phonological processing, and phonemic awareness
- ○ Avoiding reading out loud or to themselves
- ○ Increased frustration, anger, and/or anxiety around reading tasks
- ○ Avoiding homework

- *Dysgraphia*
  - ○ Difficulty with letter or number formation— forming from the bottom-up rather than top-down, segmentation of letters, or inconsistent formation
  - ○ Spacing between letters and words that is inconsistent—sometimes too much space, or maybe too little
  - ○ Sizing of letters and numbers may also be inconsistent—sometimes too big and other times too small
  - ○ Placement of letters and numbers on the line may be off—sometimes they write on an upward or downward slant or have difficulty staying in a straight line
  - ○ Poor or inconsistent pencil grip
  - ○ Difficulty with utilizing the right amount of pressure while writing—sometimes too much pressure or too little pressure
  - ○ Poor organization of thoughts and ideas when writing sentences, short stories, or essays

- *Dyscalculia*
  - ○ Difficulty with number sense and sequencing
  - ○ Weak mental arithmetic skills
  - ○ Slow to perform arithmetic and memorize math facts
  - ○ Difficulty understanding place value
  - ○ Has trouble learning to count, skips over numbers
  - ○ Has trouble understanding number symbols
  - ○ Struggles with understanding patterns (such as smallest to largest)

NONVERBAL LEARNING CHALLENGES

Alternately, individuals with nonverbal learning challenges often have greater difficulty learning and processing information that is nonverbal, while they often demonstrate strengths in language-based learning. Because most traditional schools are highly focused on language-based learning, students with nonverbal learning challenges often go unidentified, misidentified, or misunderstood. This is because such students often excel in language-based learning, so their challenges may fly under the radar until they are quite a bit older. While a nonverbal learning challenge is not identified in the DSM-5, you can think of nonverbal learning challenges as almost the opposite of a language-based learning challenge.[15,16]

Children with nonverbal learning challenges typically have greater difficulty with visual-spatial awareness, higher-order comprehension, social communication, applied learning across the board (reading, writing, and math), and executive functioning.[15,16] Of course, as with anything else, each individual with nonverbal learning challenges demonstrates their own pattern of strengths and weaknesses, and this may overlap with other diagnoses including ADHD and ASD.

Common warning signs associated with nonverbal challenges include[15,16]:

- Poor coordination or clumsy
- Trouble recognizing nonverbal cues (facial expression and body language)
- Poor fine motor skills
- Visual-spatial challenges
- Very literal or concrete, may struggle with sarcasm and social nuances
- Difficulty seeing the big picture

GIFTEDNESS AND 2E

Students who are gifted have unique strengths and challenges that can be misunderstood and misdiagnosed. **Giftedness**[17,18] is defined as having a certain intellectual ability that is significantly higher than the norm for their age and grade level. This can be reflected in a variety

Giftedness: having a certain intellectual ability that is significantly higher than the norm for a particular age and/or grade level.

of ways, including intelligence, creativity, and artistic abilities. Gift-edness often results in what is called "asynchronous development," as defined in Chapter 2, meaning that there are gaps between certain intellectual abilities and other parts of their development, like social skills, motor skills, or emotional development. This is referred to as being twice exceptional or "2E." Students who are twice exceptional are both gifted and have a diagnosis such as a learning disability, ADHD, or other vulnerability that impacts their ability to access and effectively utilize their intellectual gifts. Reconciling these gaps can be confusing and challenging for gifted students—they don't under-stand why some things come so easily to them while other tasks are so difficult. This may also make it more difficult for gifted students to make and maintain rewarding relationships. Given this, consider the strategy of "Closing the Expectation Gap" discussed in Chapter 9 when supporting gifted students.[17,18]

While gifted students may demonstrate advanced functioning in cer-tain areas (making it more difficult for them to relate to same aged peers), they may also demonstrate delayed functioning in other areas (again making it difficult for them to relate to same-aged peers). For example, a gifted student may possess advanced knowledge of vocab-ulary and ability to communicate, which makes them stand out from kids their own age and relate really well to adults. It is helpful to pro-vide gifted kids with opportunities to engage in activities with other gifted children with similar interests so that they can develop and maintain rewarding relationships.

Research suggests that 17 percent to 35 percent of children who are gifted also have a sensory processing disorder.[17] Often, this is reflected as being overresponsive to auditory input, overresponsive to tactile input, or having dyspraxia. It is hypothesized that students who are gifted take in more sensory information in their environment because their brains are taking in more information in general.[17] We have also observed that students who are gifted may be more susceptible to sensory over-load due to the added stress from their cognitive load. Students who are gifted will likely need more sleep than their peers in order to help restore their brain cells and solidify the information they are process-ing on a daily basis. Also, you might need to have some extra snacks on-hand for your gifted students, as their brains need more replenish-ing on a regular basis due to the amount of glucose being utilized.

Often students who are gifted or twice exceptional have learning needs and require accommodations but have greater difficulty accessing them because they typically function at their grade level. Gifted and 2E children face unique challenges in being accepted, supported, and allowed to reach their full potential in our society because, at times, their disabilities mask their giftedness, and at other times, their giftedness masks their disabilities.

Common warning signs associated with giftedness and 2E students include[17,18]:

- Mismatch between intellect and output
- Seemingly bored or unengaged
- Seemingly not living up to their potential
- Anxiety, worry, sadness, and frustration

OTHER COMMON DIAGNOSES THAT IMPACT LEARNING

There are of course many other diagnoses that children may have, which will impact their learning and functioning in school. We will not dive into each of them here but have included references at the end if you'd like to continue expanding your knowledge. Here are a few of the other diagnoses that you may encounter in your classroom[8-10]:

- *Processing speed* is the ability to quickly and accurately complete tasks, learn, or understand new concepts. This is particularly important in a fast-paced learning environment like school. Students with slow processing speed may seem like they're always one step behind. They may miss information or look around the room at others for cues as to what they should be doing.
- *Auditory Processing Disorder (APD)*[3] is characterized by the difficulty taking in, interpreting, and forming meaningful concepts with auditory information. This might include recognizing patterns in auditory information, telling the difference between certain sounds and words, interpreting tone of voice, filtering out important auditory information in a loud environment, and remembering what has been said. Children with APD may be misdiagnosed as having an attention problem.
- *ADHD* is a frontal lobe deficit that impacts ability to sustain attention, maintain organization, track projects and assignments, and manage workload. Often students

with ADHD have deficits in working memory and executive functioning skills. Working memory is the ability to hold information in your brain in order to utilize it for a functional task. Executive functioning skills are primarily frontal lobe skills that are necessary for impulse control, attention switching, organization, and time management, to name a few. Students with ADHD often also display "motor overflow," resulting in excessive movement, touching objects, or talking. A student may be diagnosed with ADHD primarily inattentive, ADHD primarily hyperactive, or ADHD combined type.

- *ASD* is a wide spectrum of deficits marked by social challenges and overall social, emotional, and cognitive rigidity. There is a range of cognitive function associated with ASD, depending on the severity of the diagnosis. Students with ASD may have difficulty with communication, interacting with peers, processing the sensory input in their environments, and navigating new or different environments.[8–10]

Common warning signs associated with other diagnoses that impact learning include[8–10]:

- *Processing speed*
  - Difficulty completing work on time
  - Frustration around completing academic work
  - Slow to transition
  - Makes simple errors
  - Misses social cues or social nuances

- *APD*[3]
  - Mishears what is being said
  - Difficulty following directions, especially multi-step directions
  - Difficulty understanding speech in the presence of background noise
  - Difficulty telling or retelling a story
  - Hurt feelings as a result of misinterpreting what is being said
  - May not understand sarcasm, jokes, or subtle humor
  - Trouble interpreting nonverbal cues
  - Easily distracted, difficulty maintaining attention
  - Difficulty understanding fast or rapid speech

- *ADHD*
    - Acts impulsively
    - Frequently demonstrates inattention
    - Easily distractible by things around the room
    - Demonstrates emotional dysregulation
    - Difficulty organizing work or the workspace
    - Poor time management or awareness of time

- *ASD*
    - Social challenges—may avoid interactions and/or eye contact
    - Concrete thinking
    - Inflexibility and rigidity in thoughts and behaviors
    - Difficulty with transitions
    - Difficulty with reciprocal communication
    - Sensory processing sensitivities

As mentioned above, there is an overlap between many, if not all, of the diagnoses discussed. Students with the same diagnosis may present differently and have challenges in different area. For this reason, and because each child is unique, it is important not to rush to judgment or assume a particular diagnosis. If you are seeing a combination of the signs outlined above, Chapter 10 will discuss what resources are available in order to obtain extra help in identifying and supporting students with learning disabilities.

COMMON MISCONCEPTIONS REGARDING LEARNING DISABILITIES

Now that we've explored some of the common learning differences that students in your classroom might face, it is important to debunk some misconceptions that go along with these differences[19,20]

- Children with learning disabilities have low IQs.[19,20]
    - This is not true. Children with learning disabilities have a discrepancy between their intellect and their academic output. This means that their intellect is often average or above-average, but they cannot produce work that reflects their intellect. This is a cause of considerable frustration and overwhelm for children with learning disabilities because they can feel, internally, that something is not right.

- Learning disabilities are a result of poor teaching or a lack of motivation.[19,20]
  - False. Learning disabilities are brain-based differences that, from an early age, can be identified. They require specialized, targeted, consistent, and structured intervention and academic support. Students with learning disabilities may want to learn but don't know how without appropriate intervention. The "lack of motivation" that may be seen is likely reflective of them going into the blue zone of dysregulation because they are so overwhelmed.

- Learning disabilities are easily diagnosed.[19,20]
  - Unfortunately, there is no quick and easy way to determine if a child has a learning disability. They must undergo comprehensive, extensive, and thorough psycho-educational and/or neuropsychological testing in order to get an accurate diagnosis and profile of their learning strengths and challenges. Often learning disabilities co-occur, so it is likely that a student will have more than one.

- Learning disabilities fade with time, or children can grow out of them.[19,20]
  - Learning disabilities do not just go away. You cannot grow out of them, and they are not developmental. They are with you for life. The sooner a child is identified as having a learning disability, the better. This way the child can receive early intervention services that will set them up for success—academically, socially, and emotionally. Early identification means that the child can develop strategies to compensate for their challenges and learn how to advocate for themselves so they can go on to achieve their goals.

It is important to note that one very common warning sign for all learning disabilities and diagnosable conditions is disruptive behavior. This indicates that the student has reached a state of dysregulation. Often the student functions in this state of dysregulation for the majority of the day, working hard just to "keep it together" as much as possible. A learning disability or a condition such as ADHD, ASD, and processing speed deficits can all lead to students acting out, falling behind, avoiding work, crying at school, becoming frustrated, or refusing to comply, withdrawing, or shutting down.

It is equally important to note that not all students with learning disabilities will demonstrate disruptive behavior as an indication of dysregulation—they may "freeze" or shut down similar to Pablo in the opening vignette. This coping mechanism is, again, helping them to "keep it together" during the school day despite being completely overwhelmed. These students often fly under the radar and are not diagnosed until later in life because they are not causing any "problems" in the classroom.

While we are searching for the "why" behind disruptive behavior, trying to understand why a child may be acting out, or discerning why a student may be shutting down, it is necessary to consider the warning signs listed above to determine if the child might be at risk of having a learning disability. Remember, students want to do well when they can. If we are able to identify a learning disability, or other diagnosable condition, and support the child by providing them with the appropriate interventions, their disruptive behaviors will likely also decrease. We call this "Closing the Expectation Gap" and will talk about this concept further in Chapter 9.

Reflective Activity

It's important to remember that students do well when they can, and when they have the appropriate skills and resources to do so. The behaviors some students demonstrate in the classroom may be an indication that they have a learning disability. Take a moment to think about your experiences with students who have learning disabilities.

What has been positive or rewarding?	
What has been challenging or frustrating?	
What barriers or misconceptions did you carry?	
What questions did you ask to search for the "why"?	

THE POWER OF EARLY INTERVENTION

Teachers, you are on the front lines of identifying early warning signs for students who may have learning disabilities. For students in Pre-K and kindergarten, this may be their first exposure to a great deal of academic input. While yes, there is a developmental curve to learning, you can use the common warning signs above to get a better sense of whether there are any red flags. One of the main reasons Ashley got into this line of work—working with some of the youngest populations—is because she was immensely moved by the research on the importance of early identification and intervention.

Students who are identified early as having learning challenges, and who are provided with the right intervention and support, can go on to lead very successful and rewarding lives. Anecdotal reports suggest that students who understand their learning differences early on can develop a more coherent life narrative that allows them to develop a positive sense of self, and better advocate for themselves as they get older. Students who are not identified early, on the other hand, with each passing year, fall further and further behind. This can cause them to question their self-worth and result in them being confused about their actual abilities. Not only can this be devastating to each individual student and their families, but also it can result in decreased overall outcomes because the brain is less "plastic," or able to be changed, the older we get.

While the earlier you can intervene, the better—it is never too late. Typically, this just means that progress is slower, requires more dedication, and takes longer. If you have a student in second, third, fourth, or fifth grades who you find is struggling, there is still time to make a positive impact and change the course of their life. Ashley even works with teenagers and young adults, who, for one reason or another, were not diagnosed with a learning disability when they were younger. They often went from one school to the next, receiving failing grades, never feeling successful, and subsequently developing co-occurring diagnoses like anxiety and depression. Once their learning disability was identified, it changed the way they approached education; they were able to adjust the way they learned, advocate for themselves, and receive the appropriate intervention and support. In the end, they were able to achieve success and build their self-confidence. It is never too late to start.

SUPPORTING INTEGRATION OF STUDENTS WITH INDIVIDUAL DIFFERENCES

Earlier in the chapter, we talked about using a multimodal sensory approach to integrated learning in the classroom. This is an approach that will benefit all students in your class, as well as promote more integration for students with learning disabilities. However, it is likely that students identified as having learning disabilities will need other support from you and the special education team at your school in order to achieve success. By using attuned listening and co-regulation as a foundation for implementing these strategies, you can come alongside your students and let them know someone is "in their corner." Remember, without first achieving a "just right" state of regulation, the student will continue to struggle participating in academic tasks on any level.

Strategy I: Scaffolding

Scaffolding[21,22] is the systematic way a teacher uses modeling, problem-solving, task management, and guided practice to help a student achieve a specific goal. Typically, scaffolding supports are decreased as a student progresses toward independence and "mastery." One way to think about scaffolding is as though you are constructing a building. At first, the building is fully supported with scaffolding; over time as the foundation, walls, and ceiling are built, you can take one piece of scaffolding down at a time until, finally, the building is standing on its own, without any support. The same idea holds for your students. At first, they need a great deal of scaffolding and support, until they are finally able to do the task on their own. Some students will need more scaffolding than others. Those students with learning disabilities will likely need even more support. Here are some ways you can use scaffolding in your class:

- Break tasks down into very small steps and complete one step at a time.
- Preview tasks with students ahead of time.
- Model and demonstrate in a variety of different ways.
- Check for understanding throughout the activity.
- Allow students to put concepts in their own words.
- Use dictation with students who struggle with writing.
- Make "reference sheets" to put on the student's desk.

Scaffolding: the systematic way a teacher uses modeling, problem-solving, task management, and guided practice to help a student achieve a specific goal.

Interactive Scenario

Read the scenarios and determine how you might use scaffolding to support that student. Reflect on what you expect the outcome to be once you use the scaffolding.

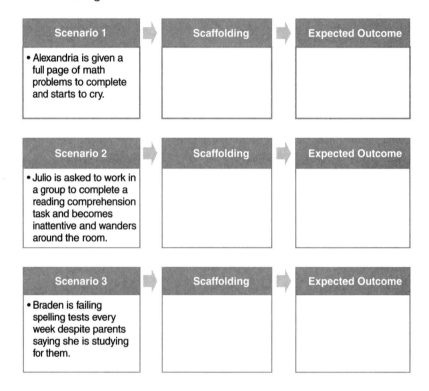

Scenario 1	Scaffolding	Expected Outcome
• Alexandria is given a full page of math problems to complete and starts to cry.		

Scenario 2	Scaffolding	Expected Outcome
• Julio is asked to work in a group to complete a reading comprehension task and becomes inattentive and wanders around the room.		

Scenario 3	Scaffolding	Expected Outcome
• Braden is failing spelling tests every week despite parents saying she is studying for them.		

- In scenario 1, scaffolding options include: using another piece of paper to display one math problem at a time, providing multiplication tables or math formulas, or allowing the student to complete every other problem. The expected outcome is that she can complete the worksheet without crying.

- In scenario 2, scaffolding options include: breaking the task down into one step at a time, allowing the student to work with a partner instead of a group, or providing a visual schedule of each step. The expected outcome is that the student engages fully in the assignment.

- In scenario 3, scaffolding options include: decreasing the number of spelling words until mastery is achieved or allowing the student to re-take the test after learning from mistakes. The expected outcome is that the student passes the spelling test.

- Allow the student to complete some of her work in class and some at home.
- Adjust the number of math problems to complete.
- Use organizational charts and diagrams to add more structure.
- Allow the student to read a passage of a book then listen to it afterward (or vice versa).
- Pair the student with a peer who demonstrates more understanding.

It is important to keep in mind that scaffolding is a step-wise process that requires monitoring and some trial and error. The type of scaffolding that worked with one student may not work with another student. While you may already use scaffolding techniques with your class as a whole, scaffolding for students with learning disabilities will look a little different. Often students with learning disabilities require a more systematic, intensive, and comprehensive step-wise approach to intervention, some of which can be applied in their general education class, while additional support will be necessary in more individualized opportunities such as special education resource specialist programs.

Strategy 2: Build Resilience

Everyone is born with a certain level of tolerance for stress. Some children are born with hardier, more robust nervous systems, while others are born more sensitive and fragile.[23–25] Those children who are born with a fragile disposition makes them even more susceptible to environmental stressors, while others are hardly impacted by their environment at all—brushing stressors off as no big deal. At the same token, not all stress is bad stress! A certain level of stress can be healthy, be adaptive, and work toward building resilience in your students.[24]

No matter what disposition we are born with, we have the capacity to build resilience throughout our lives. **Resilience** is the process of adapting well in the face of adversity, trauma, tragedy, threats, or sources of stress.[25] This is done by overcoming challenges we face when we're under an optimal level of stress.[26] Co-author Jamie often uses a strategy of having her clients rate (easy, medium, hard) how challenging they expect an activity to be prior to starting. This allows them to mentally prepare for the activity, as well as know that they may need a certain level of help to accomplish the task. After the activity is finished, Jamie has them reflect on whether or

Resilience: is the process of adapting well in the face of adversity, trauma, tragedy, threats, or sources of stress.

not the activity was as challenging as they expected. Over time they can also reflect on how an activity once rated as "hard" is now rated as "medium" or "easy."

We want students to know that some stress is good and benefits the growth of our brain, but too much stress is not good and interferes with learning.[26] Finding that "just right" zone of stress and challenge is particularly important for students with learning differences who, many times, feel like everything is hard and they are good at nothing. They may frequently experience "failure" and have a difficult time understanding why things seem to come more easily to other students. Thus, building resilience through co-regulation with a trusted teacher who responds appropriately to nonverbal cues and practices attuned listening is so critical! These students often need more reflection on their strengths, which you can facilitate by highlighting what those strengths may be.

Another part of building resiliency is reinforcing the self-worth of a student, particularly by leaning into their strengths. *We often suggest that teachers provide these students with various roles around the classroom that give them a sense of purpose and responsibility.* These can also help to break up the workload in order to maintain a more optimal level of stress. The student might help pass out papers, help collect papers, help dismiss tables/pods at the end of class, help set the timer for the independent work period, help erase the board, or take turns being the line leader. You know your classroom setup and students best, so think creatively about how you can give empowering responsibilities to your students with learning disabilities.

Here are some other ways to build resiliency in your classroom:

- Foster a growth mindset through encouraging students that they can get smarter and that there are people around them to support their learning.[26]
- Give your students a sense of internal control over challenging situations (like the rating system Jamie uses).
- Talk about stories of resiliency, and ask them to share stories of when they've felt resilient.
- Talk about strengths, and ask them to notice their own strengths.
- Positive relationships with peers and teachers can be a protective mechanism for students overcoming challenges and allow them to build more resilience.[27,28]

- Identify moments of adaptive stress, within the context of a safe, protective relationship.
- Use the strategies outlined in this chapter in regard to teaching students to search for the "why." By providing

Reflective Activity

Building resiliency is a way we overcome challenges and increase our ability to manage stressful situations. This is something that you can foster in your students—particularly those with learning differences—as well as yourself as a teacher.

In which areas of teaching do you need to foster more resilience in yourself?

- _____
- _____
- _____

With whom do you co-regulate when facing adversity or undergoing stress?

- _____
- _____
- _____

When have you encountered a challenging situation in the classroom that resulted in too much stress and thus interfered with your ability to effectively teach?

- _____
- _____
- _____

What is a story of resilience you can share with your students? Think about yourself, a family member, a community member, or someone famous.

- _____
- _____
- _____

them with strategies to learn more about themselves, empower them to become active participants in their learning, to encourage mistakes, and asking questions you will be providing them with the tools to build resiliency.

Strategy 3: Know the Limits

We all have limits. Students with learning differences may have limits that change from day to day—this is common with neurological disorders. You may need to adjust your scaffolding depending on how the student is feeling on a particular day. This should not be seen as a setback—new connections within the brain are continuing to be laid. This may also mean that a student may be more resilient one day compared to the next. This can be influenced not only by living with a learning disability on a daily basis but also by external factors like how much sleep the student received the night before, whether or not the student ate breakfast, or if the student is facing other stressors like moving to a new house.

Paying attention to their nonverbal cues and using attuned listening are necessary to understanding a student's particular limits. It is also important to hear—really hear and listen to—a student when he says he needs a break or *really* can't do something that day or requires more help. Remember that dysregulation can look like "red zone" behaviors like acting out or "blue zone" behaviors like shutting down.

It's also important to recognize your limits when supporting students with learning disabilities. It is easy to invest a lot of time and energy into students who might need more support. Set parameters for yourself both in the classroom and outside of school in terms of the time, finances, and emotional energy you exert with particular students. We know this can be hard because you want to support every student the best that you can. Remember from Chapter 3 that the goal is to be a mirror, not a sponge. Watch for burnout. While the strategies we've discussed in this chapter, and throughout the rest of the book, can certainly support students with learning disabilities, it is likely that they will need other interventions, which we will discuss in Chapter 10. Working within a healthy team of co-regulated individuals and knowing that you're not in it alone is incredibly important to your mental health; this will go a long way in helping you to stay regulated to support the students in your class.

CHAPTER 7

Handwriting That Promotes Integrated Learning

*"I like the process of pencil and paper as opposed to a machine.
I think the writing is better when it's done in handwriting."*
—Nelson DeMille

As Joshua stopped to massage his hand once again, he realized he was losing even more time on his journaling activity. He looked around to see his classmates nearing the end of the first page of the notebook or even turning to the next page in their notebook. Yet, he had barely reached the halfway mark on his paper. It wasn't that he didn't have enough to say. He was so excited to write about his recent fishing trip. It just . . . was hard getting these ideas onto paper. His third-grade teacher, Mr. Avery, had been sympathetic the first semester and thought maybe Joshua would "kick it into gear" and catch up to his peers as the school year progressed. But that wasn't happening. Mr. Avery had received reports at the beginning of the year from the second-grade teacher that maybe Joshua could use some handwriting support, but nothing was ever discussed beyond that. He was a smart kid, but his lack of handwriting efficiency was holding him back.

As it turns out, Joshua entered kindergarten with a "funky" grasp: his four fingertips in a row on the pencil with his thumb stabilizing somewhere in the middle. It was thought he would just "grow out of it" and learn to hold his pencil correctly. No such luck. While Joshua was able to meet the demands of writing early on in kindergarten and first grade with semi-legible writing, he started to feel the added pressure when he entered second grade. He just couldn't keep up, his hand was constantly cramping, and his writing was getting sloppier. Joshua was trying his best. If he "slowed down" and "focused" like he was instructed, then he was never able to complete his work and got marked down because of it. It seemed like he could never win, and it was starting to wear on him emotionally.

As you know, Joshua is not alone. Many students who could have benefitted from handwriting support early on never do, for a variety of reasons. While teaching handwriting seems to be a dying art in many school districts, we feel that handwriting still holds a valuable place in the classroom. Through our experience, teachers are seeing an increasing number of students who struggle in this area, so we felt it important to address this concern as its own chapter. This chapter will emphasize the importance of handwriting and written expression in relation to development, integration of the brain, and its impact on other areas of learning such as literacy skills. As a result, you will be better equipped to search for the "why" when a student is struggling with writing. This information will also help you to integrate various activities in your classroom to promote improved handwriting and provide adaptive strategies to students who need more assistance, especially given that writing can be a big source of dysregulation for many students that will require co-regulation.

NOTE: *The term "handwriting" will refer to the physical act of writing, while the term "writing" will encompass the entire process involved with putting ideas onto paper.*

DEVELOPMENTAL AND SENSORIMOTOR FACETS OF HANDWRITING

Handwriting is not a developmental milestone that is "hardwired" into our neurological system; it is something that must be taught and developed through a wide variety of skills, which we will explore below.[1,2] Some children catch onto handwriting better than others. *It is important to recognize that the development of handwriting has positive long-term implications for brain integration, facilitation of reading skills, comprehension of material, sustained attention, and complex thinking.*[3]

Supportive Diagram

Many developmental skills contribute to the establishment of good handwriting skills. While you may not have much influence over this in your classroom, it is important to keep in mind when considering why a student may be struggling with handwriting.

Therefore, understanding the multifaceted nature of handwriting is an integral part of teaching it in school.

Developmentally, there are many things that contribute to a child's readiness to engage in handwriting. This starts in infancy with tummy time and crawling. Tummy time and crawling mark unique periods in our lives when we are weightbearing through our hands, arms, and shoulders. This is when we develop strength in these body parts and form the arches in our hands. Shoulder strength is critical to stabilizing our arm when writing. Inadequate shoulder strength can result in leaning into the paper too much, grasping too tightly on the pencil, or fatiguing easily, to name a few. The arches in our hand help to maintain an appropriate tripod or quadripod grasp on the pencil with adequate strength.

Tummy time and crawling also develop neck strength and stability that is important for maintaining an upright posture when writing. "Proximal stability equals distal mobility" is a commonly used catchphrase in the world of occupational therapy. This means that in order for us to effectively move our wrists and fingers, we must first establish stability in our shoulders and core muscles. Children with poor postural stability (those who lean on other people or objects, prefer to lie down, have difficulty sitting in a chair) often have poor handwriting because they must focus so hard on simply sitting upright.[4] Their writing is compromised because they seek more stability by leaning on the desk, resting their head in their hand, or pushing harder on the paper—all of these negatively impact the ability of the arm to flow smoothly as a unit and the fingers to move the pencil efficiently.

As infants grow into toddlers and toddlers into children, play activities help to build even more strength and endurance in shoulder, hand, neck, and postural muscles that facilitate good handwriting skills. This includes climbing at the playground, monkey bars, crawling through tunnels, coloring with sidewalk chalk, molding clay or Play-Doh, and yoga. Fine motor skills then start to develop through activities like stringing beads, pegboard puzzles, picking up small objects, buttoning, and peeling stickers. It is in these years that the use of different tools also helps to shape their pencil grasp and ability to manipulate a pencil. Digging with a shovel, banging with a hammer, tapping with a drum stick, eating with a fork, mixing with a spoon, all serve as precursors to manipulating a writing tool. Now they are finally ready to start using crayons, paintbrushes, colored pencils, and regular pencils to learn the horizontal, vertical, circular, and diagonal strokes necessary to form letters.

Midline crossing—the ability to reach across the body—is also a critical developmental skill required for handwriting. Play activities naturally facilitate this skill as infants and toddlers want to reach something on the other side of their body. Typically, children establish a hand dominance by 2–3 years old that can be seen not only when they hold a writing tool but also when they eat with a utensil, play with a toy, or throw a ball. Crossing midline is also required when traveling from left to right across the paper, otherwise the child will need to constantly be adjusting the paper or his position in his chair to compensate. Midline crossing facilitates the horizontal integration of the brain discussed in Chapter 1, which is important for not only the development of motor skills but also the development of emotional regulation.

Then there are all the sensorimotor factors in handwriting. Holding a pencil requires modulation of tactile input from the writing tool on the fingers, discrimination of proprioceptive input to use the right amount of force, tactile discrimination and praxis to move each finger in a distinct position on the pencil, and vestibular discrimination to hold the pencil up against gravity. Manipulating a pencil requires praxis to move the fingers apart from the rest of the hand and arm, discrimination of proprioceptive input to know how much pressure to use on the pencil and paper, and vestibular discrimination to know which direction to move the pencil to form shapes and letters. Forming shapes and letters requires praxis to remember the necessary motor pattern, body awareness to understand right versus left, visual and vestibular integration so the eyes and hand can move in a coordinated manner, and visual modulation as to not get overwhelmed (or underwhelmed) with the visual input on the paper.

All of these sensorimotor skills are facilitated by various indoor and outdoor play activities. Our tactile sense is developed through exploring various textures, like sand, dirt, grass, Play-Doh, shaving cream, food, clothing, and through manipulating toys with various textures. Our vestibular sense is developed through crawling, walking, rolling, spinning, hanging upside-down, swinging, climbing, and jumping activities. Our proprioceptive sense is developed through cuddling, crawling, running, jumping, grasping, banging, hammering, digging, pushing, and pulling. Without these rich sensory experiences early on in life, some students may find it difficult to integrate their sensorimotor systems in order to successfully engage in handwriting.

Throughout infancy and toddlerhood, we are also developing visual-perceptual skills that are required for handwriting. Recall from Chapter 4 that visual-perceptual skills are higher-level cognitive skills for how we utilize the visual input received by the brain. Stacking blocks, stringing beads, puzzles, shape sorters, driving trains along a track, looking at books, cutting with scissors, and playing catch are all things that strengthen the visual-perceptual skills necessary for handwriting. Even outside play like climbing ladders, digging holes, filling buckets with sand, hopscotch, and riding a tricycle establish good visual-perceptual skills.

As you can see, handwriting is a very complex skillset that requires the development and integration of multiple sensorimotor systems. There are many things throughout a student's early life that help establish a readiness for handwriting. There are also many steps along the way where the foundational tools required to learn handwriting may go off track. *It is very important, therefore, for teachers to be aware of and sensitive to handwriting vulnerabilities. Not only will delays in handwriting impact a students' learning, and ability to keep up academically, but it will also impact them emotionally and socially—causing heightened frustration, dysregulation, and negative social comparisons.*

While you may not have much influence over these factors in your classroom, it is important to keep all these things in mind when considering why a student may be struggling with handwriting. Did Joshua skip the milestone of crawling? Does Joshua prefer sedentary activities, like reading books and playing on an iPad, rather than exploring and climbing outside? Some researchers suggest that the effort required to produce legible handwriting may take away from the attention and complexity of their thoughts, which may be the case with Joshua.[2] Being curious about the factors underlying a student's difficulties strengthens your understanding, empathy, and ultimately the teacher-student dyad; these will consequently impact the student's regulation, engagement with learning, and willingness to problem-solve strategies.

WRITING AS AN INTEGRATED BRAIN ACTIVITY

We've talked a lot about the importance of an integrated brain already in this book. Writing is no exception. Writing involves the activation of upwards of 15 different brain regions in both the right and left hemispheres.[5] Without all of these brain regions operating in an integrated manner, writing skills can suffer. Remember from Chapters 1 and 6 that the integration of different areas of the brain is an important part of facilitating academic success. Let's be clear: there are varying degrees of what defines a "successful writer," and every classroom has students with a wide range of writing skills. This goes to show that the way these brain regions are integrated can differ from student to student.

Writing can be broken down into five different skills that are driven by distinct areas of the brain. However, all of these areas must be communicating together in order to produce a final product.

- The premotor area and cerebellum are most responsible for the *fine motor skills* that comprise writing, including pencil grip, control of the pencil, finger differentiation, and motor memory of individual letter formation.
- The language areas of the brain, such as the left fusiform gyrus and right precuneus, are most responsible for **orthographic coding** whereby we must translate verbal ideas in our head to written language, as well as recognize grammar and spelling patterns.
- The occipital lobe, or visual area of the brain, is most responsible for *visual processing* that allows us to recognize different letters and words, keep within the lines, remain oriented to the margins, not reverse letters and numbers, and use proper spacing.
- The frontal lobe, or **executive function** area of the brain, is most responsible for the *organization and planning* that goes into writing a complete sentence, coherent narrative, or well-structured essay.
- The sensorimotor area of the brain is most responsible for *kinesthetic awareness* that results in the appropriate amount of pressure on the pencil and paper and the automaticity of handwriting.

Orthographic coding: the ability to visually form, store, and recall letter sequences and words, as well as understanding the structures of a written language.

Executive functions: a group of cognitive skills that are used to manage, control, organize, and integrate other cognitive functions; they include attention switching, initiating tasks, planning, thinking ahead, inhibiting behavior, and time management.

Supportive Diagram

Writing is a highly integrated activity that activates many areas of the brain. These correspond with the five main skill components that are necessary for the writing process.

(Continued)

(Continued)

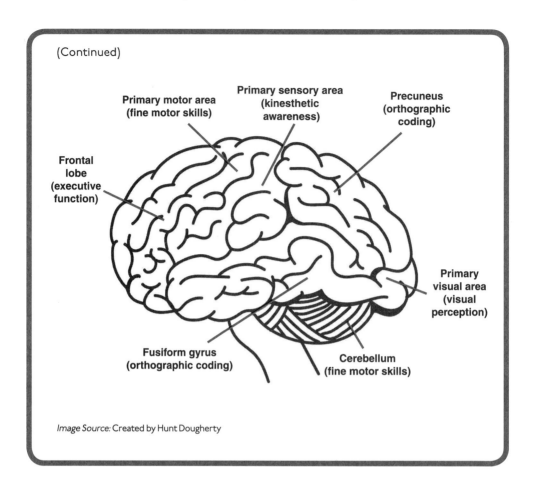

Image Source: Created by Hunt Dougherty

Research shows that the motor areas of the brain responsible for writing are actually activated when we read as well.[5] It is thought that this helps to reinforce the pattern of letter recognition and letter formation. In fact, students categorized as "good spellers" activated the writing-based motor regions of their brain whereas students categorized as "bad spellers" did not. The researchers go on to suggest that "recognizing correctly spelled real words, even if no handwriting is involved, depends on motor patterns for writing the letters in written words."[5] In addition, through neuroimaging, we know that recognition of familiar letters activated both the visual and motor areas of the brain.[6] This goes to show that reading and writing inform each other and complement each other.

As we mentioned in Chapter 6, dysgraphia is a specific learning difference that is broadly characterized as a difficulty with writing. A student with dysgraphia may experience difficulty in any combination of the five aforementioned areas. Thus, it is important to explore what might be underlying the student's difficulty with writing. Different strategies and supports will be necessary depending on which area is most impacted. Some of these strategies and supports are discussed at the end of this chapter. As a note, it is not uncommon for students with dysgraphia to also have another diagnosis, such as dyslexia or dyspraxia.

By now you may be wondering about typing—is that a suitable replacement for writing in our technology-driven world? While typing and screen time have their place in today's technology-driven society, it is undeniable that handwriting still has a valuable role in classrooms. *Typing activates far fewer areas of the brain, meaning that it is overall a less integrated activity.*[5] Research also demonstrates that typing activates more visual areas in the brain and has less distinct motor patterns; handwriting, however, activates both the visual and motor areas of the brain.[5] Handwriting inherently requires the writer to think ahead about what they want to write, organize their thoughts, consolidate information, and self-correct errors in order to avoid continually erasing, starting over in the writing process, or getting marked off for needless mistakes—these are all executive function skills that are important in many aspects of learning.[7] Typing, in contrast, requires less organization and planning because you can more readily move around text and edit what you are typing—not to mention many programs are designed to help auto-correct errors. Research consistently highlights that students perform better on tests, integrate information better, and have improved recall when writing versus typing.[8,9] Encouraging your students to take notes by hand rather than relying on typing, therefore, can be very beneficial for their overall learning. Students tend to have better attention when writing because they must slow down, think more critically, and self-monitor for errors. Thus, formulating first drafts of essays and short-answer responses via handwriting is a good practice for your students.

There are times, however, when typing can help support the learning needs of students, especially students who have been diagnosed with a learning disability. Once you learn how, typing is less labor-intensive and requires fewer motor skills than handwriting so when a large quantity of writing needs to be completed in a designated period of time typing may be a better option. Typing can be practiced when completing final drafts of essays, as most of the benefit of handwriting has been accomplished in previous drafts and brainstorming activities. Children who have language-based learning differences, as delineated in Chapter 6, often benefit from typing programs that assist with spelling, sentence construction, and idea organization, to name a few.

It is best to provide the lowest level of support possible to help your students achieve success and build their confidence, just like the other scaffolding suggestions we provided in Chapter 6. As they gain more skills and confidence with handwriting, for example, they may need to rely less on the use of the computer for typing.

As a note, students with dyslexia, dysgraphia, or attention deficit hyperactivity disorder (ADHD) often benefit from learning and using cursive handwriting rather than printing.[10] When learned properly, cursive can actually be more efficient than printing because the letters flow together with less time required to lift the pencil. It is also thought that this flow of cursive better flows with the thoughts of children with dyslexia and ADHD; the stop and start of printing can often interfere with this flow. However, we caution against teaching a student cursive writing for only a semester or entire school year before giving the student the choice between using cursive or printing. A student will naturally want to choose the style that he or she has learned for a longer period of time—printing—because it feels more comfortable even if it is less effective in the long run. We recommend that cursive be used for a similar period of time as printing before allowing the student a choice. Typically, this means teaching printing from kindergarten to second grade, teaching cursive from third to fifth grade, and allowing the student to choose once he or she enters sixth grade.

REGULATION AND HANDWRITING

Writing is hard for many students, whether it is the physical act, the organization and planning aspect, the translation of thoughts to text, or the integration of all the sensory components involved. This is true for children with and without a diagnosis of dysgraphia. Research suggests that between 5 percent and 33 percent of school-aged children struggle in some aspect of the writing process.[2] Some students take naturally to the process, while others must work hard on perfecting this skill. Meeting each student where he or she is at can be challenging as a teacher. Because handwriting is such an integrated activity that requires many higher level cognitive processes, starting with regulation is the key to success with any student. A student will not be able to "push through" and will likely even shut down, if the expectation gap of writing is too big.

Let's look back at the example with Joshua. He was excited to tell his story about a recent fishing trip but became overwhelmed as soon as he picked up his pencil. He became emotionally overwhelmed, sighed heavily, and would even fall out of his chair in an exasperated heap sometimes. Joshua's dysregulated state that was caused by writing made it even more difficult for him to learn the skills he needed in order to become a better writer. Using the skills outlined earlier in the book to support a state of regulation and calm Joshua's nervous system before diving into any more challenging work can help students to access the necessary parts of their brain needed to learn hard things. By starting with regulation, not only will you help your students access the curriculum needed to learn handwriting and written expression skills, but you will also provide them with lifelong tools such as frustration tolerance that they will take with them everywhere they go.

Students who struggle with writing often experience a large impact on their self-confidence and self-esteem.[2] They don't understand why they have so many ideas but can't seem to get them down on paper. They get frustrated that they can't keep up with their classmates, just

Reflective Activity

Writing can be a challenging activity for many students for a variety of reasons. Think about a current or past student who has struggled with writing, and consider the following:

How were you able to co-regulate with the student?
- _____
- _____
- _____

How could you foster small moments of writing success with this student?
- _____
- _____
- _____

What would you do differently with this student, given the information in this chapter?
- _____
- _____
- _____

What were you able to do to remain regulated when interacting with this student?
- _____
- _____
- _____

like Joshua in the opening vignette. They are embarrassed that other peers or teachers can't read their writing, even though the answer is correct. They may also compare themselves negatively to their peers— "Why can she write so well and my handwriting is such a mess?" Building self-esteem through small moments of success is critical for children who have difficulty with writing. Take the time to co-regulate with these students. Acknowledge that writing can be challenging. Encourage them to do what they can. Provide them with tools to support their needs, as discussed in the next section. A positive teacher-student dyad can go a long way in facilitating regulation so that the student can access the complex skills required for writing.

We also recognize that writing can be a particularly triggering activity for you as a teacher. Maybe you feel like you've presented the same rules of punctuation over and over again, and students still are not capitalizing the first word in a sentence or ending it with a period. Maybe your students only complete the bare minimum of writing necessary but won't expand their thoughts beyond that? No matter what the instigating factor, it is important to find ways to help yourself regulate around writing so that you can then co-regulate with your students.

FACILITATING IMPROVED HANDWRITING

Learning to write takes practice; there's no doubt about it. Practice is how our brain strengthens new motor patterns and, in turn, makes automatic motor pathways so we don't have to think about our movements during handwriting.[10,11] We have talked about this before using the phrase "neurons that fire together, wire together." I bet you can form all the letters of the alphabet with your eyes closed while someone else is talking in the background—all because of your motor memory and automaticity after years and years of practice. As we mentioned in the beginning of the chapter, we feel that due to the integrative nature of handwriting, it is important to continue to teach this skill in the classroom. With that, there are things you can do to help your students be more successful when writing.

When students learn a new symbol or form of writing, they must concentrate more because the motor pattern is not yet automatic. This is why practice is key to establishing good writing habits, and why establishing good writing habits early on is critical. If a student has poor writing habits, such as an inefficient pencil grasp or segmented letter formation, the more these motor patterns are ingrained and become automatic, the more challenging it is to re-wire the brain with new motor patterns. Just think about a baseball player having to change his batting stance after three years of playing versus six months of playing. In fact, handwriting skills tend to develop the most rapidly between the ages of five and seven years (kindergarten and first grade), so intervening early is important.[1]

In addition to practicing the physical act of forming letters and numbers appropriately, there are many other skills that need to be built and strengthened in order for students to be successful in writing legibility and efficiency. Even when you are not directly practicing handwriting, you can still be doing various classroom activities to support the foundations of successful handwriting.

Strategy 1: Prioritize Positioning

Remember: "Proximal stability equals distal mobility." Establishing strong muscles close to the body, such as shoulder, back, neck, and core muscles, will facilitate stronger motor control in the hands and fingers. When decreased proximal stability is present, children must focus so hard on keeping their body still that they cannot adequately perform precise, fluid movements necessary for handwriting. While building proximal stability happens primarily outside the classroom through play-based activities, there are some things you can integrate into your classroom to facilitate stronger proximal stability. This may be more and more necessary as screen time replaces time that students would typically be climbing, running, and exploring outside. Many of these activities can serve as a movement break, as discussed in Chapter 5.

1. Yoga: poses such as bridge, downward dog, triangle, frog, and tree are great to start with. Focus more on the quality of the poses than the quantity of time the poses are held. As students show they can maintain the quality of the pose, then start to challenge them to hold each pose for a longer period of time.

2. Balancing on one foot: try this on the right leg, left leg, and with eyes closed. Encourage students to stand like a flamingo without wrapping their foot around their opposite leg, holding their foot with their hand, or holding onto something nearby.

3. Superman position: students should lie on the floor on their stomachs with their arms and legs stretched out (i.e., in full extension). When you say "go," they should lift their arms, legs, and head off the floor to pretend like they're flying through the air. Hold this position for as long as possible—see if you can set new class records each time.

4. Rollie-pollie bug position: students should lie on the floor on their backs with their arms crossed over their shoulders and their knees bent. When you say "go," they should lift their feet off the ground and bring their head up to their knees, similar to doing a crunch or sit-up. Hold this position for as long as possible—see if you can set new class records each time.

5. Wheelbarrow walks: students need to partner up and decide who will go first as the "wheelbarrow" (student A). Student A will put her hands on the ground while Student B will lift up Student A's feet. Student A will walk on her hands around the perimeter of the classroom in the direction you instructed. Student B and Student A will then switch.

Positioning of the chair and desk (or table) must be considered as well. The ideal position in a chair for tabletop activities, handwriting included, is 90-90-90: 90° (an "L" shape) at the hips, 90° at the knees, and 90° at the ankle with feet flat on the floor.[1] If the chair is too small, then the student will slouch back and will try to find a comfortable position for her legs. If the chair is too large, the student will not feel supported and may sit on the edge of the chair to put his foot on the floor. The height of the desk or table also influences posture, shoulder stability, and wrist stability. The ideal table height should allow for the elbows to rest comfortably at a 90° angle (an "L" shape). If the desk or table is too short, then the student will feel the need to hunch over or lean on his arms for stability, thus compromising the fluidity of their handwriting. If the desk or table is too high, then the student will need to reach up and may not see their work as well. We all know that students come in a wide variety of sizes, so different sized chairs, desks, and tables—or chairs, desks, and tables that can be adjusted—may be necessary to support their positioning needs. If you cannot change the height of chairs or desks, then consider the following ideas to support the positioning needs of your students:

1. Place phone books wrapped in duct tape, sturdy shoeboxes, or upside-down plastic bins under the student's feet.

2. Allow the student to sit on a core disc or other type of cushion to raise the seat.

3. Have the student use a slantboard to elevate the desk surface.
4. Place a thick textbook on the desk to elevate the surface.
5. Allow the student to stand.

Alternative seating options have gained popularity in classrooms over the years, and rightly so. Sometimes chairs just don't provide the support a student needs to engage in learning, including handwriting. But how do you know which alternative seating option a student should use? And what are the best alternative seating options out there? Chapter 5 addresses some alternative seating options for children with different sensory needs, but there are also some considerations for children who need handwriting support. As with most supportive devices, you may need to experiment with which seating option is best for a particular student.

Supportive Diagram

Positioning while sitting at the desk is an important part of a student's handwriting quality. Proper positioning supports the student's posture, shoulder stability, and wrist stability, all of which are important for the fluidity of handwriting. Adjusting the heights of your student's tables, desks, and chairs can help support their individual needs. Remember the 90-90-90 rule!

Image Source: Created by Hunt Dougherty

1. TheraBand on the front legs of the chair: use this for students who need extra proprioceptive feedback to their body, for students who like to sit on one leg in their chair, or for students who shift their positions in their chair.
2. Ball chair: use this for students who switch between sitting and standing, for students who shift their positions in their chair, or for students who need extra movement.
3. Wobble stool: use this for students who have trouble focusing, for students who shift positions in their chair, or for students who rock back and forth on the front/back legs of the chair.

Now that proximal stability has been established, positioning of pencil in the hand should be addressed. The most functional grasp patterns, according to research, are the dynamic tripod, lateral tripod, dynamic quadripod, lateral quadripod, and the adjusted or modified tripod grasp.[12] These grasps allow for the pencil to rest in the thumb webspace (i.e., the space between the thumb and index finger), allow for fluid movement of the fingers, and decrease the pressure load on the hand. This does not mean that students who have alternative grasp patterns will not or cannot have legible, efficient handwriting without any notable difficulties.[12] However, it does mean that *most* students will benefit from using one of these grasp patterns because of the long-term implications for endurance, speed, and legibility as writing demands increase. This is the circumstance in which Joshua finds himself in the opening vignette. Focusing on his pencil grasp in earlier years would have prevented many of the challenges he is now facing in third grade where he must produce a much larger volume of writing. Plus, we cannot predict whether there will be future consequences on the student's ergonomics that may cause unintended injury.

Consider utilizing some of these strategies and activities to help support the pencil grasps of your students:

*   Use modeling clay and putty to strengthen hand muscles.
*   Use tweezers and chopsticks (you can put stickers on them to indicate where fingers should be placed).
*   Pinch the tip of the pencil with thumb and index finger, and then flip it backwards.
*   Use broken crayons and small pencils (like "golf pencils"), especially for pre-K and kindergarten students.

Supportive Diagram

These represent the most functional pencil grasp patterns that should be emphasized during handwriting.

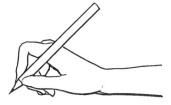

Dynamic Tripod

Dynamic Quadripod

Lateral Tripod

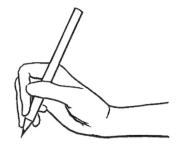

Lateral Quadripod

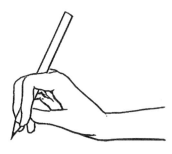

Modified Tripod

Image Source: Created by Hunt Dougherty

- Hold a pom pom, cotton ball, or small rubber ball (with the middle, ring, and pinky fingers) in the same hand as the pencil.
- Make a "tennis ball monster" by cutting a two-inch slit in a tennis ball and squeezing open to "feed" him small objects

(remember to squeeze with the thumb on one side of his "mouth" and index and middle finger on the other side of his mouth).

- Practice "sequential finger touching"—touch each finger to the thumb individually; repeat both forward (index finger to pinky) and backward (pinky to index finger) with each hand. As students progress, have them do both hands at the same time and then challenge them to do each of these with their eyes closed. Studies have found that this skill is a predictor of handwriting legibility.[5]

For students who are struggling with the positioning of the pencil, you might consider changing the pencil they are using or adding a pencil grip. Using the least restrictive accommodation is recommended early on in learning handwriting, such as pre-kindergarten through first grade. This allows the student to achieve a functional grasp without depending too much on the accommodation. As the student shows progress in her ability to hold the pencil functionally without an adaptive pencil or pencil grip, then you can more readily remove it. However, once a student enters second grade and is still having difficulty achieving an appropriate grip, such as Joshua, then it is recommended that a more supportive accommodation be used in order to combat the poor motor habits already in place and more aggressively address the concern. These are the accommodative pencils and grips, *in order from least supportive to most supportive*, that Jamie typically recommends:

- Broken crayons or golf pencils (these are good for naturally facilitating a tripod or quadripod grasp)
- Jumbo grip pencils
- Triangular pencils
- Handi-writer (you can also just use a thin hair tie wrapped around the wrist and end of the pencil)
- EZ grip
- Start Right grip
- Pinch grip
- Crossover grip (this grip would be a good starting place for Joshua)
- Grotto grip
- Writing claw grip

Interactive Scenario

Consider how you can support the positioning needs of the students in the following scenarios. What accommodations might the student need? What expected outcome do you anticipate?

Scenario 1	Accommodation	Expected Outcome
• Calvin, a second grader, is tall for his age. He often leans his head in his hand when writing.		

Scenario 2	Accommodation	Expected Outcome
• Jaime, a Kindergartener, holds his pencil with a fisted grasp.		

Scenario 3	Accommodation	Expected Outcome
• Karla, a fourth grader, often switches positions when sitting and rocks back in her chair.		

- Scenario 1: Calvin could benefit from a taller desk or using a slantboard to elevate his writing surface. This would set him up for a better upright posture when writing.

- Scenario 2: Jaime could benefit from using broken crayons or golf pencils. This would facilitate a more functional grasp by preventing him from using his entire fist.

- Scenario 3: Karla could benefit from using a wobble stool. This would still allow her some movement, but she would be better able to focus on writing.

Strategy 2: Make It Multisensory

Just like it is important to integrate multisensory activities in your classroom instruction to support the learning needs of students, so is using multisensory activities to facilitate handwriting. As explored above, most of the sensory systems are necessary to perform the motor task of handwriting; this includes the visual, tactile, proprioceptive/kinesthetic, vestibular, and auditory systems. One study found that sensorimotor experiences in the classroom increased the visual processing of preschool students learning how to recognize letters, concluding that "learning by doing" through motor and sensory activities lay important foundations for writing.[13] Programs like *Handwriting Without Tears* have gained much attention over the years because of their success in using a multisensory approach to handwriting.

- Visual-perceptual activities:
  - Do mazes, connect-the-dots, and color-by-numbers.
  - Do crossword puzzles, word searches, and word scrambles.
  - Play "I Spy" games and worksheets.
  - Build with tangrams and parquetry blocks.
  - Form large figure-eights, infinity signs, and rainbows in the air or on paper.
  - Do jigsaw puzzles.

- Tactile activities:
  - Form letters in shaving cream using fingers.
  - Form letters in finger paint.
  - Form letters in sand (wet, dry, kinetic).
  - Form letters with Play-Doh and clay.
  - Form letters with pyramid-shaped sponges on chalkboards.
  - Form letters with pyramid-shaped sponges in paint.

- Proprioceptive activities:
  - Write letters using sidewalk chalk or on chalkboards.
  - Write letters on sandpaper; try out different grits.
  - Write letters in Play-Doh or clay.
  - Form letters with toothpicks and marshmallows.

- Vestibular/Movement-based activities:
  - Form letters with your body individually.
  - Form letters with your body with a partner.
  - Write letters in the air with your index finger.
  - Write letters in the air with your foot.
  - Form letters using wood pieces (see *Handwriting Without Tears* curriculum).
  - Practice sequential finger touching.

- Auditory activities:
  - Sing songs about phonics.
  - Say mnemonics while forming letters (e.g., "The letter E goes down, across, across, across").
  - Clap, snap, or stomp to different phonetics of each letter.
  - Sing song about letter formation (see *Handwriting Without Tears* curriculum).

Strategy 3: Break It Down

As we mentioned, writing is a process that involves many steps. Some students find it difficult to manage all of those steps all at once. For example, they may have a lot of ideas and stories to tell but not know where to start, how to create a cohesive narrative, how to keep their thoughts straight, or how to best manage their time. Or they may get so hung up on whether or not their spelling is accurate or if they are remembering all the punctuation and grammar rules. Or they may never move beyond "sounding it out" to recognizing familiar words and word patterns. This is particularly true for students who struggle with executive functioning and orthographic coding aspects of writing.

In order to support the executive function needs of students, consider the following:

NOTE: Often, but not always, executive function difficulties are seen in students with a diagnosis of ADHD and/or learning disabilities.

- Integrate brainstorming sessions into your writing periods. These are quiet times where the student is simply coming up with ideas and following her imagination, activating parts of the brain that cannot be accessed when engaged in other activities.[14] You can encourage students to jot down words, phrases, or pictures to help them remember their ideas but nothing beyond that.
- Use organization charts and outlines to aid with the sequencing of ideas and mapping out a plan. This can eliminate the frustration of having to re-order entire paragraphs of writing. It can also help students stay focused on the main idea and not "go off the rails."
- Use thought bubble organizers to break down the writing process. The central bubble serves as the main idea with spokes coming off the main idea with supporting ideas. These should be one-word or short phrases, enough to trigger the student's memory when revisiting the diagram.

- For younger students, statements like "First . . . then . . ." can help create a linear thought process. Use these statements to create a cohesive narrative and sequential ideas.
- Practice other sequencing-based tasks in the classroom in order to flex students' executive functioning skills. Some ideas include origami, following multistep instructions, art activities, step-by-step drawing, board games, and following a recipe.
- Help students estimate the amount of time they think certain steps in a writing task will take them to complete. This will teach them time management that is an important part of not feeling overwhelmed or not getting too distracted when writing. Some students may need verbal reminders as to when they should be moving on to the next step.
- Place a visual timer, like the Time Timer, where your students can see it. This will help them better organize their time by visualizing how much time is remaining for a particular task.

In order to support the orthographic coding needs of students, consider the following:

NOTE: *Often, but not always, orthographic coding difficulties are seen in students with a diagnosis of dyslexia.*

- Focus on phonological awareness without looking at any words. Have the students imagine what the letters look like when they are going through phonics. This will help them to better "sound out" a word rather than solely relying on memory of sight words.
- Create a "word bank" list for high-frequency words or specific topic vocabulary the student will be using when writing. This will support their spelling needs to decrease the demands they feel when writing.
- Help students find patterns when spelling certain words, and when there are exceptions to the patterns (which is true a lot in English!). Place a "reference sheet" of these patterns on their desk for them to reference when writing.
- Encourage students to self-edit their written work by identifying a certain number of words they think they

Reflective Activity

Looking back on the three supportive strategies listed for writing, consider the following:

> **Which strategies do you already incorporate into your classroom?**
>
> _____   _____   _____

⬇

> **Which strategies do you feel could benefit the majority of your students?**
>
> _____   _____   _____

⬇

> **Which strategies do you feel could benefit a specific student?**
>
> _____   _____   _____

spelled incorrectly. Start with a smaller number so the student does not feel defeated or overwhelmed. This will help you identify patterns of errors the student is making and also help support the student in recognizing his errors. You can work through the correct spelling of those specific words together, as well as key in the student on the patterns you are noticing (when age-appropriate).

• Have writing periods where you encourage the student to only focus on their writing and not on their spelling or grammar.

As always, the language that you use when supporting these students is critical. It is important to affirm their feelings, not give them more feedback than they can handle, and point out their strengths and improvements. In this way, you are providing co-regulation that will support the teacher-student dyad, improve their self-confidence, and help them improve their writing abilities.

Keep in mind that students with learning disabilities, as outlined in Chapter 6, may also struggle with writing for other reasons, such as language-processing or word-retrieval vulnerabilities. Some writing difficulties are more subtle than others. As always, be curious and continue to search for the "why." It is important to note that if you have a student with particular difficulty writing that requires more assistance than you can provide, then you should refer her to a specialist who can help identify the concerns, such as an occupational therapist, neuropsychologist, speech and language pathologist, or educational therapist. We will discuss more about these resources in Chapter 10.

CHAPTER 8

Considerations for Specialty Teachers

"Everyone thrives most in his or her own unique environment."
—Marilu Henner

Isaac trudged slowly into the gymnasium yet again already looking fatigued before physical education (PE) class began. Ms. Radishaw knew it was going to be another challenging day for Isaac. Ever since they started the unit on dance two weeks ago, Isaac just wanted to goof off. He would fall to the floor intentionally and purposefully mess up. Up until this point, Ms. Radishaw would approach Isaac individually to correct his errors and would reprimand him in front of the class in order to get him back in line. She could tell that dance was harder for him, but it couldn't be *that* hard—they were only learning basic dance steps and every other student seemed to catch on quickly.

Ms. Radishaw thought to herself, "I'll give him two more chances today and then I'm going to do something about it." Sure enough, Isaac exhausted his two chances only 10 minutes into class. But today when Ms. Radishaw approached him, he not only fell onto the floor but also started to cry. "I just can't do it, Ms. Radishaw. I'm a terrible dancer," Isaac commented. "You can do this, Isaac. You're just not focusing or trying hard enough," Ms. Radishaw replied.

What Ms. Radishaw should consider doing next is asking "why" Isaac was having such consistent difficulty in executing the dance steps. Was he having difficulty keeping up with the music? Was he struggling with processing the verbal directions? Was he demonstrating a deficit in motor coordination? Was he having difficulty working through his frustration tolerance or feelings of embarrassment? Was he overstimulated with all the noise? Specialty classes provide unique and rich sensory experiences for children. Such classes may also present certain challenges for particular students. It is clear that Isaac was having difficulty with integration on some level, requiring support, collaboration, and creative problem-solving[1] in order to develop a solution.

Teachers of specialty classes, we love your creativity, flexibility, and passion for enriching the lives of your students. Whereas core classroom teachers typically remain with a certain group of students throughout the year, you are in the unique position to have the opportunity to work with most, if not all, of the students in your school. You have many more children on your radar, for a shorter amount of time than typical classroom teachers. You may end up working with kindergarteners and fifth graders in the same day—and because of this, your knowledge of developmental needs is vast. This can be an exciting and fun way to engage with students; however, it can also present distinct challenges, especially for children who have particular differences and needs.

We know that there are many resources[2] out there already for teachers of specialty classes, so we will keep this brief, spending time discussing how some of the strategies described throughout this book apply to you. This chapter will explore the various factors that can influence regulation, attention, and participation in specialty classes, as well as ways to facilitate improved performance. We recognize that specialty classes provide many opportunities and some challenges. They take place in unique environments and provide students with exposure to many different sensory inputs. Teachers of specialty classes are able to offer students access to a wide array of enrichment activities that some students may not have access to, or experience otherwise. Because of the range of ages and developmental stages of students that you work with on any given day, and the unique aspects of your job, we would love to spend a few minutes discussing how the concepts in this book apply to the amazing work that you do.

It is important to note that the information in this chapter contains many generalizations and should only serve as a starting point for your curiosity.

Students with specific diagnoses, such as sensory processing disorder, attention deficit hyperactivity disorder (ADHD), and autism spectrum disorder (ASD), all have unique strengths and vulnerabilities that must be considered. However, we do want to highlight that specialty classes might be more supportive or challenging for certain students (even those without a diagnosis), and we want to encourage you to explore "why" so that you can better engage with those students.

A NOTE ABOUT RELATIONSHIPS AND REGULATION IN SPECIALTY CLASSES

Because all students have individual learning styles, sensory preferences, emotional responses, and academic needs, they will have varying responses to the differing learning environments and demands of specialty classes. A student who struggles in PE, for example, may excel in library or art. A student who shuts down, or freezes, in their more academic core classroom may end up coming to life in their art, music, and PE classes. It, of course, depends on each student's unique needs and individual differences, which will determine why they are successful in certain classroom settings and have difficulty in others. This information, in and of itself, can be a valuable piece of the puzzle during our search for the "why." This is also why teachers of specialty classes need to be a part of the conversation when developing a plan for students who are struggling. Often, specialty teachers are left out of the conversation, feel less supported than other teachers, and may have greater difficulty directly applying these concepts to their distinct learning environments.

While students typically only see teachers in specialty classes one to two times per week, the relationships developed in these environments do impact learning. In fact, specialty teachers have the opportunity to really reach students who may be struggling in regular classroom settings. If a child has a particular affinity for art, athletics, reading, or languages, specialty classes can be a time where they excel, feel a sense of pride, accomplishment, success, and mastery. This is extremely necessary for students who may be struggling in other aspects of academia. Allowing students to feel a sense of success in your class is vital to their sense of self-esteem, self-worth, sense of belonging, and development of self-efficacy. If you know that a particular student requires extra support outside your class, it is particularly important to provide labeled (specific) praise when you see them thriving in another environment like your specialty class.

Reflective Activity

Think back to your specialty classes when you were in elementary school. Recall a specific teacher who you had in PE, art, or music, for example.

> **What made that teacher stand out or seem different from the others?**
> _____

⬇

> **How do you remember feeling in that particular specialty class?**
> _____

⬇

> **What was special, challenging, or memorable about the specialty teacher?**
> _____

Other times, however, because of the additional sensorimotor inputs, changes in routine and classroom settings, and unique learning demands, students with special needs may have greater difficulty in specialty classes. They will need even more co-regulation through the teacher-student dyad in order to fully participate in a specialty class. Focusing on developing relationships with your students, particularly those who may be struggling in your class, is an important foundation for their success in your class. It will help you search for "why" they may be struggling. This chapter will review concepts already discussed in this book, and help specialty teachers apply co-regulation techniques, as well as explore the unique sensorimotor and learning-based factors that may arise, *keeping in mind that all students are different and the generalized observations may not apply to all students with certain diagnoses.*

SENSORIMOTOR FACTORS IN SPECIALTY CLASSES

As outlined in Chapters 4 and 5, sensorimotor integration is a key piece to a child's regulation and ability to produce efficient movements and

Reflective Activity

Look back on the information provided in Chapter 4 and 5. Consider the unique sensorimotor aspects of your specialty class, and how they may result in a particular student having difficulty or excelling in your class.

Primary Sensorimotor Inputs	Possible Challenges	Possible Successes
• _____	• _____	• _____
• _____	• _____	• _____
• _____	• _____	• _____

meaningful responses. While sensory input abounds in core classrooms, it is even more prevalent in specialty classrooms and environments. As we now know from Chapters 4 and 5, students may be triggered by certain sensorimotor input that makes functioning and regulation more difficult for them. They also may be regulated by sensorimotor input that actually makes functioning in specialty classes easier, and more successful, for them.

Physical Education

PE actively engages the sensory and motor systems more than any other class at school. In particular, balance and coordination-based activities like standing on one foot, jumping jacks, learning dance steps, jumping rope, imitating poses, riding a bicycle, and climbing all require good sensorimotor processing. Ball sports and games rely on eye-hand coordination so that the eyes can follow a ball through the air and then move toward a ball to catch it without losing balance or losing track of the ball. Students also must have adequate strength and endurance to participate for the entire class without becoming fatigued. They must use the right amount of force when throwing or kicking a ball.

Let's face it. Gymnasiums are also loud and echo tremendously. It can be difficult to hear your own voice, which makes listening to instructions even more challenging. This level of noise can be overwhelming for anyone. Gym mats, rubber balls, and other equipment all have distinct smells, especially when those odors are contained inside. Not to mention how stinky 30-plus students can get after running around (or removing their shoes, if necessary, for a particular activity). The texture of different balls, equipment, mats, grass, to name a few, provides a wide variety of tactile input.

So far, that means that PE requires a great deal of vestibular, proprioceptive, and visual integration to engage in a wide variety of motor-based activities, and provides considerable auditory, olfactory, and tactile stimulation. PE also has a unique impact on the arousal system because it requires a high degree of regulation switching. This means that students must go from being quiet and listening to instructions, to being physically engaged or competitive in a game, to going back to listening instructions or waiting their turn, to again being "in the game."

You can see now how much is going on in terms of sensorimotor input in one PE class. You can imagine how some students who may struggle with balance, eye-hand coordination, endurance, or even auditory sensitivity might be impacted. For students, like Isaac in the vignette above, PE is highly dysregulating and frustrating because of the level of coordination required for many activities. Some students who are dysregulated may resort to "fight or flight" behaviors by avoiding activities, refusing to participate, running around the gym, or yelling. Other students who are dysregulated may resort to "freeze" behaviors by falling onto the ground, hiding in a corner, or appearing lethargic (despite entering the gymnasium with adequate energy).

Physical fitness and athletic abilities are also closely tied to social and emotional functioning. Students who are more athletic are often viewed more favorably, while those who lack coordination or endurance may be viewed as weak. This can impact students in terms of peer relationships, developing self-esteem, and a sense of self-worth. Children who experience difficulty with motor coordination may resort to "silly" behaviors as a way to mask or hide their vulnerabilities. This silly behavior reduces the social demands of appearing athletically adept and the risk of social ridicule. Some children would rather be viewed by their peers as silly, than be identified as weak or uncoordinated athletically.

For some students, PE is a regulating activity and helps to reset their attention after sitting in a classroom for an extended amount of time. This is because of the amount of sensory input, particularly vestibular and proprioceptive, that PE provides. Such students may see PE as an escape from the routine demands of academic work and a means to tap into their athletic self. This may be the environment in school where the student most thrives.

Art

The beauty of art lies in the colors, shapes, and mediums that students can manipulate. Naturally this creates visual stimulation. It also creates tactile stimulation from touching the materials: sponges, cotton balls, clay, oil pastels, glue, tissue paper, foam all have a different texture and may leave different residue on the hand. Keep in mind that all the various art supplies have distinct smells that, particularly when confined to a classroom, can get to be quite pungent.

Drawing, painting, building, sculpting, and many other artistic endeavors require a large degree of fine motor coordination. This may involve manipulating a writing tool, using scissors, tearing paper, and pinching clay with just the right amount of force.

This means that art provides visual, tactile, and olfactory stimulation, as well as requires vestibular, proprioceptive, and tactile integration to engage in fine motor coordination. Again, there are going to be those children who thrive in this environment, and those who are overwhelmed by the multitude of sensorimotor task demands put on them. Students with tactile and visual sensitivity, for example, may get easily overwhelmed and enter their "fight or flight" zone of regulation. This may mean throwing materials, smearing textures every which way, refusing to touch something, or wanting to look out the window. Or a dysregulated student may enter the "freeze" zone of regulation whereby he might put his head on the table, not be able to make a decision, or close his eyes.

Yet, for some students, the freedom to manipulate things with their hands and interact with a variety of textures will be calming and help them to regulate through this creative freedom. They might have strong fine motor skills compared to their gross motor skills, which allows them to "show off" what they can do with their hands despite not being great at sports. This may be the environment where the student develops a true sense of himself.

Music

It probably comes as no surprise that the sensory system most impacted in music class is the auditory system. The loudness of instruments and singing. The different frequencies of instruments and music. The unfamiliar sounds of instruments and songs. All of this in a confined space.

There are some other more subtle sensory aspects to consider in music as well, such as the smells, tastes, and textures associated with different instruments. Wood smells and feels far different than plastic, which also differs from brass. Then factor in the body coordination of tapping, hitting, shaking, clapping, or stomping to a specified beat. For older students, there is also a fine motor coordination component required to learn how to play instruments. Learning where your fingers are supposed to go and when you are supposed to move them (without constantly looking at them) requires a high level of body awareness. Plus, there is considerable visual stimulation once reading music comes into play—all of those notes on the paper can get quite overwhelming for some students.

To review, that's auditory, tactile, visual, olfactory, and gustatory stimulation on top of the vestibular and proprioceptive integration required to coordinate movements with appropriate body awareness. That's a lot of sensorimotor input in one class! Students with auditory sensitivity and poor coordination are the most likely to demonstrate challenges in this environment. They may cover their ears, run around the room, hum to themselves, play out of turn, bang too hard, or just sit there disengaged. For students who enjoy auditory input, feeling different instruments, and can easily coordinate their fingers, music may be the environment where they build self-confidence and find a "just right" challenge they can learn to master.

Library

Visiting the library is particularly unique as a specialty class in that it is lacking many sensory inputs. The library may be a very calming and regulating place for students who become overwhelmed easily by sensory input. However, it can prove challenging for students who need certain sensory input in order to be more regulated, for students who have difficulty remaining quiet and still, or for students who have difficulty reading.

That said, the primary sensory input at the library is visual. Looking through the aisles and aisles of books can be exciting for some students and overwhelming for others. The book jacket colors and titles on the spine may become jumbled or dizzying. A more subtle sensory input that a library offers is the smell of books, both old and new. Some students find this comforting and alluring while others can barely crack open the pages because the smell is too repugnant.

So we can see that the library is often lacking in auditory, vestibular, proprioceptive, and tactile input, while at the same time offers much visual stimulation and olfactory stimulation. You may see students get dysregulated by moving all around the library, jumping up and down, taking books off the shelves unnecessarily, or making noises to themselves due to the lack of sensory input. Or you may see students get dysregulated by rubbing their eyes, looking at a blank wall, pulling the first book they see off the shelf, or plugging their nose due to the sensory stimulation.

Lunch/Recess

Similar to the gymnasium, the cafeteria often has an intense amount of auditory input: the echoes that resound from the various conversations, the banging of trays and utensils and lunch containers, and the pitter patter of feet. Plus there is usually a loud air conditioner or heater humming in the background that makes it difficult to hear.

Then there are all the smells and tastes. Eating is one of the most stimulating sensory experiences in which we engage on a regular basis. The smell of the school-provided lunch and the smells from other students' lunches (tuna fish sandwich, anyone?) adds to the complexity of the eating experience. And because 80 percent to 90 percent of what we taste is actually what we smell, it can negatively impact a student's appetite.

Visually there is a lot to take in as well. It seems like many cafeterias are in continual motion. Students opening their lunches and containers. Students walking to their seat with their trays. Students raising their hands to ask a question. Students being dismissed to throw away their trash. Not to mention choosing what to eat first in your own lunch!

So far, that's a large amount of auditory, olfactory, gustatory, and visual stimulation. Then you add to it the fine motor coordination required to open containers, unwrap packages, and use utensils. Plus you need to maintain adequate postural stability to stay sitting on a bench or in a chair. This means the vestibular, proprioceptive, and tactile systems must be working together as well. No wonder some students get completely overwhelmed with eating lunch and choose to only eat a few bites, only eat the foods they *really* like, switch between standing and sitting, or use only their hands when eating.

Then they are released outside to recess. Much like the sensorimotor demands of PE, recess requires students to engage their vestibular and proprioceptive systems to engage in a variety of movement-based activities. Swinging, going down the slide, running, riding a tricycle or bicycle, climbing the play structure, jumping, and hanging upside-down on the monkey bars are all good examples. For many students, this unstructured free play at recess can be regulating, providing their bodies with the input they need to refocus in the classroom.

Despite being outside in an unconfined space, the noise level of students at recess can still be resounding. Not to mention there may be uncontrollable environmental sounds such as a nearby train, factory, or construction site. And there are usually plenty of whistles being blown. Often, recess also allows students to play in sand, dig in the dirt, roll in the grass, and find treasures in nature. Students may bump into each other, brush up against one another, or tag each other on the back. Recess can be a large source of visual stimulation as well—ball sports, jump ropes flailing, watching a large number of peers run around, and all the colors on the play equipment.

All said and done, that means recess requires vestibular and proprioceptive integration to engage in a wide variety of motor-based activities, and provides considerable auditory, tactile, and visual stimulation. While recess and breaks are a necessary and important part of the day, they can mean different things to different students. This is why students' play might look very different at recess. Some may choose to engage their tactile systems more and stay in the sand box; others may choose to engage their proprioceptive systems more and stay on the monkey bars; and others may choose to remove themselves from everything and play cards with a peer off to the side.

For those of you who are responsible for watching students during breaks and recess, we salute you! This is likely an active and potentially overwhelming time with so many children in a large open space—it can be difficult to keep track of everything that is going on. While most students will likely thrive in this environment, there may be some who struggle. Similar to PE, the physical demands of recess and breaks can cause anxiety related to social ridicule about appearing weak or uncoordinated. Students who are impacted in this way may look lonely: be wandering around the outside of the yard by themselves, be sitting on benches by themselves or playing in the grass, sand, or dirt, independently. Or students may get utterly overwhelmed with the amount of auditory and visual stimulation required to keep up with their peers during structured games, resulting in yelling or hitting. There is truly a tricky balance of supporting students in their sensory needs as they reset to enter the classroom and making sure that students feel safe and connected.

LEARNING DIFFERENCES UNIQUE TO SPECIALTY CLASSES

Students with learning disabilities, ADHD, and other diagnosable conditions may excel and find your specialty class to be a place of refuge for them. If this is the case, you, as their specialty teacher, can use this as an opportunity to connect with them, build their sense of self-esteem, and help them to develop a sense of belonging, acceptance, and connection at school. While this may be true in some instances, we felt it would be helpful to identify some potential challenges that students with learning differences and unique challenges may experience in specialty classes.[3]

While we make many generalized statements below regarding functioning in various specialty classes, it is important to remember that all students' learning needs are different and unique. What is true for one student with ADHD or dyslexia, for example, may not be true for another student with the same diagnosis.

Physical Education

PE can be challenging for students with learning disabilities if they struggle with listening to instructions, processing order of instructions, speed of processing information, and adjusting behaviors accordingly. It requires a high degree of attention to listen to and attend to the instructions being given, especially with multistep instructions involved in many sports games and motor-based activities. It requires students to keep up with processing the instructions that are given, to sequence the physical movements, and to track when they are supposed to do the specific instructions. And many times games and activities have exceptions to the rules, which add another layer of mental flexibility and ability to quickly process when that exception may apply. For students who struggle with auditory processing, processing speed, attention, and transitions, it can be difficult for them to keep up with what is being asked of them.

Art

Art is more of a creative and intuitive activity that can be challenging for students who think more linearly and have difficulty coming up with their own ideas. It is not uncommon for students with learning challenges to be perfectionists—trying to exert some semblance of control over their environment—which can impact how they manage their time and wrestle with the notion that beauty also lies in imperfection.

Art projects often require the ability to attend to instructions, follow sequences, and utilize executive functioning skills to initiate tasks appropriately, follow steps, and maintain a level of organization. This can be particularly challenging for students with ADHD. They may get lost in all the choices, not know what to do next, rush through their project, or underestimate the amount of time something may take.

Music

Similar to art, music taps into creativity. However, as students progress in learning how to play instruments, a high level of integration between multiple brain regions is required to learn how to read music and then actually play the instrument to a beat.[4] Children with auditory processing disorders, slow processing speed, and attentional deficits can have difficulty following instructions, going step-by-step, and attending to what they are required to do. Not to mention they may be notoriously off-beat or struggle with pitch. While learning to play an instrument is incredibly beneficial for brain integration, students with learning disabilities can potentially demonstrate higher levels of frustration when first learning to play.

Foreign Language

For children with language-based learning disabilities and auditory processing disorders, learning a new language can be incredibly challenging. Such students are likely already having difficulty learning their language of origin, let alone a completely new language. This can be incredibly triggering and overwhelming for such students. Memorization demands in foreign language classes can also be challenging, which may require accommodations and modifications to be made. As students get older, children with language-based learning disabilities typically respond well to completing an American Sign Language (ASL) class as a foreign language requirement because ASL relies more heavily on visual and motor processing, which can be a strength for some students with language-based learning disabilities.

Library

For children with language-based learning disabilities, library may be an overwhelming class for them. If, for example, a child is not reading at the same level as peers, they may begin to compare themselves negatively to others. If reading is a challenging task for them, even just walking into the library may increase their "flight or fight" nervous system responses. Reading and learning how to read can be a very vulnerable process for students, especially for students who have learning disabilities; this increases the chances of them becoming dysregulated in certain situations. This may look like frustration, acting out, or goofing off; or shutting down, putting their head down on the table, crying, or refusing to engage. For students with ADHD, choosing a book from the library may be overwhelming and they may become distracted by books that may be inappropriate for their reading level. They may need more direction on where to look for a book and more pointed guidelines on what to look for when selecting a book.

Lunch/Recess

Lunchtime is a wealth of social interaction that is welcomed by many students. But for some, keeping up with peer conversations, engaging socially, understanding social norms, and navigating this unstructured time may be overwhelming. This may be especially true for students with auditory processing disorder, slower processing speeds, and ASD.

Recess and breaks may be thought of as a time to just let children go and do their own thing, but they can actually create complex interactions and challenges that are important to stay on top of. There are a few things to look out for and consider. Some students need the opportunity to run free and socialize after sitting still for so long. They require the proprioceptive and vestibular input of running, jumping, climbing, and swinging in order to remain regulated for the rest of the day.

However, unstructured social interactions and physical activities that occur during recess and breaks can cause more anxiety and

Supportive Diagram

Recess can be one of the most challenging times of day, particularly for the teachers and aides who are monitoring the students. It can also be a time in which students can learn valuable skills such as navigating conflict, building social interaction, and practicing emotional regulation. By co-regulating with students who are struggling at recess, you can help facilitate positive experiences and interactions by considering the following:

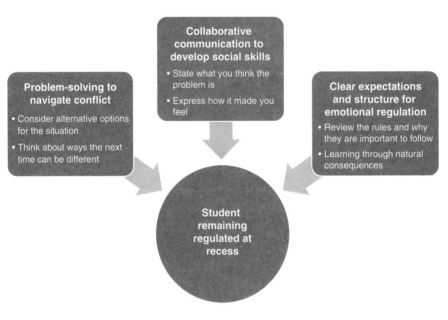

frustration for many students with slower processing speeds, social challenges, ASD, ADHD, and lower impulse control. Because of what we know about the nervous system when threatened (as discussed in Chapter 1), certain students may go into the "blue zone"—shutting down, withdrawing, or isolating themselves—because they do not know how to initiate social interactions with peers or navigate certain physical tasks. Other students may respond by entering the "red zone," struggling with impulse control by hitting, pushing, kicking, or calling names.

Due to the nature of recess—so many students in typically a large space with less adult supervision—it can be a recipe for distress. Recess, lunch, and breaks can also be an incredibly valuable opportunity to help students learn how to navigate conflict, build social skills, and practice emotional regulation if addressed correctly. Thus, it is important that lunch and recess staff become familiar with the principles outlined in this book to facilitate regulation and skill-building. Providing clear expectations, creating structure, encouraging collaborative communication, and assisting in problem-solving are all great places to start! Refer to Chapters 2 and 9 for ways you can do this.

BOOSTING REGULATION AND PARTICIPATION IN SPECIALTY CLASSES

All of the strategies that we've discussed in the book thus far are applicable to your specialty classes. The ultimate goal is to increase the amount of regulation that students feel in order to better participate in your unique learning environment. Given the nature of the frequency and structure of your classes, there are some other strategies that are important for you to consider. These strategies can also support your regulation as you strive to teach a large number of students with varying sensorimotor and learning needs.

Strategy 1: Find a Connection Point

Collaborating and connecting with teachers more involved with the students as well as with students themselves will go a long way in fostering the ever-important teacher-student dyad. *Because you work with so many students for shorter periods of time, you may not feel as though you know students well enough to provide valuable information—but you do. As we mentioned, a student's behavior and functioning in your class is an important piece of the puzzle. You have a unique lens and environment that may help students get the support they truly need to succeed in school.* Isaac, for example, may have never been identified as having a motor coordination challenge if Ms. Radishaw hadn't recognized his difficulty in her class and started searching for "why." Refer back to Chapters 2 and 3 on the principles of regulation and the teacher-student dyad as a starting point.

Your collaboration with the core teachers of students who are showing particular difficulty in your class is especially important. Ask if they've noticed similar behaviors, and discuss strategies they have found that work well. Ask if that student has a 504 plan or Individualized Education Plan, even if it does not include accommodations or goals for your specific class. You may learn something about the student that will give you a sense of why that student may be struggling in your class. Or you may be better able to relate to the challenges she faces on a daily basis that may result in dysregulation. Keep the door of communication open both ways. Let the core teacher know what positives, negatives, improvements, or setbacks a particular student has that day. Offer insight as to why you suspect that might be, given the activities in your class. Remember that you are an important part of the team.

Secondly, work toward connecting and collaborating with the students. You work with so many children on a weekly basis, and chances are you will not jive with every student who comes into your class—that's ok. It is still important to work toward building a relationship that is trusting and safe. This is especially true for students who may need some extra support in your specific learning environment. Take some extra time to say "hi" to these students, ask how their day is going, develop a handshake with them, or send an extra dose of specific praise their way. Let them know they are seen and heard. In our vignette above, Ms. Radishaw could say to Isaac, "I see that you are really having a hard time sticking with these new dance moves. I can see how frustrating and overwhelming this is. Learning new things is hard."

Once you develop a positive teacher-student dyad, it will help your student to feel more connected and motivated to work with you to find a solution. When you notice him struggling, you can then partner with him to solve the problem. In our vignette above, Ms. Radishaw can first take a moment to connect with Isaac, joining with him in his distress, saying something as simple as "When I first learned these moves, they were really hard for me too." Or, "learning new dance steps can be really hard at first; it can take some time to get used to. The more we practice, the easier it gets! Let's think together about how to make this less stressful."

Strategy 2: Creative Problem-Solving

Luckily, because you are a teacher of a specialty class, you are also probably very creative, curious, and excellent at thinking outside the box. If not, that's ok—we can help! Once you've recognized a problem, asked the right questions, and used the teacher-student dyad

Interactive Scenario

Taking the example of Ms. Radishaw and Isaac in the opening vignette:

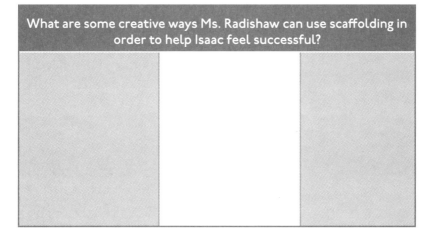

What are some creative ways Ms. Radishaw can use scaffolding in order to help Isaac feel successful?

Ideas may include:

- Break down the dance into smaller steps.

- Give him more frequent breaks.

- Create a simple song or numbering system for the dance steps so they are more easily remembered.

- Work with him one-on-one for a few moments to model the steps next to him.

- Slow down the tempo of the dance.

to connect with your student to help them regulate, you can now move into some creative problem-solving strategies. The strategies of scaffolding in Chapter 6 and accommodation in Chapter 9 are both applicable here. It may just look a bit different in specialty classes. Because there is sometimes more flexibility in specialty classes, there can be more options when it comes to creative problem-solving. Some students do better when they are placed in nontraditional roles, particularly when traditional roles and expectations are too challenging for them. Partner with your students to come up with a new solution.

Below is a list of other creative problem-solving strategies that may be useful in your specialty class:

- PE
  - Assign the student the role of a referee.
  - Assign the student the role of permanent goalie/catcher/pitcher.
  - Break down instructions into smaller, more manageable chunks.
  - Yell out reminders for instructions that a student may frequently forget.
  - Give the student more frequent breaks.

- Art
  - Allow students to wear gloves.
  - Allow a student to help pass out art materials.
  - Allow a student to help organize art materials.
  - Provide two to three examples of finished products.
  - Break down projects into smaller, more manageable tasks.
  - Provide a template for students to use if desired.

- Music
  - Use noise-cancelling headphones.
  - Sit next to the student to help her "keep the beat."
  - Label music with colors or letters to make it easier to read.
  - Place stickers on instruments for where fingers should be placed (the students can put corresponding stickers on their fingers if desired).

- Foreign Language
  - Decrease memorization demands.
  - Make language activities more visual and "hands on".
  - Create songs that help students better connect with the language.
  - Make connections between English and the foreign language being taught.

- Library
  - Make reading levels private.
  - Provide cushions, pillows, or core discs as seating options.
  - Have a smaller bookcase with fewer books displayed for certain students to access.

- o   Allow a student to help check out books.
- o   Give a student the job of putting books back on the shelves.

- Lunch/Recess
  - o   Set up a table where a small group of children can sit to interact.
  - o   Start a lunch club where a small group of students can eat just outside the cafeteria or in a teacher's office.
  - o   Provide "conversation cards" at lunch tables to assist in social interaction.
  - o   Distribute dry erase boards or chalkboards for students to play tic-tac-toe or hangman when they finish eating.
  - o   Give students special "jobs" or roles during more unstructured time outside.
  - o   Give students a structured task to complete like "go find five friends who like the color purple."
  - o   Give little "scavenger hunts" where students have to find three leaves, two sticks, and one flower.
  - o   Provide extra time notifications to students who have difficulty transitioning from recess.

Strategy 3: Create Consistency and Clear Expectations

Children (and adults) do well when they know what to expect. Consistency creates comfort. Because specialty classes do not occur every day, and the schedule itself is sometimes inconsistent, this can be difficult for some students. Helping students know what to expect and when can help reduce anxiety and difficulty with transitions, and allows the students to plan and problem-solve for the future.

Consistency will also support you as a specialty teacher. Communicating with students' regular teachers can give you insight into what works and what doesn't work. This is especially true regarding the language that you use with the students. There may be specific phrases, clapping patterns, or communication methods that the teacher uses consistently in her classroom that you can implement in yours. If there is a certain strategy that works for a student in one classroom setting, attempt to keep it consistent across settings.

Other ideas regarding consistency include:

- Students respond well to schedules, particularly written schedules, as they are familiar with these in their regular classrooms. Have a schedule posted at the beginning of each class and draw your students' attention to it, in case they need to reference it.
- When creating rules, use similar wording to that used in their core classes. This may mean you need a separate set of rules for each grade level to better connect with them.
- In the beginning of the year, it might be beneficial for the core teacher to stay in the specialty class for the first 5 to 10 minutes of the class in order to help with the transition.
- Use the same format of "circle time" or "group meetings" to open the class, allowing everyone to connect and check in before starting the activities in class. This can help to set the tone, put something familiar into place, and give you an idea of how certain students are doing that day.
- If possible, visit different classrooms throughout the year during their morning meeting time in order to better connect with certain students.

Remember that you are a valued member of the academic team and have much insight to offer. The classes you offer are a valuable part of facilitating integrated learning and drawing on students' unique talents. Your ability to apply the principles and strategies discussed in this book will go a long way in facilitating regulation, creating meaningful relationships, and supporting students with a wide variety of learning needs. Start small by implementing a few changes in your classes, and then build from there. And don't forget to take time to reflect on your own regulation and ways you can draw support from other teachers and staff.

CHAPTER 9

Redefining Behavior Plans

*"If we teach today's students as we taught yesterday's,
we rob them of tomorrow."*

—John Dewey

Katie, a 10-year-old girl in fifth grade, attended a large public school in the middle of her city. She had a history of difficulty focusing and getting work done. Notes on her report cards and progress reports often indicated that Katie was a bright student with lots of potential, and that she was social and eager to engage with others, but that she would often call out in the middle of class when she was not supposed to. She had difficulty remaining seated, would rock back in forth in her chair, stand up at her desk, fidget with pencils and erasers, yell out unrelated or inappropriate comments, and make many simple errors on her academic work. Her teachers and parents felt that Katie was not living up to her potential and found that her symptoms seemed to be getting worse. Katie's teacher, Ms. Mackenzie, found herself redirecting Katie more frequently every day. "Katie—be quiet, no more talking." "Katie, sit still." "Katie, stop distracting your friends." "Katie, please focus on your work."

The constant prompting was becoming frustrating and overwhelming for Ms. Mackenzie and irritating to Katie, who began to roll her eyes or scowl every time she was redirected. Katie got into even more trouble at recess, resulting in scuffles with friends, throwing sticks and rocks at others when she was mad, kicking them when things did not go her way, and yelling out mean comments. Other parents began to complain about how Katie's behavior was impacting their children. Ms. Mackenzie decided to ask for help and called for a student support team meeting with Katie's parents, school psychologist, and other relevant individuals to attend. During the meeting, Katie's parents were tearful and overwhelmed, commenting that Katie had recently been diagnosed with attention deficit hyperactivity disorder (ADHD) and a sensory processing disorder. Her parents were exasperated and exclaimed that they did not know what to do, but that they were working with professionals outside of school and were happy to try anything within school that might help. Ms. Mackenzie and Katie's parents worked on developing a behavior plan.

They identified target behaviors and decided on rewards. Katie was set up to earn stars when she was able to sit still and quietly, not engage in aggressive behaviors toward peers, and complete her work. If she was able to earn a certain number of stars each day, and at the end of the week, then her teachers and parents decided that she would be able to pick out a new toy or game over the weekend.

Over the first few days, it seemed as though the behavior plan was working. Katie was earning stars and building up to the big prize at the end of the week. However, after the first days, Katie began to lose steam. She wasn't able to manage her impulses and stop her body from moving and fidgeting. She wasn't able to keep her mind focused on the work she was doing. At recess, she couldn't stop herself from feeling big feelings when things didn't go her way, and she didn't know what to do instead. Ms. Mackenzie found herself resorting to strong prompting and redirecting again, which was not working. Katie began to feel defeated, developing a sense of shame, which caused her to then feel a sense of worthlessness and ineffectiveness, impacting her self-esteem. She began making comments such as "I'm a loser," "No one likes me," and "I'm never going to be able to do this." It was becoming clear that Katie had skill deficits that were impacting her ability to even use the behavior plan effectively.

A NOTE ABOUT BEHAVIOR PLANS

Behavior plans that focus on rewards, in some cases, can be very helpful, and if done right, are extremely effective. We have all worked with students who are easily motivated by receiving rewards, and they respond well to relatively simple behavioral charts. Students who respond well to behavior charts often already possess foundational skills that allow them to meet the goals presented within the plan. Such a student's lower brain is likely already generally regulated, and he is able to more readily access the upper parts of his brain that allow him to understand and utilize behavioral charts successfully. Behavior charts can help such students to stay on task and on track, allowing them to meet their goals, obtain the reward, and develop motivation to continue working. Over time, such behavior plans can be phased out as the student's motivation increases. However, there are students who do not respond well to this strategy, and in some cases, this strategy actually makes behaviors worse, impacting a student's sense of self-esteem and self-worth, as we see in the example with Katie.

Our aim in this chapter and throughout this book is not to suggest that one way is better than the other, or that behavior management should always be handled in a certain way. We are hoping to build an awareness about individual differences and help teachers to identify strategies that will work well for all students. Our goal is to help build an awareness of what is underlying the behavior and to use that information to help guide interventions that will be most impactful for each student. In this chapter, we will discuss why traditional behavior plans do not work well for all students, and what to do when they are ineffective.

We hope to expand students' motivation and desire to learn from earning the next sticker or reward, to being motivated by learning itself. We also hope to redefine behavior plans through the lens of *relate to regulate* using the teacher-student dyad, and closing the expectation gap by determining how to *accommodate to regulate*. It is important to remember, though, that in order for us to use any of these skills, we first need to be regulated ourselves. From what we know about the brain, if we are not in a regulated state, we will not be able to access the upper part of our brain that allows us to successfully use the skills outlined in this chapter. If you find yourself in a stressed out state of mind prior to engaging in the strategies outlined in this chapter, take a moment for yourself to use the skills outlined earlier in the book to find a state of regulation in yourself so that you can best access your own problem-solving skills.

STRUCTURE, APPROPRIATE BOUNDARIES, AND CLEAR EXPECTATIONS

One of the most common confusions we hear from parents, teachers, and professionals we work with is understanding how to maintain firm boundaries, guidelines, and expectations while holding them within the protective confines of the dyad, in a supportive, regulated, and validating way. It seems that often parents and professionals confuse such strategies outlined in this book with becoming too permissive. That is not the case. All children, and especially children with special needs, sensory processing, and learning differences, require consistency, predictability, and clearly outlined structure, expectations, and routines.

We have seen many programs that attempt to integrate social-emotional and relational strategies that become too permissive and end up with children displaying even more behavioral problems than before. One way to understand this concept in a simple way—which you can use to also explain to children—is that all emotions are ok! Any feeling that you are feeling is healthy and appropriate. There are no "bad" or wrong feelings. It is ok to feel whatever it is you are feeling. However, not all behaviors are ok. It is ok to feel mad, for example, but it is absolutely not ok to yell, hit, scream, or throw things when you are mad. Those behaviors are unsafe for you and for everyone around you, and those behaviors have natural consequences, so we are going to work with you to help you learn how to be mad (sad, worried, etc.) in a safe way. In summary, while all emotions are ok, not all behaviors are. There is no excuse for unsafe behavior, and we will work together to ensure that everyone stays safe. That said, it is important to keep in mind the developmental expectations of regulation skills that we outlined in Chapter 2 as we move through this chapter. Depending on their developmental level and chronological age, a student may need more co-regulation and guidance to navigate the difference between their emotions and behaviors.

As we continue to explore the often-confusing line of holding structure and boundaries within the context of a protective relationship, it will first be helpful to review the different styles discussed when talking about parenting as well as classroom management. They include permissive, authoritarian, authoritative, and detached.[1-3] You may already be familiar with these terms, so we will reference them quickly here:

- *Permissive* teachers are often described as being very nice, maybe even too nice. They often feel a strong desire to have students like them, and have difficulty setting limits. They are often warm and supportive but struggle with setting clear expectations and following consistent guidelines. They may ignore disruptive behavior or handle it in a way that is not effective. This often leads to a classroom that feels out of control, where students do not feel safe, and where learning is difficult. Permissive teachers are often high in terms of level of warmth and support but low in terms of providing clear expectations, structure, boundaries, and guidelines. Research has shown that this is not the most effective way to manage a classroom.[1-3]

- *Authoritarian* teachers often have very high demands, expectations, structure, and guidelines, to the point where it may come off as punitive, shaming, or blaming. The authoritarian style of classroom management is, in effect, the opposite of permissive. Those with an authoritarian style often rate very low in terms of providing warmth and support for their students. While this style may result in more behavioral compliance of students in the classroom, it also often leads to high rates of stress, anxiety, low self-esteem, and distress in both teachers and their students.

- *Detached* teachers have neither high levels of warmth nor clear expectations. They may have difficulty engaging with students at all, often feeling as though they are going through the motions just to get through the day.

- *Authoritative* teachers demonstrate a high level of warmth while also holding high expectations and structure for their students. This is the most ideal strategy to manage the classroom. However, this takes practice, time, and ongoing support from those around you. It is not easy. Authoritative styles provide warmth and supportive relationships with their students, but their students also

Supportive Diagram

As teachers, it is important to remember that you can maintain firm boundaries, guidelines, and expectations while holding them within the protective confines of the teacher-student dyad, in a supportive, regulated, and validating way. When social-emotional and relational strategies become too permissive, students may end up displaying even more behavioral problems than before. *The most effective teaching style is one that adopts an authoritative stance, a healthy combination of warmth, structure, clear expectations, and support.*

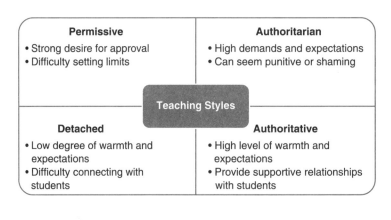

Permissive	Authoritarian
• Strong desire for approval • Difficulty setting limits	• High demands and expectations • Can seem punitive or shaming

Teaching Styles

Detached	Authoritative
• Low degree of warmth and expectations • Difficulty connecting with students	• High level of warmth and expectations • Provide supportive relationships with students

know that the teacher is the boss, and what she says goes. Students understand the clear expectations, and what the demands of the classroom are. Both students and teachers feel more successful and empowered when this strategy is used.

As outlined above, the most effective teaching style is one that adopts an authoritative stance: a healthy combination of warmth, structure, clear expectations, demands, and guidelines. For many of us who work with children, this is easier said than done! It takes practice, time, patience, and support from those around us. It is also important to realize that our state of regulation may also dictate which teaching style we adopt. If we are in a flight or freeze state, we may look more detached or permissive, for example. If we are in a fight state of regulation, we may look more authoritarian.

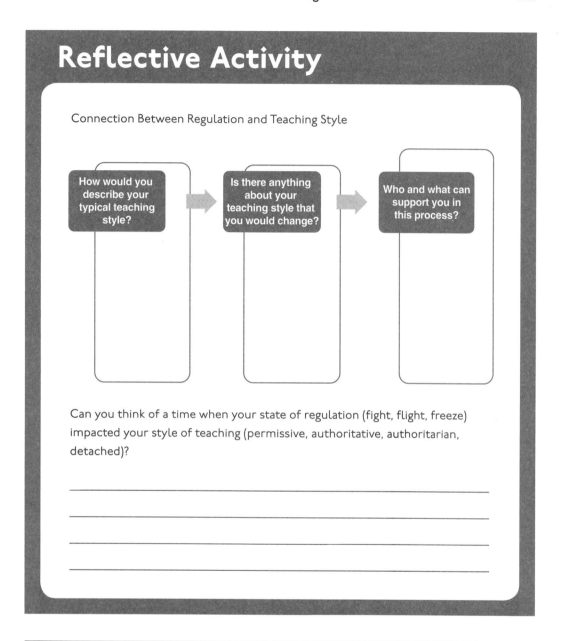

Reflective Activity

Connection Between Regulation and Teaching Style

| How would you describe your typical teaching style? | Is there anything about your teaching style that you would change? | Who and what can support you in this process? |

Can you think of a time when your state of regulation (fight, flight, freeze) impacted your style of teaching (permissive, authoritative, authoritarian, detached)?

_____

_____

_____

_____

 online resources Available for download at **resources.corwin.com/ClassroomBehaviors**

You may be wondering: how can I adopt the authoritarian teaching style and effectively set appropriate expectations and boundaries? This will be discussed in more depth as we explore the difference between natural and punitive consequences, focus on ways to praise, and identify how our state of regulation impacts the style with which we work.

NATURAL VERSUS PUNITIVE CONSEQUENCES

Another common confusion we'd like to address is understanding the distinction between natural and punitive consequences. All behaviors, actions, and choices have natural, or logical, consequences. If, for example, we don't go to work, then we won't make money. If we don't turn in our homework assignment, we won't get a good grade. If we don't water our plants, they will die. Additionally, if we exercise, we will be healthier and have more energy, and if we are trustworthy, we will have many positive relationships in our lives. These are all examples of natural, or logical, consequences to our choices, decisions, and actions we make throughout our lives.

It is necessary for students to learn the impact their choices, decisions, and behaviors have on others as well as on their own lives. **Natural consequences**[4,5] also serve as a way to learn important lessons about the impact of their behaviors. It is important to use natural consequences in order to teach students about the impact of their behaviors but also use them as a way to identify and teach an underlying skills deficit.

We want to emphasize the importance of using natural consequences within the confines of a safe, co-regulatory relationship. Establishing a positive teacher-student dyad is therefore a necessary step before using natural consequences. We also want to emphasize that natural consequences will evolve as a student develops regulation and social-emotional skills. Thus, the developmental expectations of regulation highlighted in Chapter 2 will be an important reference as you hold natural consequences in mind. A fourth-grade student, for example, will likely need less guidance to understand the concept of natural consequences than a first grader.

Natural consequence: the results of an action, behavior, choice, or decision that someone makes. They help us learn the difference between adaptive and maladaptive behaviors and choices.

If, in a pre-K classroom, a child throws the scissors, a natural consequence is that she can no longer use them until she can learn how to use them safely, while also using *scaffolding* with the child to support her in learning how to use them safely. Scaffolding is a strategy we discussed more in-depth in Chapter 6. Recall that scaffolding is the systematic way a teacher uses modeling, problem-solving, task management, and guided practice to help a student achieve a specific goal. Typically scaffolding supports are decreased as a student progresses toward independence and "mastery." As a teacher, you can hold the boundary of no longer being able to use the scissors while expressing to her that you understand how frustrating it is to learn how to cut with scissors:

> I know learning how to cut with scissors can be really hard and frustrating. I see how mad it is making you. It made you so mad that you threw them. You are showing us that you cannot use the scissors safely right now, because you just threw them, and they almost hit your friend. You are not going to use them until you can show us that you are able to use them safely, *and* I will help you learn how to use them, so it no longer feels so frustrating.

This is an example of how teachers can hold a firm boundary, validate, and also search for the "why," which will help to identify what skill the child needs to learn in order to be able to complete the task successfully.

The following steps were used in this scenario:

1. Hold the boundary of the natural consequence (she cannot use the scissors).
2. Validate the child's emotional experience (using scissors is really hard and frustrating!).
3. Develop an awareness of what might be causing the frustration around using scissors (perhaps the student has an underlying fine motor delay that is impacting her ability to learn how to use the scissors effectively).
4. Identify ways to scaffold and support the student around learning how to cut with scissors safely and effectively (provide the student with adaptive scissors then slowly transition to typical scissors).

In another example, Juan, a fifth-grade boy who attended a rigorous college preparatory private school, continued to fail one math test after another. He was doing the work in class, but because math was hard for him, he was not practicing at home, or turning in his math homework. He was also not studying for his math tests. His difficulty with math caused him to enter a freeze state of regulation. His response to this state of regulation resulted in him avoiding the work for as long as he could. This impacted his ability to learn the math concepts, and the natural consequence of this behavior was for him to fail his math tests.

Luckily, his teacher recognized that Juan was not being lazy or defiant; she realized that math was actually triggering a dysregulated nervous system response. The teacher maintained the natural consequence of him receiving a failing grade on his math tests, while also scaffolding support for him to help decrease his dysregulation when confronted with a challenging math test. She worked with him after school to teach him new strategies to study and understand the math concepts. She allowed him to take the test home and practice the concepts until he was ready to re-take it for an average of his two scores. When Juan was ready, he re-took the test and received an A.

In this scenario, the teacher held firm to the natural consequence of Juan receiving a failing grade for tests he did not study for but provided him with an opportunity to achieve success while also scaffolding him to address the underlying skills deficit. Not only was Juan held accountable for his previous decision not to study, but he was also given the opportunity to learn new strategies so that he would not become flooded next time around. This is a good example of how teachers can hold natural consequences while still providing students with the strategies and skills they need to learn and achieve their goals.

Alternatively, **punitive consequences**[4,5] are used more in the form of punishment. They often "don't fit the crime" and seem out of proportion to whatever the behavior or decision was. Usually punitive consequences are a result of the teacher being in a dysregulated state. They also often do not focus on addressing the underlying skills deficit or teaching any new skills. For example, a punitive consequence may look like a detention, suspension, time out, or staying in for recess.

Punitive consequences: a form of punishment that is usually unrelated to the behavior. It often results in feelings of anger, shame, and frustration and no skills building occurs.

If, for example, the young pre-K student above who threw the scissors was put in time-out or had to stay in for recess to clean the classroom, that would be a punitive consequence. If Juan, who was failing math tests, was removed from the soccer team until he pulled his grades up, that would be another example of a punitive consequence. There would be no way for the students to learn the skills that they needed, they would not feel supported or understood, and this may result in them feeling angrier at the adults in their lives, ultimately leading to higher levels of frustration and a greater degree of disconnection in the teacher-student dyad. Additionally, it would likely cause continued distress for the teacher by getting stuck in a maladaptive regulation-response cycle (see Chapter 3).

Supportive Diagram

Natural consequences serve as a way to learn important lessons about the impact of their behaviors. Punitive consequences are used more in the form of punishment and often seem out of proportion to the behavior or decision.

Let's take the example of a student throwing scissors:

Punitive consequences	Natural consequences
• Sitting in the corner for 30 minutes staying in for recess, and mopping the floors • Writing "I will not throw scissors" on the board 100 times • Losing privileges unrelated to scissors such as staying in for the next week, or losing free play time with peers.	• Not using scissors until she can use them safely, while also teaching her how to use them safely • Providing her with adaptive or safety scissors to practice using them correctly • Validate her emotional experience of frustration around using scissors and discuss the impact her unsafe behaviors have on others. Explaining she cannot use them until she is able to demonstrate that she can use them responsibly

Punitive consequences often tend to create feelings of shame, guilt, and blame in our students.[6] They tend to focus on enforcing compliance through external means of control resulting in students doing better only because they fear punishment and are attempting to avoid it. *Natural consequences, however, build on the knowledge that students do well if they can, and students naturally want to do well. Natural consequences support students in doing better not only by them learning about the consequences of their actions but also by providing them with functional skills to improve their capabilities.* Natural consequences often result in supporting students in developing intrinsic motivation to learn new skills, develop self-control, and feel safe and secure within the confines of the teacher-student dyad and classroom community because there are clear boundaries, expectations, and guidelines.

Reflective Activity

We have all experienced consequences for our actions throughout life. Take time to reflect on the difference between natural consequences and punitive consequences you received in elementary school.

Think back to a moment in your childhood when you were grounded, were punished, lost a privilege, had to stay in for recess, or got a detention.

What do you remember from this experience. What did you learn? Do you think you learned the lesson the adults in your life wanted you to learn?

Now think back to when you were a child, and identify an adult in your life who you felt really understood you, was there for you, and helped you.

What qualities did this individual have that helped you? What skills did this individual help you develop?

_____

_____

THE POWER AND PERIL OF PRAISE

The last piece we'd like to clarify in this chapter pertains to using praise and identifying strengths in an appropriate way. Research has shown that when praise is not used correctly, it can have the opposite intended result.[7] Praise, when used incorrectly, can lead to decreased self-esteem, a lowered sense of self-worth, and negatively impacted overall self-image. It can decrease motivation and the frequency of positive behaviors. We'd like to take a moment here to clarify why this is and specify how to use the power of praise to our advantage.

Praise, when conducted correctly, not only increases the frequency of the positive behavior that was praised but also enhances the teacher-student dyad, improves regulation, and builds perseverance, resiliency, and self-esteem.[7] Although many of these suggestions seem intuitive, common sense, and straightforward, they are actually harder in practice than they may seem. Both authors, Ashley and Jamie, continue to find themselves doing this incorrectly with their own children and the children they work with, having to constantly catch themselves and adjust.

- *Be authentic and sincere:* While younger children tend to respond well to frequent and demonstrative praise, research[8] suggests that starting in older elementary school, students are able to differentiate between sincere and overly affirmative praise. In fact, one way to actually *decrease* self-esteem, positive effort, and your credibility as a teacher is to engage in overly positive or over-the-top praise too frequently. Ensure that your praise is accurate, authentic, and sincere. If it is over-the-top, students will begin to realize over time that you are not being authentic, and they will either not believe you or not be able to live up to the hype.

- *Specific praise is best:* Be conscientious about the way you praise. General praise such as "good job!" or "way to go!" is too general and not beneficial. This type of praise, over time, tends to get tuned out, and is not useful because the student does not typically know what you are specifically praising. In order to praise effectively, ensure that the praise is specific—that it identifies exactly what you are praising. Some examples include:

  - "I love how you are waiting patiently for your turn— this really shows how patient you can be!"
  - "I can tell how much your group members enjoy working with you because you are really listening to them and asking such thoughtful questions."
  - "I like that you are sitting criss-cross with your hands in your lap. This tells me that you are ready to learn."
  - "I see that you wrote down all your homework assignments in your agenda. Thank you for doing that."

- *Focus on the process and progress[9]:* Try to hone in on the energy that the student puts into the work, and not the outcome (or the grade). Praise the focus, effort, or determination. Recognize that achievement is a process. Using "I" statements also helps the student know that you are really focusing on her and noticing what she is doing. Some examples include:

- ○ "I see how you are working really hard to focus on the details of the work you are doing."
- ○ "I love your determination—I can tell you do not give up easily."
- ○ "I can see that you are working really hard to take this problem step by step; that is a great strategy."
- ○ "I can tell the students really enjoyed your presentation; they were all so active and engaged in the discussion."
- ○ "I enjoy the thought you put into your essay; your creative writing and passion for the subject was really evident."

Just as we all have individual differences in learning, we have individual preferences in receiving praise. Research has shown that younger children tend to enjoy being complimented publicly, while older elementary students and teenagers prefer "private praise."[10] While this is generally the case, Ashley has worked with many younger children who become very uncomfortable when being praised publicly. As with getting to know any one of your students' learning styles, it will take time to determine how to praise in a way that will be most meaningful to each of them.

Reflective Activity

The foundational concept is that teachers and adults in children's lives need to be able to relate to them to support their level of regulation. While this is the case, teachers also need to hold the structure, boundaries, and expectations of the classroom in a firm, yet warm way. Take a moment to think a little bit more in depth about how your state of regulation may impact your

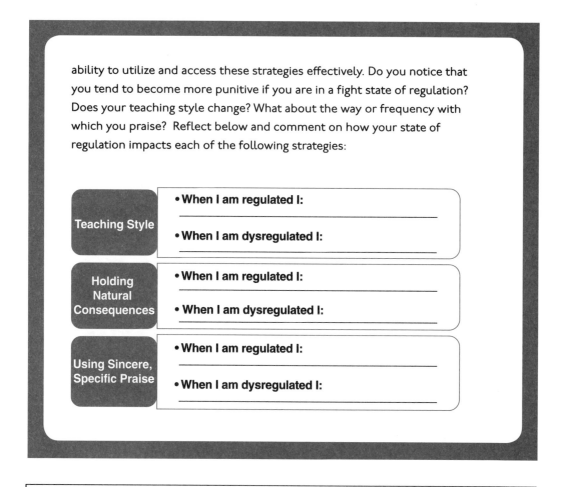

ability to utilize and access these strategies effectively. Do you notice that you tend to become more punitive if you are in a fight state of regulation? Does your teaching style change? What about the way or frequency with which you praise? Reflect below and comment on how your state of regulation impacts each of the following strategies:

Teaching Style
- **When I am regulated I:**
  _____
- **When I am dysregulated I:**
  _____

Holding Natural Consequences
- **When I am regulated I:**
  _____
- **When I am dysregulated I:**
  _____

Using Sincere, Specific Praise
- **When I am regulated I:**
  _____
- **When I am dysregulated I:**
  _____

online resources ⬎   Available for download at **resources.corwin.com/ClassroomBehaviors**

Now that we have cleared up some common confusions and misconceptions regarding structure, boundaries, and expectations; natural versus punitive consequences; and use of praise, we can better understand that all children have meltdowns, at one point or another, no matter what. *You, as a teacher, can use all the strategies outlined in this book, and you will still have students who meltdown, have crying spells, act out, are disruptive, defiant, frustrated, sad, or worried.* This is because, as we've discussed, our emotional responses are brain-based reactions to our state of regulation and nervous system response. Because of this, it is helpful to understand more about meltdowns and how to help a student when you find yourself in the midst of a meltdown.

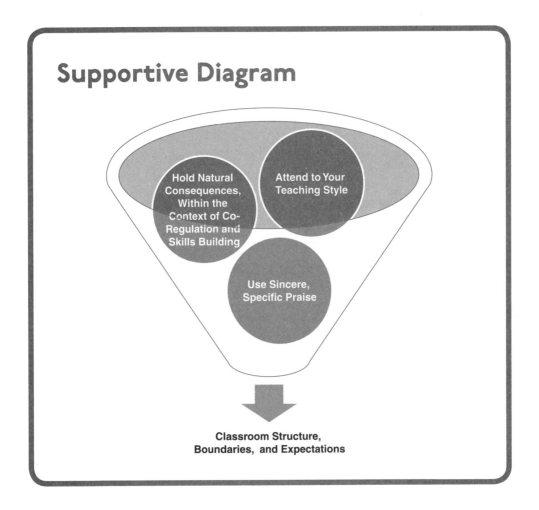

Supportive Diagram

Hold Natural Consequences, Within the Context of Co-Regulation and Skills Building

Attend to Your Teaching Style

Use Sincere, Specific Praise

Classroom Structure, Boundaries, and Expectations

THE LIFESPAN OF A MELTDOWN AND IN-THE-MOMENT STRATEGIES

As we've mentioned, despite our best laid plans and efforts, all children have meltdowns or experience emotional distress at some point—it is just to be expected. We've discussed states of regulation and their responses, but it may be helpful to break down "the meltdown" a bit more, especially as we redefine behavior plans. Understanding the common lifespan of a meltdown, which we have adapted here,[11] can help you know that it is temporary and utilize strategies not to escalate with your student. Because of those mirror neurons that we discussed in Chapter 3, we know how easy it is for our students' emotional states to rub off on us. If we better understand what is happening in a meltdown, it is easier to prevent those mirror neurons from causing us to escalate with the students we work with.

As seen in the meltdown curve diagram, there is usually something that triggers a meltdown. It could be anything: certain sensory input, a social interaction, a frustrating academic task, the need for a snack. Much of what we discuss in this book includes ways to search for the "why" or identify what is the vulnerability that may be underlying the behavior, as well as underlying any one particular trigger. *However, keep in mind that sometimes the specific trigger may not immediately proceed the meltdown—there may be a delayed response. Sometimes the final "trigger" is more like the "straw that broke the camel's back" rather than the actual "why" behind the behavior.* A student may be working so hard all day to keep it together, that they finally burst over what may seem like a very small or unimportant event. When triggers seem inconsistent or difficult to identify, this can be one reason why. This is also why it is important to continue searching, even after certain triggers may have been identified. As we've discussed in Chapter 1, after a trigger is identified, it is necessary to stay curious, dig a little deeper, and begin to make hypotheses about the vulnerabilities that may be underlying behaviors *and* their triggers. Keep this in mind as we explore how to navigate a meltdown in the moment, after a student's vulnerability has been triggered.

Once a student is triggered, they begin to escalate along the curve and enter a nervous system response of either fight, flight, or freeze. At that point, there is a brief period of time, called the *Window of Opportunity,* when you can engage in "in the moment" strategies to help the student regulate before the escalation becomes too severe. It is helpful to pay attention to more subtle "yellow zone" cues of dysregulation as a way to prevent a more severe meltdown. The yellow zone is when a student is beginning to get dysregulated, but in the early stages, early enough to intervene in time to prevent a major meltdown. If you recall from Chapter 2, signs of the yellow zone include frustration, initial stress, slight nervousness, or silliness. This is the Window of Opportunity.

If this doesn't work, you can then just plan to "ride it out" in a safe way until the child reaches a state of calm again. Oftentimes this means using the co-regulation techniques we discussed in Chapter 2 to help the student feel safe and supported. Once the student returns to a calm state, you can discuss skill-building strategies to prepare and plan for the next time the student is triggered again. This is when the learning, skill building, and teaching happens, not in the moment of dysregulation or during a meltdown, but after. As discussed, one reason that traditional behavior plans may not work is because they

Supportive Diagram

Understanding the life of a meltdown by following the "meltdown curve" can help decrease the severity of the situation and facilitate the use of strategies to get back to a regulated state. This is especially important for students who repeatedly struggle with regulation in the classroom.

Meltdown Curve

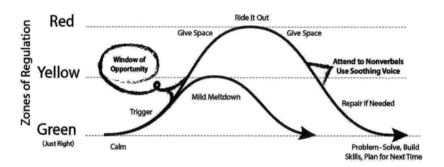

Image Source: Created by Hunt Dougherty; adapted from Buron and Curtis (2012).

do not address the fact that there is an underlying skill or vulnerability that the student has not yet been able to master. If we are able to identify what this skills vulnerability is and provide them with the tools to navigate the situation more effectively, within the context of a safe, co-regulating relationship, then their behavior, regulation, and overall ability to learn will improve. We can use our newly defined behavior plans as a tool to help students learn new skills.

As mentioned previously, and seen in the diagram of the meltdown curve above, "in-the-moment" strategies can be used during the Window of Opportunity. Again, because each child is different, and each situation is unique, not every strategy is going to work for every child. This often takes trial and error, planning, and practice. You will need to be in a state of regulation yourself, use attuned listening, and check your nonverbals when implementing these. If you are able to identify certain students' patterns of vulnerabilities, you can use that information to help inform the "in-the-moment" strategy as well. Some "in-the-moment" options that may be helpful to use during this small Window of Opportunity include the following:

- Breathe in for four seconds and out for six (longer exhale).
- Breathe in through your nose like you're smelling a rose, and out through your mouth like your blowing out a candle.
- Squeeze and relax our muscles (pretending we are cooked spaghetti and uncooked spaghetti).
- Squeeze all your muscles individually from your nose to your toes.
- Press your hands together.
- Notice colors—look around the room and identify three things that are red (green, blue, etc.).
- Notice sounds—sit quietly and notice three things you can hear that you wouldn't otherwise notice.
- Identify a safe quiet place and person the student can spend time with.
- Take a walk.
- Do jumping jacks, chair push-ups, or wall push-ups.
- Get a glass of water.
- Eat a snack.
- Take a few minutes to read a book or do a puzzle (for students who find such activities calming).
- Utilize the quiet sensory nook in the classroom.
- Validate the student's emotional experience.
- Join with the student on something they are interested in.
- Identify and utilize strengths; use the power of praise.
- Allow the student to engage in a quiet activity that is preferred or of interest to him.

In Chapter 2, we discussed strategies to build into the daily routine. These include being aware of the daily schedule, knowing that children need frequent breaks, using the Breathe Body Begin method, and integrating "mindful moments" into your class. These strategies can be integrated throughout the day to increase brain-based regulation for all students. The goal of utilizing these strategies on a regular basis is to decrease the frequency and intensity of meltdowns, preventing the need for "in-the-moment" strategies.

Reflective Activity

Look at the list of "in-the-moment" strategies, and consider your own ideas for "in-the-moment" strategies:

What are some strategies you have found that work for students in your classroom?

_____   _____   _____

What are some strategies you would like to implement for students in your classroom?

_____   _____   _____

PUTTING IT ALL TOGETHER: A NEWLY DEFINED BEHAVIOR PLAN

We now know that in order for children to feel safe enough within their relationships to become regulated, we need to relate to them, which leads to regulation. However, as adults, we need to be regulated ourselves in order to relate to the people in our lives. This is, in essence, a dynamic cycle between our ability to regulate to relate, as well as relate to regulate.[12–14] The strategies outlined in the beginning of this book and in this chapter provide a foundation as a way to use the teacher-student dyad as a way to better understand the dynamics that occur between the teacher and the student. It additionally provides ways to use the relationship to better support students in developing regulation skills, which ultimately leads to more successful learning. It also provides reflective opportunities for teachers to build insight and awareness into their own states of regulation.

We hope that we have now clarified some common misconceptions, as well as discussed what *all* children need in order to achieve success. So far, we discussed the importance of *all* children needing ongoing nurturing relationships; a foundation of physical and emotional safety; the need for access to developmentally appropriate, sensory-rich experiences; and safe, regulated adults in their lives.[15] Specifically in this chapter we explored how to hold appropriate structure, boundaries, and expectations; clarify natural versus punitive consequences; use specific praise; and better understand meltdowns that all children have, all of which will help to search for "why" a behavior is happening and to better address behaviors that might arise in your class.

The strategies we outline below are designed more specifically for children who have been identified as having disruptive or challenging behavior who require some sort of intervention. Recall from Chapters 5 and 6 the difficulties that students with sensory processing disorders (SPDs) or other learning

Supportive Diagram

This new model outlines the important aspects to consider when creating a behavior plan. The inner layers of the model should be established before moving to the outer levels.

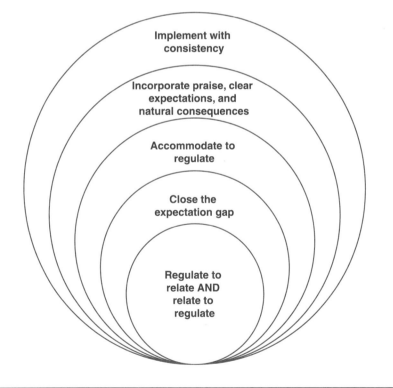

Implement with
consistency

Incorporate praise, clear
expectations, and
natural consequences

Accommodate to
regulate

Close the
expectation gap

Regulate to
relate AND
relate to
regulate

disabilities face on a regular basis that may lead to dysregulation when participating in scholastic activities. It's no wonder these students may display an increased number of behaviors that require your attention and thoughtful intervention. These may be students who already have an Individualized Education Plan (IEP) or 504 plan in place, or students who just need some extra consideration to feel seen, heard, and successful.

There are many who have provided valuable insights into changing behavior plans in school such as Dr. Ross Greene, Ph.D.,[16] and Dr. Mona Delahooke, Ph.D.[17] We have taken concepts discussed throughout the book, as well as from prior research, and integrated them into a cohesive plan to redefine behavior plans. In order to do so, we have outlined three important strategies to consider when developing a behavior plan for a specific student.

Strategy I: Close the Expectation Gap

Often when we see students who are exhibiting considerably disruptive behaviors in the classroom setting, that is an indication of a certain "expectation gap." An **expectation gap** can be defined as the difference between expectations of the classroom environment and the student's ability to meet those expectations. This gap signifies that a student *cannot* meet the necessary expectations set for her, such as the opening scenario with Katie, not that the student is overtly refusing to meet them. Often the student's nervous system arousal is heighted to the point where she cannot perform the necessary academic demands, no matter how hard she tries. When we take a moment to search for the "why," as outlined in Chapter 1, we can then better understand the expectation gap, know where it is coming from, and see why it is causing such disruptive behaviors. It is then that we can identify an appropriate plan moving forward.

As with Katie, who had recently been diagnosed with ADHD, we know that many of the classroom expectations are going to be difficult for her to reach. By nature, ADHD, which is a brain-based neurological difference, makes it more difficult for Katie to manage her impulses and her motor overflow. She often very likely feels extremely uncomfortable in her body, feeling as though she is always on the go, feeling out of control and as though she is constantly overwhelmed by her own internal state. Because she has also been diagnosed with an SPD, she is often overwhelmed by her external environment: crowded spaces, noisy environments, and busy visual fields all cause her to have even more difficulty regulating to a point where she is unable

Expectation gap: the difference between the expectations of the classroom environment and the student's ability to meet those expectations.

to learn. While thinking about vulnerabilities, it is also important to remember to identify the strengths of the child and ways to support the child by allowing her to use her strengths to develop skills that are more challenging for her.

If we look at Katie's expectation gap, it is very wide. The demands of her environment are way up here, and her ability to meet them are way down here. She is a having difficulty using and accessing her strengths because her expectation gap is so wide that she is going into a state of dysregulation. We will use Katie's example to walk through her expectation gap. In order to *identify the expectation gap*, ask two questions:

1. *What are the expectations (demands) in the classroom environment that the student is unable to meet?*

Expectations can be broken down into three different categories including academic, social/relational, emotional/behavioral. Of course, every class, and every grade, is going to have different demands, expectations, and benchmarks that each student is expected to meet.

*   Academically: Katie is expected to sit still during teacher-led lectures.
*   Socially: Katie is expected to raise her hand when she'd like to participate.
*   Behaviorally: Katie is expected to play appropriately and independently at recess and during unstructured time.

2. *What are the skills that the student is lacking that impact his or her ability to meet the demands of the environment?*

Again, this is going to vary depending on the grade of each student and the particular expectations of your learning environment, and will help to identify any potential vulnerabilities the student may have:

*   Katie is having difficulty with motor overflow (remaining seated when expected to do so).
*   Katie is having difficulty with impulse control (calling out over other students and the teacher).
*   Katie is having difficulty integrating sensory input (covering her ears when there is a lot of noise).
*   Katie is having difficulty regulating her big feelings (becoming aggressive during recess).

Supportive Diagram

Asking questions can help to identify and close the expectation gap in order to better support a student. Using this as a basis for a behavior plan can reduce the demands placed on the student and build skills for the student in order to better access and participate in academic activities.

Identify the Expectation Gap

- What are the expectations the student is unable to meet?
- What are the skills the student is lacking to meet the expectation?

Close the Expectation Gap

- What expectations can you reduce to meet the needs of the student?
- What skills can you teach to decrease the impact of his or her vulnerabilities?

By answering the two questions above, we are better able to understand Katie's "expectation gap," which indicates that her vulnerabilities are greatly impacting her ability to meet the demands of the classroom. In order to develop strategies to *reduce* the expectation gap, we have to identify ways we can *accommodate* in order to *regulate*. In order to determine the answer, we need to ask more questions. *Ask the following two questions to determine how to close the expectation gap*:

1. *What expectation demands in the environment can we reduce to meet the needs of the student?*

To decrease the demand that she needs to sit during all teacher-led lessons, consider the following:

- Allow Katie to use a standing desk, wiggle seat, or TheraBand.
- Provide Katie with more frequent breaks; allow her to take a walk, get a glass of water, or even just stand up and stretch when she needs to.
- Provide Katie with a quiet, nondistracting fidget she can keep in her desk.

To decrease the demand of calling out over other students and becoming dysregulated by noise, consider the following:

- Identify a safe place and a safe person Katie can meet with when she is dysregulated and disrupting the classroom.
- Provide noise-cancelling headphones.
- Identify a cozy corner in the classroom, and provide her with a list of simple mindfulness strategies she can use.
- Decrease assignments if Katie is overwhelmed; have her complete every other problem on the math worksheet, for example.

To decrease the expectation of independently navigating unstructured time, which results in aggressive behaviors, consider the following:

- Give Katie structured tasks to complete during unstructured time.
- Provide her with a special job or task to complete during this time (e.g., find five friends who like the color purple).

   2. *What skills can we teach the student to decrease the impact of his or her vulnerabilities and so that he or she can meet the demands of the environment?*

It is important to note that some of these skills she may be able to access at school, while others she can access outside of school. This will be discussed further in Chapter 10.

- Katie will benefit from mindfulness-based skills to increase regulation, impulse control, and internal control over her motor overflow.
- Katie will benefit from social skills training to increase her ability to navigate unstructured social time.
- Katie will benefit from occupational therapy to support her in developing sensorimotor integration.

Reflective Activity

Identifying and closing the expectation gap is an important part of developing a behavior plan for a student. Think about a student in your class who is struggling with disruptive behaviors. Consider the following:

How big is the student's expectation gap?	Are their disruptive behaviors triggered by this gap?	What state of regulation might this gap cause them to experience?	How does the student's dysregulation impact your regulation?	How is your state of regulation impacting that of the student?

online resources ⬏ Available for download at **resources.corwin.com/ClassroomBehaviors**

Now that we have a better understanding of the expectation gap, this will help us better understand what might be underlying the disruptive behaviors. We can then form hypotheses about what is going on and how to help. *From here we want to tie in the idea of regulation. How is this expectation gap impacting the child's regulation?* Does this expectation gap trigger their threat response? Next, we can look at the teacher-student dyad. How does the student's state of regulation impact that of the teacher? How is the teacher's state of regulation impacting that of the student?

Strategy 2: Relationship + Accommodation = Regulation

Once we have a better idea of the student's expectation gap and how that "gap" is impacting the state of regulation in both the teacher and the student, we can input that information into our newly defined behavior plan and develop a plan of action that focuses on developing three things:

1. The co-regulation of the dyad (regulation/response cycle)
2. Underlying skills vulnerabilities of the student as well as the student's strengths
3. How to lower the demands of the environment (accommodate) and increase the student's skill level internally (scaffolding skills)

While the ultimate goal of the behavior plan is to increase the student's engagement in the learning process, we know that the student must attain and maintain a state of regulation first in order for learning to happen. As we have discussed, when you *relate to regulate*, for most typically developing children, this is enough to allow you and your student to reach a state of co-regulation and optimize their learning potential. For students who are not typically developing and may have learning challenges, ADHD, autism spectrum disorder, or an SPD, not only do you have to *relate to regulate*, but as we discussed in Chapter 5, you also have to *accommodate to regulate*.

Once you have developed insight and awareness into your own state of regulation and how it impacts that of your students, you can integrate these two concepts, relate to regulate and accommodate to regulate, to redefine behavior plans. You can see that we do not use rewards, sticker charts, or other "external motivators." We focus on internal states of regulation, co-regulation between the teacher and the student, ways to reduce the demands of the environment, and ultimately ways to build the student's internal resources and skills, which will close the expectation gap, increase learning, and improve a sense of success for all involved.

Along every step on the way, it is important to remember to *identify ways to praise and integrate strengths*. Starting and ending with strengths in any situation is a great way to decrease defensiveness and allow others to feel supported, heard, and understood. What are some ways to praise Katie from our vignette above? What are some of Katie's strengths that we can implement into her behavior plan?

Supportive Diagram

When creating behavior plans, it is important that you focus on the regulation of the student by identifying expectation gaps, relating to the student, and providing appropriate accommodations for the student to experience success. Ultimately this will result in the student increasing her engagement in the learning process. Remember that this is a process that needs to occur over time. This process occurs best when the teacher has already developed insight and awareness into his or her own state of regulation and how that impacts the regulation of his or her students.

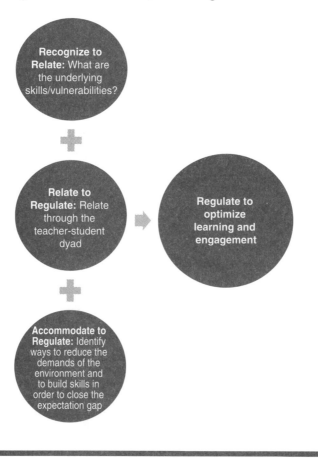

Recognize to Relate: What are the underlying skills/vulnerabilities?

Relate to Regulate: Relate through the teacher-student dyad

Regulate to optimize learning and engagement

Accommodate to Regulate: Identify ways to reduce the demands of the environment and to build skills in order to close the expectation gap

Below are some steps you can take to consider the necessary relationship and accommodations a student may need in order to be regulated enough to learn.

- **Step 1: Recognize to relate:** Search for the "why?" What is the underlying skills deficit that is causing the challenging behaviors? Once we understand that the student is not intentionally trying to be defiant, oppositional, mean, or rude, and that she may have a brain-based, neurological difference, we can better understand the situation, relate to the student, and validate his or her emotional experiences. Use this time to identify strengths as well.

- **Step 2: Relate to regulate:** Use the teacher-student dyad to reach a state of co-regulation. Once we better understand the underlying vulnerabilities, and the reasons underlying the disruptive behaviors as we did in step 1, we can then move toward using the power of the teacher-student dyad to reach a state of co-regulation with our student, using the strategies outlined in this book. The co-regulation strategies you identify as helpful can be included in the behavior plan.

- **Step 3: Accommodate to regulate:** Once we've begun to develop an empowering teacher-student dyad with our student, we can use the *expectation gap* strategies to identify what accommodations need to be provided to lead toward regulation. We are supporting our student by providing them regulation through the teacher–student relationship, and also through accommodations in their environment. Once both pieces have occurred, the student should have many opportunities to obtain a regulated state, enough to begin learning the internal skills they need to learn in order to meet the demands of the environment.

It is important to recognize that this is a process. You will likely need to move through these steps multiple times throughout the day with a student, especially in the beginning stages of implementing the behavior plan. As the student begins to build more skills and the expectation gap is closed, these steps may become less and less frequent. *Remember that the ultimate goal is not compliance but a curiosity for learning that is driven by a regulated state and appropriate classroom demands.*

Strategy 3: Implement with Consistency

The concepts in this chapter may seem counter-intuitive and go against the norms that are typically implemented in your school. It takes patience and practice to shift ways of thinking and doing. This is what we hope we've done throughout this book so far. We understand that in many academic settings, there are institutional policies and practices in place that may feel helpful and supportive—or they may feel daunting and overwhelming. We hope that there may be one or two things that you can take with you from this different way of thinking and begin implementing at your setting. Just as with doing anything new, the more you practice, the easier it gets. The more consistently you are able to use the skills outlined in this book, the more positive change you will see! We understand that riding the tide of change takes time. It is not going to happen overnight, but it will happen little by little, and this lens is already starting to help make changes in certain schools.

If you resonate with the information in this book, but don't feel as though you have the power, resources, or support to make a change in your setting, know that you are not alone. You may feel like, as an individual, you do not have enough power, influence, or support to make a change. *This is not so: it starts with you!* There are steps you can take to feel empowered to make a change in your community. *Make a change by connecting with others, educating and advocating, and integrating the ideas in this book into the work that you do.*

- *Connect with others:* If you feel as though the concepts discussed in this book are helpful and meaningful to you, but find that you are alone in your community, or are surrounded by others who take a different approach, you can find a way to connect with others. Luckily, in this day and age, a simple Google search will help you connect with others with similar viewpoints. There are professional agencies and groups, academic institutions, and professional members that hold this viewpoint. You can join professional groups or agencies that can help you become more connected with resources and support networks that have a similar lens.
- *Educate and advocate:* If you feel empowered to speak out, you can use your platform to educate others. Provide them with the research that backs up the concepts in this book; learn more about the brain and how the brain impacts regulation and learning. Spread the news about integrating this model into the classroom. The more we talk about these concepts, discuss their efficacy, and use them in our day-to-day work, the more others will learn about them and see the positive changes that are being made, and the more we will be able to redefine behavior plans.

Reflective Activity

We understand that you may have multiple students in your class who have expectation gaps big enough that they need to be supported by a behavior plan. It is important to think about how you, as a teacher, are able to navigate this challenge. This will look different for each teacher and each classroom.

What are certain ways you are able to support all of your students who have behavior plans throughout the day?

What are certain limitations or barriers to supporting multiple behavior plans?

Which times of the day do you anticipate will be the most challenging to support multiple behavior plans?

How do you anticipate it would work to implement some of the strategies outlined in this chapter into a student's behavior plans?

Who can you talk with to help with consistent implementation and advocating for a redefining of behavior plans?

- *Use one strategy a day:* Even if you don't have the power or opportunity to make big changes in your setting right now, that is ok. Think about ways you can make little changes; identify one strategy that you can use a day. Once this becomes more comfortable, think about ways to integrate this information into IEPs and 504 plans. Change is possible, it can happen, and it starts with you!

Next we will explore ways you can access additional support for students, as well as ways you can support parents of students with additional needs. This will give you another opportunity to connect with those around you and use the strategies in this chapter to make a difference in the lives of your students.

CHAPTER 10

Supporting Students Who Need Additional Help

"Better than a thousand days of diligent study is one day with a great teacher."

—Japanese Proverb

First grade had been challenging for Eliza in many ways. In kindergarten, she had "gotten by" with her reading skills, but now she was starting to fall behind. Writing demands also started to pick up, and she was already seeing herself as having terrible handwriting. In gym class, she couldn't catch a ball, often being made fun of by other peers. All of her friends were playing soccer at recess, but she just wanted to play house like in kindergarten. It was like she couldn't win. She was trying as hard as she could, but would she ever be good at anything in school?

After many months, Eliza began to avoid certain activities at school and perform the "bare minimum." Her attention span, particularly for reading and writing, was very limited, and she would often get out of her seat to play with nearby toys. Eliza's language arts teacher, Mrs. Lawson, had 34 other students in her classroom who were also learning to read and write. How could she invest even more time in Eliza to help her develop these skills? Mrs. Lawson knew that these things were challenging to many students, but Eliza was so stubborn when it came to even trying. Even after working hard to co-regulate with Eliza and establish a positive teacher-student dyad, Mrs. Lawson felt like little progress was being made.

Mrs. Lawson recognized that maybe Eliza had some underlying challenges that had not yet been identified. Maybe the support Eliza needed was beyond what she could provide in the classroom? She knew that the school had resources in place to support students like Eliza, but she never had to access them before. First, however, she felt it important to hold a meeting with Eliza's parents in order to further discuss her observations and gain their insight. While these meetings usually evoked anxiety in Mrs. Lawson, she knew this step was critical to continue searching for the "why."

As we've discussed, one of the most important pieces of protecting yourself emotionally as teachers, protecting your students' needs, and protecting and developing the teacher-student dyad is knowing when to ask for help, what type of help is needed, and how to go about getting the right type of help. We understand that each school environment has their own policies and procedures in place when it comes to navigating getting extra support for students. This likely varies from setting to setting, public to private, and even district to district. Navigating this process likely feels different for everyone. Some schools may have an excellent system in place, where for others this process may feel overwhelming, confusing, or frustrating. Whatever the case may be, we understand that there are likely different systems and steps in place at each of your academic settings that need to be navigated in a certain way. While this is the case, it can be helpful to know what resources exist and which professionals are out there who can help.

Most times, the first step in this process is to meet with the student's parents, as Mrs. Lawson did in the opening vignette. Again, this may look different depending on your school environment. We want to emphasize the importance of involving parents in this process, through the building of a *teacher-parent dyad*. We also want to provide some helpful strategies that can be utilized when meeting with parents in order to ease the process.

UNDERSTANDING SUPPORTS WITHIN YOUR SCHOOL

Just as we talked about the brain being both "linked" and "differentiated" in Chapter 1, it is important for professionals to be the same. This means that even though we all have our unique specialties and lenses, we need to collaborate in order to best support students who

Supportive Diagram

Knowing the key professionals who can help support students is important as you consider the individual differences of each student. The professionals who are included on a student support team should be both "linked" and "differentiated"—meaning they are in close communication with other professionals while still holding their unique specialties and lenses.

have extra needs. Often there are many pieces to the puzzle—sometimes these pieces come together quickly, while at other times they are laid out slowly. Whatever the case, it is important that all professionals who are included on the student's support team are in communication with each other on a regular basis.

As you navigate the supports in your school, there are likely several key professionals to whom you can reach out. There may be some professionals with whom you've regularly interacted while others you have not. You may find it helpful to bring some of your concerns, insights, and observations to the professional who you suspect could best support the student before meeting with parents. It is important to understand their unique roles so that you can accurately recommend who might need to be included on the team. Some of them are outlined here:

- *Psychologists* provide mental health support to students who are experiencing emotional or social distress. They can provide interventions, resources, skills, and tools to students who need help with navigating strong emotions such as anxiety, frustration, anger, sadness, or depression. They can also provide support around developing social skills, entering into social situations, and navigating interpersonal relatedness. Common areas of difficulty within the school environment include anxiety, frustration around academic tasks, difficulty with social functioning, as well as emotional and behavioral dysregulation. If you are at a public school, then school psychologists can often conduct testing as part of the Individualized Education Plan (IEP) process and are typically involved in developing goals for IEPs. They can also be involved in helping to develop a 504 plan.
- *Occupational therapists* support students in their ability to participate in daily school activities, including academic achievement, self-care skills, social skills, recess activities, and behavioral organization. They might provide support to teachers to help students better access curriculum, suggest alternative seating options to maximize attention, provide assistive technology that will aid in a student's learning, or build specific skills that allow the student to better engage in the educational experience. Common areas of difficulty within the learning environment include fine motor skills like handwriting, cognitive impairment, visual-

perceptual problems, difficulty staying on task, difficulty
with organization, or inappropriate sensory responses.
Within the school district, occupational therapists can
also be a part of the IEP team, helping to determine
which students may benefit from receiving occupational
therapy services.

- *Speech and language pathologists* work with students who
  have difficulty with communication that impacts their
  educational performance. This may include voice disorders,
  fluency problems, articulation, or language disorders.
  They help students to understand and use basic language
  concepts, support their reading and writing skills, increase
  students' understanding of texts and lessons, and facilitate
  social skill development. Common areas of difficulty within
  the school environment include difficulty expressing
  thoughts and ideas, difficulty understanding and following
  directions, trouble communicating with peers, poor ability
  to read nonverbal cues, or limited vocabulary. Speech
  and language pathologists can also be an integral part of
  the IEP team.

- *Physical therapists* provide services to students who
  have difficulty safely physically navigating the school
  environment or who need more support in their motor
  performance. There are a wide variety of environments
  within the school that a student may need to navigate,
  including classrooms, hallways, stairs, buses, bathrooms,
  gymnasiums, auditoriums, playgrounds, and field trip
  destinations. Common areas of difficulty in the school
  environment include difficulty maintaining sitting balance,
  difficulty climbing the play structure at recess, inability
  to catch or throw a ball in physical education activities,
  learning to use assistive devices for mobility (e.g., walker
  or wheelchair), or unsafe navigation of the classroom
  or hallways.

- *Educational therapists* are educators who provide
  individualized support to students with learning
  differences, using their knowledge of the emotional,
  social, neurological, academic, and behavioral aspects of
  learning. They equip students with strategies and tools
  to be successful learners, better access the information
  in academic curriculum, and build skills to narrow the
  gap of their learning differences. They are also trained in
  other structured, intensive curriculums and interventions

for students with learning disabilities. Common areas of difficulty within the learning environment include dyslexia, dysgraphia, language processing, auditory processing, visual processing, organizational skills, or attention-related difficulties.

- *Audiologists* provide comprehensive evaluations to determine if a student has an auditory processing disorder related to the higher-level cognitive processes associated with hearing. They go beyond assessing whether or not a child can hear, like the beeping tests performed at the pediatrician. Common areas of difficulty within the learning environment include difficulty following multistep directions, difficulty understanding how to do a task, poor ability to retell a story, difficulty with reading fluency or reading comprehension, trouble keeping up with peer conversations, or misinterpreting social cues. *NOTE: Audiologists will typically refer to a speech and language pathologist and/or occupational therapist for ongoing intervention once the evaluation is complete.*

- *Developmental optometrists* work specifically with the child population regarding a wide variety of vision needs. They go beyond assessing whether or not a child requires corrective lenses. This can include oculomotor skills, which are related to the coordination of the eye muscles, and visual-perceptual skills, which are related to the higher-level cognitive processes associated with vision. Common areas of difficulty within the school environment may include difficulty following along when reading; losing place when reading; fatigue when reading or writing; complaints of blurred vision or headaches; difficulty copying information from the board; poor ability to stay between the lines when writing; frequent reversals of letters; misaligning numbers in math problems; or difficulty finding objects in his desk, cubby, or backpack. A student like Eliza would be a good candidate for a referral to a developmental optometrist.

If you work in a public school setting, you are likely familiar with the processes of establishing a Student Support Plan, 504 plan, or IEP for a student, so we will only briefly outline them here.

- *Student Support Team (SST):* An SST is typically formed when a student is first identified as having difficulties in the classroom. It is usually the "first line of defense." This

Reflective Activity

Having a multidisciplinary team to support a student who needs additional support can help alleviate some of the pressure you feel as a teacher.

Take a moment to think about your school's policies around providing help for students.	
How has this process been for you?	With which professionals have you interacted before?

team is designed to further explore the student's academic, behavioral, and social-emotional progress in school. After certain needs are identified, the SST can propose strategies, accommodations, and interventions that can be implemented without needing a more formalized plan.

- *504 plan:* A 504 plan is typically developed for a student with a diagnosis or disability that is impacting their functioning at school. Section 504 has a broader definition of "disability" than the Individuals with Disabilities Education Act, so some children who wouldn't typically meet the full criteria for an IEP are able to obtain support through a 504 plan. A student does not need to go through any additional testing to qualify for a 504 plan. A student with a 504 plan may have an anxiety disorder, attention deficit hyperactivity disorder, high-functioning autism, depression, or other disability that impacts their functioning but not to the point of qualifying for special education services through an IEP. Students with 504 plans often receive services and environmental supports/accommodations such as extended time, preferential seating, and more frequent breaks.

- *IEP:* This process can be initiated by the parent, teacher, or school personnel. Meeting with a parent before recommending an IEP is an important and necessary step. Typically, SST meetings are initiated prior to deciding whether or not an IEP is warranted. The IEP evaluation process may include any number of specialists, including those listed above. In order to qualify for an IEP, a student must first undergo an evaluation with the school, or district's, school psychologist and special education team, which may include an occupational therapist, speech and language pathologist, and other professionals on the team deemed necessary. This evaluation process will help to determine if the student meets the criteria for special education services. If the student does in fact meet the criteria, then the student will qualify for additional special education services, which may include RSP pull-out classes in certain subjects, modifications, accommodations, or other services deemed necessary.

In private schools, this process can vary greatly. While public schools have certain funding sources set aside to provide services for students with disabilities, private schools do not have the same requirements. For that reason, private schools vary greatly from the types of support they are able to provide. The best way to navigate this is to learn more about your school's policies and go from there.

ACCESSING EXTERNAL SUPPORTS

Unfortunately, there may be cases where internal supports are not available, not able to be accessed, or not adequate.

- Some private schools do not have internal support available depending on their funding. In this case, they must rely on the resources available in the community in order to help students. This also puts the onus more on parents in order to follow through with accessing those resources.

Typically, private schools still have an SST or equivalent individual or group of professionals who can guide you and parents through the process to get the student the support he needs.

- It may be that the accommodations provided by a 504 plan are not adequate to support the student's needs, yet the dysregulation being experienced by the student does not qualify for special education under an IEP.

- Sometimes the student is not performing poorly enough to qualify for services despite clearly having difficulty in the classroom. He may be meeting the grade-level expectations academically but still exhibiting considerable difficulty with regulation throughout the school day. This is often the case with students who have asynchronous development or are considered 2E.

- Sometimes students have needs impacting their educational performance that cannot be adequately identified or addressed using the internal supports available. For example, with Eliza, a developmental optometrist or vision specialist is probably the best referral for her, but not all schools have this professional on staff.

In these cases, the student may need supplemental services outside of those provided within the school environment, or the student may need to access all of her services outside of the school environment. Thus, it is important to build relationships with professionals in the community who are trusted and who align with your educational approach. It is best practice to recommend two to three professionals in each area of need so that parents can make their own decisions about who to contact. Professionals who contract with insurance companies and those who are fee for service (that is, they do not take insurance) should be delineated.

Again, most schools likely have policies in place when it comes to their teachers making recommendations for outside support. Most public schools may be limited in what they can recommend, while private schools typically have lists of trusted providers where families can go to receive services. While there are additional services in your community, depending on what the needs are of the family and the student, it is best to ask your school administrators or staff about the policies and resources already in place that they can recommend or provide.

Once you've identified that a student needs extra support and have followed the appropriate policies and procedures of your school in addressing your concerns, it is likely that somewhere within that process, a meeting with the parents will take place. Before we jump into strategies that are useful when meeting with parents, we first want to address the teacher-parent dyad.

ESTABLISHING A TEACHER-PARENT DYAD

Just as a teacher-student dyad is important for establishing a safe, trusting relationship that facilitates learning, it is important to consider the development of a teacher-parent dyad. The **teacher-parent dyad** is also a protective relationship that focuses on the reciprocal impact of each other's regulation. We recognize that some parents do not serve as primary caregivers for certain students. For the sake of simplicity, we use the term "parent" broadly to encompass anyone serving as the student's caregiver. As Mrs. Lawson highlighted in the vignette, meetings with parents can often be anxiety-provoking for teachers. Maintaining a regulated state is important so that you can also facilitate the regulation of the parent. *Use your mirror neurons: when you are at ease and set a calm, collaborative tone, then the parents will likely follow.*

It may seem that this dyad can be tricky to establish because of the limited time you may have with parents. Introducing the idea of being curious about their child's learning at the beginning of the school year can set the tone. Sharing with parents, at Back to School Night, for example, about how to foster a sense of curiosity in learning, asking questions, and searching for the "why" when it comes to their child's learning, can help parents become active participants in engaging in their child's learning process. Just as it does not take much time to build a positive teacher-student dyad with the vast majority of children, it also does not take much to develop a positive teacher-parent dyad. Again, think of mini-moments you can engage in with parents to build that positive, protective, preventive relationship.[1]

Teacher-parent dyad: a protective relationship between the teacher and the parent that focuses on how the state of regulation of the teacher and parent impact each other.

You may notice that some parents trigger dysregulation in you more readily than others. Parents are hard-wired to protect their children, which can often be interpreted as being defensive. It is therefore important to validate the feelings of the parent. Let the parents know

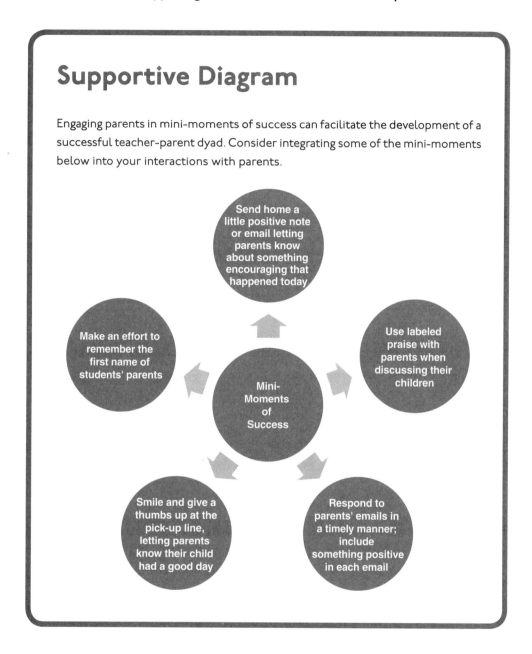

Supportive Diagram

Engaging parents in mini-moments of success can facilitate the development of a successful teacher-parent dyad. Consider integrating some of the mini-moments below into your interactions with parents.

Send home a little positive note or email letting parents know about something encouraging that happened today

Make an effort to remember the first name of students' parents

Use labeled praise with parents when discussing their children

Mini-Moments of Success

Smile and give a thumbs up at the pick-up line, letting parents know their child had a good day

Respond to parents' emails in a timely manner; include something positive in each email

what they are already doing well to support their child. For many of you who have been present in an IEP, SST, or 504 plan meeting, you know that emotions can run high. There are of course many times where these meetings result in incredibly positive, heartwarming, encouraging, and supportive opportunities for parents and educators to collaborate on ways to best support their children and students. Unfortunately, such meetings can also be stressful, anxiety provoking, and overwhelming for everyone involved. *While everyone enters into such meetings with the same goal in mind—to best help the student—individuals on the team may have different ideas and beliefs about how to go about achieving this goal.*

Developing a positive teacher-parent dyad from the beginning of the school year is a preventative and protective measure teachers can take to reduce the anxiety many parents experience regarding their children's learning. Such a dyad can serve as a protective relationship that works toward building a collaborative, safe working alliance with them.[1] If parents feel safe and connected with their child's teacher, it will be easier for them to remain regulated when they engage. *Interestingly, most of the strategies we describe in this book also work for adults. Give them a try with your friends, partners, spouses, and others in your life. Give them a try on your students' parents.*

Reflective Activity

Consider a time when you've had a positive interaction with a parent, as well as a time when you've had a negative interaction with a parent. Reflect on the questions below.

	Positive Interaction	Negative Interaction
What was your state of regulation?		
What was the state of regulation for the parents?		
What was the outcome of the meeting?		
How was the teacher-parent dyad established?		

Know that it is not uncommon for students to display certain behaviors at school but not at home. Often this is reflected in the differing demands, expectations, and structure that are present in each environment. It may also be reflected in the varying degree of sensory inputs. It can be difficult for parents to understand why you are describing a "completely different child" than the one they know. Remind them that you are a partner with them in this process. And that this *is* a process. You both have a shared goal in mind: their child's well-being and educational experience. Encourage parents to keep asking questions and searching for the "why," just as you have been doing. *When both parties approach the situation with curiosity, then it is possible for a mutual understanding to be reached.*

Throughout this process, it is important to let parents know that their insights and understanding of their child are valued. We will talk more about highlighting the student's strengths below, but know that this is an essential component. Affirm to parents that they truly are the experts when it comes to knowing their child. At the same time, you as teachers have much to offer parents because of the many hours you interact with and observe their children. You see them in a different light.

Sometimes parents are not ready to hear the information you are presenting. It is important that you keep your observations objective and not jump to any diagnostic conclusions, especially without any formalized assessment completed. While there is an element of timing to sharing your concerns, it is also important to keep the student's best interests at hand. We frequently experience this as therapists. Throwing a lot of information at a parent all at once can be overwhelming and too much to process. But holding back information can be damaging to the child down the line, especially if the child does not receive much-needed interventions. *It is a delicate balance of offering your professional observations and recommendations without overwhelming or dysregulating parents to a point where they cannot "take in" the information. This is why forming a positive teacher-parent dyad is so important.*

Remember that not all the parents with whom you interact have had positive school experiences themselves.[2] These past experiences may influence their attitude and approach when meeting with you. They may not know what a positive teacher-parent interaction looks like because they rarely had positive teacher-student interactions while in school. Some parents may have their own history of experiencing

Supportive Diagram

Acknowledging how a parent might be feeling can establish empathy and facilitate co-regulation. Here are some validating phrases that you can use when communicating with parents. Again, the tone of voice and nonverbal communication in which you say the following comments will also make a world of difference.

Try these . . .	Avoid these . . .
"We are going to talk about a lot today. Please feel free to ask any questions and express any concerns or worries you have at any moment. We will walk through this together, every step of the way."	"Your child is not grasping the concepts and is falling further and further behind—are you doing any work with them at home?"
"I know this is a lot of information, and I imagine it may feel overwhelming."	"Your child talks nonstop to her friends during class. I don't think she hears anything I'm teaching."
"Your child has been making so much progress! I see how hard she is working, and how much she is learning. There are still certain areas where we need to focus, and we can continue to do this together."	"We still have a lot to work on. Your child has not met these goals."
"I understand that what you are observing at home does not match with what we are observing at school. Let's look at some of the reasons why this may be the case."	"My class is very structured, and I have clear expectations for each student. Your child isn't rising to the challenge even though I know he is capable."

racism or bias and are worried that their children are going to undergo similar experiences. This may make it harder for them to engage with and trust professionals or authority figures. *Thus, it is important to check your cultural biases when interacting with parents.* Some parents may be more difficult to schedule meetings with due to the logistics of getting time off work, transportation, or childcare—this does not mean they are less dedicated to their child.[2] There are some cultures that focus more on the academic outcomes of the student while others focus more on the overall well-being of the student.

PREPARING FOR A PARENT MEETING

Now that we have considered the teacher-parent dyad, we can look toward preparing for the meeting with the parents. The preparatory work that you put in prior to meeting with parents can not only ease your anxiety but also make parents feel more supported in the long run. These strategies can be helpful during parent-teacher conferences, SSTs, 504 plans, or IEP meetings.

Strategy 1: Collect Information

Teachers need to have a strong sense of the student before sitting down with the parents. This means having clear and specific ways to communicate your concerns. Gathering work samples that effectively illustrate your concerns is critical. As we mentioned above, the demands of the classroom are different than the demands at home, so the samples you provide may not reflect what the student can accomplish at home. Know that many students with sensory processing disorders, learning differences, and behavioral challenges show inconsistency in their performance—when the conditions are "right" they can rise to the challenge.

When gathering information and specific examples of both strengths and areas of vulnerability, it is important to communicate with other teachers who work with the student. Do other teachers share the same observations? What have other teachers found that works well with that student? Are there different times of day or different topics where the student is more successful? Remember to communicate not only with core teachers but also with specialty teachers. As outlined in Chapter 8, some students may thrive in certain specialty classes because it caters more to the way they process information or integrate sensorimotor input. Or a specialty teacher may observe the opposite—that certain activities are quite challenging for that student due to the learning and sensorimotor demands of their particular class.

In the case of public schools, it is important for the teacher to establish an educational need for services before recommending an IEP. This means the student must be performing below average or below grade level in certain areas. The student may also be demonstrating considerable emotional distress or disruptive behaviors that are impacting his or her ability to access the curriculum. Collecting evidence that demonstrates this educational need will help the process move along more quickly. This also reflects that you are an advocate for helping the student get the support she needs.

As you continue to put together information, it is important to provide parents with tangible ways that you are already working to support the student in the classroom. This includes things that have worked well and things that have not. *Letting parents know that students do well when they can and when they have the right support in place is important.* Reflect back to parents that the behaviors you are seeing are likely the result of an underlying skills vulnerability. This goes back to establishing the teacher-parent dyad where you both are asking questions to search for the "why."

Strategy 2: Start and End with Strengths

When you sit down to meet with parents, it is important for both parties—teachers and parents—to start with the strengths of the student.[3,4] Ashley likes to call this the "strengths sandwich." Start and end with strengths. Ask the parents to highlight the strengths and interests of their child. You can then share the strengths that you see within the school environment, how those strengths complement what the parents see at home, and the ways you've seen the student grow. While it can sometimes be challenging for the teacher or parent to identify strengths, especially in times of crisis or distress, this sets an important tone for the meeting.

Remember that we are all human—we all make mistakes, we all need extra support at times, and we all are continuing to grow and develop. Students are no exception. When you approach your meeting with

Supportive Diagram

When participating in any meeting regarding a student—whether a parent-teacher conference, SST, or IEP—it is important to focus on strengths. All of this is embedded in a positive teacher-parent dyad. Consider using a "strengths sandwich" format with the following components:

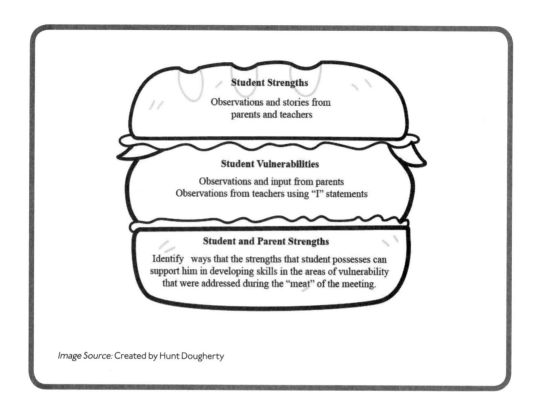

Student Strengths

Observations and stories from
parents and teachers

Student Vulnerabilities

Observations and input from parents
Observations from teachers using "I" statements

Student and Parent Strengths

Identify ways that the strengths that student possesses can
support him in developing skills in the areas of vulnerability
that were addressed during the "meat" of the meeting.

Image Source: Created by Hunt Dougherty

online
resources ▶   Available for download at **resources.corwin.com/ClassroomBehaviors**

parents using a strengths-based approach, you convey that you are a partner with them in this process. It is possible to both lean into the strengths of the student while at the same time recognizing their vulnerabilities. By starting with strengths, it also helps to put parents at ease, reduce their anxieties a certain degree, and decrease their dys-regulation. It supports parents by allowing them to notice that you also see positives in their child, which helps begin to move parents from a *reactive to a receptive* state of mind.

One of the ways that you can do this, aside from simply listing the student's strengths, is by sharing specific stories about how you see these strengths reflected in the school environment. Highlight the ways you notice the student's individuality and how that adds to the classroom dynamics. Relate yourself to the student, and convey the relationship that you have developed with her. For example, Mrs. Lawson might communicate that Eliza has a wonderful imagination that allows her to tell detailed stories other students delight in listening to. You might comment on how you also enjoy being the storyteller at family gatherings, and that your love of storytelling is what prompted you to major in English. You can then share with her parents how the love of storytelling is something that you and Eliza have really been able to share together.

During the "meat" of the meeting, when sharing concerns, it is always helpful to *start with the parent's experience* to see what their concerns are and how they have been addressing them at home. This is where you include the information you have gathered that highlights the student's vulnerabilities and areas of growth that are needed, as outlined in the strategy above. Remember to use "I statements" when talking about students' challenges at school, and avoid comments that may be experienced by parents as blaming, shaming, or labeling, such as "I've seen how hard he is really working, and my concern is that he is not grasping the concepts despite frequent repetition," or, "I love her creativity and spontaneity; she is so full of life and fun to have in class. However, her talking over her peers is really getting in the way of her learning."

After sharing your concerns, you want to end the meeting by again reflecting on the strengths of the student. Think about the ways his strengths can actually support his vulnerabilities and challenges. Ask the parents to share how they see the child's strengths as contributing to the action plan. With Eliza, her strength of telling detailed, imaginative stories can help to fuel her passion for writing even though this process is difficult at this time. Use this time to identify ways that the child's strengths can really help them to be adaptive, be resilient, and experience positive outcomes. For example, "I know we have identified a lot to work on today, but I am so excited because I have seen his determination to get through hard things, and I know he can do this too," or, "I love how strong willed she is, and I know that if we can channel that in the right direction, she will be able to achieve all of her goals!" *By identifying the strengths of the parents as well, the parents may leave the meeting feeling empowered, as well as knowing that they have some concrete action steps that they can take to begin moving forward.* "He is so strong, and so resilient; he has thoughtful and dedicated parents, and a great team in place here, we will get through this together."

Interactive Scenario

Read the short vignettes below, considering that you are meeting with the student's parents to discuss your concerns. Identify the student's strengths and ways you can frame his strengths as a way to support his vulnerabilities.

> Jonah, a first grader, is struggling with peer relationships, particularly during unstructured time like recess. He often becomes verbally abusive and physical when he feels something is not "fair" or someone "cheated." Peers have started to say they, are afraid of him.

- Strengths:

- Way to support vulnerabilities:

> Eliana, a fifth grader, can often be seen doodling intricate drawings during creative writing time. When asked about her drawings, she has an elaborate story behind them. However, she often avoids writing them down and refuses to share them with any other students.

- Strengths:

- Way to support vulnerabilities:

> Josh is a third grader who has difficulty staying focused on his work, his desk and backpack are messy, and he often loses his assignments. His teacher notices that he often fidgets with things and prompts him frequently to pay attention. Josh is athletic and well-liked by his peers—he likes looking out the window and thinking about playing outside.

- Strengths:

- Way to support vulnerabilities:

■ Jonah has a clear sense of justice and values fairness. He may do well serving as a referee during sports games, at least until he can better participate in the game itself. Affirm that justice is an

(Continued)

(Continued)

important concept while recognizing that it can be challenging to understand that not all situations can end in justice.

- Eliana is a creative thinker who has good ideas for stories. Using her drawings as a jumping-off point for her writing will be beneficial. Encouraging her to break up her drawings into different parts of a story and then writing a caption about each is a good way to leverage her strengths. Affirm that writing is a multistep process that is challenging for many students.

- Jeremiah is a student with a strong imagination and desire to do well, he is very social and enjoys playing sports, and he feels badly when he loses things. Support him by providing him with some organization strategies that he can relate back to the rules/regulations of different sports. Encourage him to verbally process his thoughts with other peers whenever possible, as this will help him stay focused and provide him a social outlet.

Strategy 3: Allow Time for Processing

Remember that not all parents will respond the same way to the information you provide. Some may take instant initiative, while others may need more time to process what has been discussed. Not all parents have the same resources. It is helpful to have a clearly delineated plan for parents based on your professional knowledge and experience. Creating a "road map" of sorts communicates your confidence and understanding of what the student might need, as well as lifting the burden of parents having to figure out this plan by themselves. It may be that the parents take a few detours along the way, but we have found as therapists that most parents appreciate the pointed direction.

Another way to facilitate the processing of information provided during your meeting is to leave time for questions and input from parents throughout your meeting, as well as designated time at the end of the meeting. Some parents may come in with many questions or may develop questions along the way. Other parents may not even know what questions to ask. Make sure to stop at various times throughout the meeting to verify that parents understand the terminology, ask what input they might have, and allow them to raise any questions or concerns. These steps will help them be active participants in the process.

By maintaining the teacher-parent dyad after the meeting has ended, you will be able to follow up with them on what information the parent still needs. Encourage the parents to continue asking questions along the way. Keep your door (and inbox!) open; let them know you are listening.

Through out the course of this book, we have covered so much ground, explored a variety of topics, and discussed a multitude of strategies. We understand that this may feel overwhelming. In reading this book, you are likely searching for help, answers, and a new way of looking at behavior. We hope that if there is anything that you take with you, it is that you know you are not alone. We are here to provide a supportive community of professionals that allows for self-exploration, self-acceptance, vulnerability, and the opportunity to build awareness into ourselves and those who we work with. No one is perfect, no one knows everything, and we all make mistakes. Through maintaining a curious and open stance, we can allow ourselves to grow, adapt, change, and make space for new outcomes. Start with your state of regulation: What do you need to re-enter a state of calm? What questions can you ask right now to solve the problem, better understand yourself or your student, and search for the "why"? Once you are able to access this frame of mind, it will open up new avenues for creativity and innovation in supporting the regulation and learning that has the potential to profoundly impact the lives of your students.

References

CHAPTER 1

1. Boyle, C. A., Boulet, S., Schieve, L. A., Cohen, R. A., Blumberg, S. J., Yeargin-Allsopp, M., . . . Kogan, M. D. (2011). Trends in the prevalence of developmental disabilities in US children, 1997-2008. *Pediatrics, 127*(6), 1034–1042.
2. Horowitz, S. H., Rawe, J., & Whittaker, M. C. (2017). *The state of learning disabilities: Understanding the 1 in 5*. National Center for Learning Disabilities.
3. Siegel, D. J. (2012). *The developing mind: How relationships and the brain interact to shape who we are* (2nd ed.). The Guilford Press.
4. Siegel, D. J., & Payne Bryson, T. (2011). *The whole-brain child: 12 revolutionary strategies to nurture your child's developing mind*. Bantam Books.
5. Voss, P., Thomas, M. E., Cisneros-Franco, J. M., & de Villers-Sidani, É. (2017). Dynamic brains and the changing rules of neuroplasticity: Implications for learning and recovery. *Frontiers in Psychology, 8*, 1657.
6. Fuchs, E., & Flügge, G. (2014). Adult neuroplasticity: More than 40 years of research. *Neural Plasticity, 2014*, 541870.
7. Perry, B. D., & Pollard, D. (1997). *Altered brain development following global neglect in early childhood*. Paper presented to Society for Neuroscience: Proceedings from Annual Meeting, New Orleans, LA.
8. Perry, B. D. (2004). *Maltreated children: Experience, brain development, and the next generation*. W. W. Norton.
9. Bick, J. B., Zhu, T., Stamoulis, C., Fox, N. A., Zeanah, C., & Nelson, C. A. (2015). Effect of early institutionalization and foster care on long-term white matter development: A randomized clinical trial. *JAMA Pediatrics, 169*(3), 211–219.
10. Siegel, D. J. (2007). *The mindful brain: Reflection and attunement in the cultivation of well-being*. W. W. Norton.
11. Badenoch, B. (2008). *Being a brain-wise therapist: A practical guide to interpersonal neurobiology*. W. W. Norton.

CHAPTER 2

1. Greene, R. W. (1998). *The explosive child: A new approach for understanding and parenting easily frustrated, "chronically inflexible" children*. HarperCollins Publishers.
2. Dobson, C., & Perry, B. D. (2010). The role of healthy relational interactions in buffering the impact of childhood trauma. In E. Gil (Ed.), *Working with children to heal interpersonal trauma: The power of play* (pp. 26–43). The Guilford Press.
3. Siegel, D. J. (2012). *The developing mind: How relationships and the brain interact to shape who we are* (2nd ed.). The Guilford Press.
4. Badenoch, B. (2008). *Being a brain-wise therapist: A practical guide to interpersonal neurobiology*. W. W. Norton.

5. Lilas, C., & Turnbull, H. (2009). *Infant/child mental health, early intervention, and relationship-based therapies: A neurorelational framework for interdisciplinary practice.* W. W. Norton.

6. Perry, B. D., & Dobson, C. D. (2009). Surviving childhood trauma: The role of relationships in prevention of, and recovery from, trauma-related problems. *Journal of CCYP, a Division of British Association for Counseling and Psychotherapy*, 28–31.

7. California Department of Education. Retrieved from https://www.cde.ca.gov/sp/cd/re/itf09socemofdemor.asp

8. Greenberg, M., Kusche, C. A., Cook, E. T., & Quamma, J. P. (2009). Promoting emotional competence in school-aged children: The effects of the PATHS curriculum. *Emotions in Developmental Psychopathology, 7*, 117–136.

9. Rosenbalm, K. D., & Murray, D. W. (2017). *Promoting self-regulation in early childhood: A practice brief* (OPRE Brief No. 2019-79). Office of Planning, Research, and Evaluation, Administration for Children and Families, US Department of Health and Human Services. Retrieved from https://fpg.unc.edu/sites/fpg.unc.edu/files/resources/reports-and-policy-briefs/PromotingSelf-RegulationIntheFirstFiveYears.pdf

10. Office of Planning, Research, & Evaluation. (2015, February 13). *Self-regulation and toxic stress: Foundations for understanding self-regulation from an applied developmental perspective.* Retrieved from https://www.acf.hhs.gov/opre/resource/self-regulation-and-toxic-stress-foundations-for-understanding-self-regulation-from-an-applied-developmental-perspective

11. Whiting, J. W. M. (1981). Environmental constraints on infant care practices. In R. H. Munroe, R. L. Munroe, & B. B. Whiting (Eds.), *Handbook of cross-cultural human development.* Garland STPM Press.

12. Nelson, C. A., & Bosquet, M. (2000). Neurobiology of fetal and infant development: Implications for infant mental health. In C. H. Zeanah, Jr. (Ed.), *Handbook of infant mental health* (pp. 37–59). The Guilford Press.

13. Saarni, C. (1999). The development of emotional competence. *The Canadian Child and Adolescent Psychiatry Review, 13*(4), 121.

14. Morelock, M. J. (1992). Giftedness: The view from within. *Understanding Our Gifted, Open Space Communications, 4*(3), 11–15.

15. Snel, E. (2013). *Sitting still like a frog: Mindfulness exercises for kids (and their parents).* Shambhala.

16. Ortner, N., & Taylor, A. (2018). *My magic breath: Finding calm through mindful breathing.* HarperCollins.

17. Willey, K. (2017). *Breath like a bear: 30 mindful moments for kids to keel calm and focused anytime, anywhere.* Rodal Books.

18. Porges, S. (2009). The Polyvagal theory: New insights into adaptive reactions of the autonomic nervous system. *Cleveland Clinical Journal of Medicine, 76*(supplement 2), S86–S90.

19. Schore, A. (2000). Attachment and the regulation of the right brain. *Attachment & Human Development, 2*(1), 23–47.

CHAPTER 3

1. Brazelton, T., & Greenspan, S. I. (2000). The irreducible needs of children: What every child must have to grow, learn, and flourish. *Journal of Family and Consumer Services, 93*, 9–10.

2. Neuman, I. D. (2007). Oxytocin: The neuropeptide of love reveals some of its secrets. *Cell Metabolism, 5*(4), 231–233.

3. Becker-Weidman, A., & Hughes, D. (2008) Dyadic developmental psychotherapy: An evidence-based treatment for children with complex trauma and disorders of attachment. *Child & Adolescent Social Work, 13*, 329–337.

4. Hughes, D. (2003). Psychological intervention for the spectrum of attachment disorders and intrafamilial trauma. *Attachment & Human Development, 5*, 271–279.

5. Bretherton, I. (1992). The origins of attachment theory: John Bowlby and Mary Ainsworth. *Developmental Psychology, 28*, 759–775.

6. Lilas, C., & Turnbull, H. (2009). *Infant/child mental health, early intervention, and relationship-based therapies: A neurorelational framework for interdisciplinary practice.* W. W. Norton.

7. Perry, B. D., & Dobson, C. D. (2009). Surviving childhood trauma: The role of relationships in prevention of, and recovery from, trauma-related problems. *Journal of CCYP, a Division of British Association for Counseling and Psychotherapy*, 28–31.

8. Kilner, J. M., & Lemon, R. N. (2013). What we know currently about mirror neurons. *Current Biology, 23*(23), R1057–R1062. doi:10.1016/j.cub.2013.10.051

9. Iacoboni, M. (2008). *Mirroring people: The science of empathy and how we connect with others.* Picador.

10. Edelwich, J., & Brodsky, A. (1980). *Burnout: Stages of disillusionment in the helping professions.* Human Sciences Press.

11. Gallery, M. E., Eisenbach, J. J., & Holman, J. (1981). *Burnout: A critical appraisal and proposed intervention strategies* (Unpublished manuscript). Department of Special Education, Western Michigan University.

12. Martelli, M. F. (1994). *Crisis survival rules: Emotional control strategies.* Retrieved from http://villamartelli.com/P_Crisis%20Control.pdf

13. Hebb, D. O. (1949). *The organization of behavior.* Wiley & Sons.

14. Siegel, D. J. (2001). Toward an interpersonal neurobiology of the developing mind: Attachment relationships, "mindsight," and neural integration. *Infant Mental Health Journal: Official Publication of the World Association for Infant Mental Health, 22*(1–2), 67–94.

15. Tronick, E. (1986). Interactive mismatch and repair: Challenges to the coping infant. *Zero to Three, 6*, 1–6.

16. Winnicott, D. (1953). Transitional objects and transitional phenomena. *International Journal of Psychoanalysis, 34*, 89–97.

17. Tronick, E., & Beeghly, M. (2011). Infants' meaning-making and the development of mental health problems. *American Psychology, 66*(2), 107–119. doi:10.1037/a0021631

18. Milke, M., Nomaguchi, K. M., & Denny, K. (2012). *How does the amount of time mothers spend with children matter.* University of Maryland.

CHAPTER 4

1. Hanscom, A. J. (2016). *Balanced and barefoot: How unrestricted outdoor play makes for strong, confident, and capable children.* New Harbinger Publications.

2. Gainsley, S. (2011). Look, listen, touch, feel, taste: The importance of sensory play. *HIghscope Extensions, 25*(5), 1–5.

3. Loman, M. M., Wiik, K. L., Freen, K. A., Pollak, S. D., & Gunnar, M. R. (2009). Postinstitutionalized children's development: Growth, cognitive, and language outcomes. *Journal of Developmental & Behavioral Pediatrics, 30*(5), 426–434.

4. Fiese, B. H., & Winter, M. A. (2010). The dynamics of family chaos and its relation to children's socialemotional well-being. In G. W, Evans & T. D. Wachs (Eds.), *Chaos and its influence on children's development: An ecological perspective* (pp. 49–66). American Psychological Association.

5. Kinnealey, M., Pfeiffer, B., Miller, J., Roan, C., Shoener, R., & Ellner, M. L. (2012). Effect of classroom modification on attention and engagement of students with autism or dyspraxia. *American Journal of Occupational Therapy, 66*, 511–519.

6. Fisher, A. V., Godwin, K. E., & Seltman, H. (2014). Visual environment, attention allocation, and learning in young children: When too much of a good thing may be bad. *Psychological Science, 25*(7), 1362–1370.

7. Broring, T., Konigs, M., Oostrom, K. J., Lafeber, H. N., Brugman, A., & Oosterlaan, J. (2018). Sensory processing difficulties in school-age children born very preterm: An exploratory study. *Early Human Development, 117*, 22–31.

8. Lin, S. H., Cermak, S., Coster, W. J., & Miller, L. (2005). The relation between length of institutionalization and sensory integration in children adopted from Eastern Europe. *American Journal of Occupational Therapy, 59*(2), 139–147.

9. Wilbarger, J., Gunnar, M., Schneider, M., & Pollak, S. (2010). Sensory processing in internationally adopted post-institutionalized children. *Journal of Child Psychology and Psychiatry, 51*(10), 1–10.

10. Onyper, S. V., Carr, T. L, Farrar, J. S., & Floyd, B. R. (2011). Cognitive advantages of chewing gum. Now you see them, now you don't. *Appetite, 57*(2), 321–328.

11. Schulz, A., & Vogle, C. (2015). Interoception and stress. *Frontiers in Psychology, 6*, 993.

12. Mayer, E. (2016). *The mind-gut connection: How the hidden conversation within our bodies impacts our mood, our choices, and our overall health.* Harper Wave.

13. Ayers, A. J. (2005). *Sensory integration and the child: Understanding hidden sensory challenges.* Western Psychological Services.

14. Norris, E., van Steen, T., Direito, A., & Stamatakis, E. (2019). Physically active lessons in schools and their impact on physical activity, educational, health and cognition outcomes: a systematic review and meta-analysis. *British Journal of Sports Medicine.* Advance online publication. doi:10.1136/bjsports-2018-100502

15. Benes S., Finn, K. E., Sullivan, E. C., & Yan, Z. (2016). Teachers' perceptions of using movement in the classroom. *The Physical Educator, 73,* 110–135.

16. Active-Play, Active-Learning (APAL) University of Texas Health Science Center at Houston. School of Public Health. (2008). Retrieved from https://sph.uth.edu/research/centers/chppr/research/project.htm?project=fcc3acb5-4611-44ea-ab9c-e3f5052a8f2d

17. Learning Without Tears. Retrieved from https://www.lwtears.com/

CHAPTER 5

1. Fisher, A. V., Godwin, K. E., & Seltman, H. (2014). Visual environment, attention allocation, and learning in young children: When too much of a good thing may be bad. *Psychological Science, 25*(7), 1362–1370.

2. Ayers, A. J. (2005). *Sensory integration and the child: Understanding hidden sensory challenges.* Western Psychological Services.

3. Miller, L. J., Anzalone, M. E., Lane, S. J, Cermak, S. A., & Osten, E. T. (2007). Concept evolution in sensory integration: A proposed nosology for diagnosis. *American Journal of Occupational Therapy, 61*(2), 135–140.

4. Chang, Y. S., Gratiot, M., Owen, J. P., Brandes-Aitken, A., Desai, S. S., Hill, S. S., . . . Mukherjee, P. (2016). White matter microstructure is associated with auditory and tactile processing in children with and without sensory processing disorder. *Frontiers in Neuroanatomy, 9,* 169.

5. Owen, J. P., Marco, E. J., Desai, S., Fourie, E., Harris, J., Hill, S. S., . . . Mukherjee, P. (2013). Abnormal white matter microstructure in children with sensory processing disorders. *Neuroimage: Clinical, 2,* 844–853.

6. Schaaf, R. C., Benevides, T. W., Blanche, E., Brett-Green, B. A., Burke, J., Cohn, E., . . . Schoen, S. A. (2010) Parasympathetic functions in children with sensory processing disorder. *Frontiers in Integrative Neuroscience, 4,* 4.

7. Schoen, S. A., Miller, L. J., Brett-Green, B. A., & Nielsen, D. M. (2009). Physiological and behavioral differences in sensory processing: A comparison of children with Autism Spectrum Disorder and Sensory Modulation Disorder. *Frontiers in Integrative Neuroscience, 3,* 29.

8. Ahn, R. R., Miller, L. J., Milberger, S., & McIntosh, D. N. (2004). Prevalence of parents' perceptions of sensory processing disorders among kindergarten children. *American Journal of Occupational Therapy, 58*(3), 287–293.

9. Cronin, A. (2003). *Asynchronous development and sensory integration intervention in the gifted and talented population.* Davidson Institute for Talent Development. Retrieved from http://www.davidsongifted.org/search-database/entry/a10251

CHAPTER 6

1. Nielsen, J. A., Zielinski, B. A., Ferguson, M. A., Lainhart, J. E., & Anderson, J. S. (2013). An evaluation of the left-brain vs right-brain hypothesis with resting state functional connectivity magnetic resonance imaging. *PLoS ONE, 8*(8), e71275.

2. Siegel, D. J. (2012). *The developing mind: How relationships and the brain interact to shape who we are* (2nd ed.). The Guilford Press.

3. Braun, B. Retrieved from https://www.auditoryprocessingctr.com/about-capd

4. Paolicellim, R. C., Bolasco, G., Pagani, F., Maggi, L., Scianni, M., Panzanelli, P., . . . Gross, C. (2011). Synaptic pruning by microglia is necessary for normal brain development. *Science, 333*(6048), 1456–1458.

5. Meyer, A., Rose, D. H., & Gordon, D. (2014). *Universal design for learning: Theory and Practice.* CAST Professional Publishing.

6. Drake, S. M., & Burns, R. C. (2004). *Meeting standards through integrated curriculum.* ASCD. Retrieved from http://www.ascd.org/publications/books/103011/chapters/What-Is-Integrated-Curriculum¢.aspx

7. Siegel, D. J., & Bryson T. P. (2011). *The whole-brain child: 12 Revolutionary strategies to nurture your child's developing mind.* Delacorte Press.

8. Wolf, M. (2008). *The proust and the squid: The story and science of the reading brain.* Harper Perennial.

9. Franklin D. (2018). *Helping your child with language-based learning disabilities: Strategies to succeed in school and life with dyslexia, dysgraphia, dyscalculia, ADHD, and processing disorders.* New Harbinger Publications.

10. American Psychiatric Association. (2014). *Diagnostic and statistical manual of mental disorders. DSM-V.* American Psychiatric Publishing.

11. Shaywitz, S. E., & Shaywitz, B. A. (2005). Dyslexia (specific reading disability). *Biological Psychiatry, 57.* doi:1301–1309. 10.1016/j.biopsych .2005.01.043

12. Dohla, D., & Heim, S. (2015). Developmental dyslexia and dysgraphia: What can we learn from the one about the other? *Frontiers in Psychology.* Advance online publication. doi:10.3389/fpsyg.2015.02045

13. Hawke, J. L., Olson, R. K., Willcutt, E. G., Wadsworth, S. J., & DeFries, J. C. (2009). Gender ratios for reading difficulties. *Dyslexia, 15,* 239–242. doi:10.1002/dys.389

14. Shalev, R. S., Auerbach, J., Manor, O., & Gross-Tsur, V. (2000). Developmental dyscalculia: Prevalence and prognosis. *European Child & Adolescent Psychiatry, 9,* S58–S64.

15. Tanguay, P. B. (2001). *Nonverbal learning disabilities at home.* Jessica Kingsley Publishers Ltd.

16. Davis, J., & Broitman, J. (2011). *Nonverbal learning disabilities in children: Bridging the gap between science and practice.* Springer-Science and Media Limited LLC.

17. Cronin, A. (2003). *Asynchronous development and sensory integration intervention in the gifted and talented population.* Davidson Institute for Talent Development. Retrieved from http://www.davidsongifted.org/search-database/entry/a10251

18. Webb, J. T., Amend, E. R., & Beijan, P. (2016). *Misdiagnosis and dual diagnoses of gifted children and adults: ADHD, bipolar, OCD, Asperger's, depression and other disorders* (2nd ed). Great Potential Press Inc.

19. Joshi, M. R. (2003). Misconceptions about the assessment and diagnosis of reading disability. *Journal of Reading Psychology, 24*(3–4), 247–266.

20. PBS News Team. (2012). *Five misconceptions about learning disabilities.* Retrieved from https://www.pbs.org/newshour/health/five-misconceptions-about-learning-disabilities

21. Vygotsky, L. S. (1962). *Thought and language.* MIT Press. (Original work published 1934)

22. Vygotsky, L. S. (1978). *Mind in society: The development of higher psychological processes.* Harvard University Press.

23. Boyce, T. W. (2019). *The orchid and the dandelion: Why some children struggle and how all can thrive.* Penguin Random House LLC.

24. American Psychological Association. (2020). *The road to resilience.* Retrieved from https://www.apa.org/helpcenter/road-resilience

25. Harvard University Center of the Developing Child. *Toxic stress.* Retrieved from https://developingchild.harvard.edu/science/key-concepts/toxic-stress/

26. Dweck, C. S. (2008). *Mindset: The new psychology of success.* Ballantine Books.

27. Haft, S. L., Myers, C. A., & Hoeft, F. (2016). Socio-emotional and cognitive resilience in children with reading disabilities. *Current Opinion in Behavioral Sciences, 10*, 133–141.

28. Brooks, R. B., & Goldstein, S. (2002). *Raising resilient children: Fostering strength, hope, and optimism in your child.* McGraw-Hill.

CHAPTER 7

1. Feder, K. P., & Majnemer, A. (2007). Handwriting development, competency, and intervention. *Developmental Medicine & Child Neurology, 49*(4), 312–317.

2. Dinehart, L. H. (2015). Handwriting in early childhood education: Current research and future implications. *Journal of Early Childhood Literacy, 15*(1), 97–118.

3. Brown, M. (2018). *In a digital age, handwriting is still important for long-term academic success.* Today's Modern Educator. Retrieved from https://todaysmoderneducator.com/2018/05/08/digital-age-handwriting-still-important-long-term-success/#.XhUGNkdKjIU

4. Flatters, I., Mushtaq, F., Hill, L. J., Holt, R. J., Wilkie, R. M., & Mon-Williams, M. (2014). The relationship between a child's postural stability and manual dexterity. *Experimental Brain Research, 232*(9), 2907–2917.

5. Richards, T. L., Berninger, V. W., Stock, P., Altemeier, L., Trivedi, P., & Maravilla, K. (2009). Functional magnetic resonance imaging sequential finger movement activation differentiating good and poor writers. *Journal of Clinical Experimental Neuropsychology, 31*(8), 967–983.

6. Kiefer, M., Schuler, S., Mayer, C., Trumpp, N. M., Hille, K., & Sachse, S. (2015). Handwriting or typewriting? The influence of pen- or keyboard-based writing training on reading and writing performance in preschool children. *Advances in Cognitive Psychology, 11*(4), 136–146. https://doi.org/10.5709/acp-0178-7

7. Rosenblum, S., Aloni, T., & Josman, N. (2010). Relationships between handwriting performance and organizational abilities among children with and without dysgraphia: A preliminary study. *Research in Developmental Disabilities, 31*(2), 502–509.

8. Duran, K. S., & Frederick, C. M. (2013). Information comprehension: Handwritten vs. typed notes. *Undergraduate Research Journal for the Human Sciences, 12*(1).

9. Smoker, T. J., Murphy, C. E., & Rockwell, A. K. (2009, October). Comparing memory for handwriting versus typing. *Proceedings of the Human Factors and Ergonomics Society Annual Meeting, 53*(22), 1744–1747. SAGE Publications.

10. Deuel, R. K. (1995). Developmental dysgraphia and motor skills disorders. *Journal of Child Neurology, 10*(1_suppl), S6–S8.

11. Longcamp, M., Zerbato-Poudou, M. T., & Velay, J. L. (2005). The influence of writing practice on letter recognition in preschool children: A comparison between handwriting and typing. *Acta Psychologica, 119*(1), 67–79.

12. Schwellnus, H., Carnahan, H., Kushki, A., Polatajko, H., Missiuna, C., & Chau, T. (2012). Effect of pencil grasp on the speed and legibility of handwriting in children. *American Journal of Occupational Therapy, 66*(6), 718–726.

13. James, K. H. (2010). Sensori-motor experience leads to changes in visual processing in the developing brain. *Developmental Science, 13*(2), 279–288.

14. Zomorodi, M. (2017). *Bored and brilliant: How spacing out can unlock your most productive and creative self.* St. Martin's Press.

CHAPTER 8

1. Greene, R. W. (2008). *Lost at school: Why our kids with behavioral challenges are falling through the cracks and how we can help them.* Scribner.

2. Center for Responsive Schools, Inc. (2016). *Responsive classroom for music, art, PE and other special areas: The go to guide for busy special area teachers!* Author.

3. Baker, J. M., & Zigmond, N. (1995). The meaning and practice of inclusion for students with learning disabilities: Themes and implications

from the five cases. *The Journal of Special Education, 29*(2), 163–180. doi:10.1177/002246669502900207

4. Atterbury, B. W. (1985). Musical differences in learning-disabled and normal-achieving readers, aged seven, eight and nine. *Psychology of Music, 13*(2), 114–123. doi:10.1177/0305735685132005

CHAPTER 9

1. Bassett, J., Snyder, T. L., Rogers., D. T., Collins, C. L. (2013). Permissive, authoritarian, and authoritative instructors: Applying the concept of parenting styles to the college classroom. *Individual Differences Research, 11*(1), 1–11.

2. Bamas, M. (2001). "Parenting" students: Applying developmental psychology to the classroom. *Teaching Psychology, 27,* 276–277.

3. Baumrind, D. (1966). Effects of authoritative parental control on child behavior. *Child Development, 37,* 887–907.

4. Bailey, S. J. (2009). *Discipline: A parent's guide for school-age children.* Montana State University Extension.

5. Gutierrez, E. (2012, April 26). *Natural and logical consequences: How implementing them leads to better discipline in children.* Michigan State University Extension.

6. Akin-Little, K. A., Eckert, T. L., Lovett, B. J., & Little, S. G. (2004). Extrinsic reinforcement in the classroom: Bribery or best practice. *School Psychology Review, 33,* 344–362.

7. Kern, L., & Clemens, N. H. (2007). Antecedent strategies to promote appropriate classroom behavior. *Psychology in the Schools, 44,* 65–75.

8. Barker, G. P., & Graham, S. (1987). Developmental study of praise and blame as attributional cues. *Journal of Educational Psychology, 79*(1), 62–66. doi:10.1037/0022-0663.79.1.62

9. Brophy, J. (1981). Teacher praise: A functional analysis. *Review of Educational Research, 51,* 5–32.

10. Burnett, P. C. (2001). Elementary students' preferences for teacher praise. *Journal of Classroom Interaction, 36*(1), 16–23.

11. Colvin, G. T., & Sugai, G. M. (1989). *Managing escalated behavior.* Behavior Associates.

12. Siegel, D. J. (2012). *The developing mind: How relationships and the brain interact to shape who we are* (2nd ed.). The Guilford Press.

13. Brandt, K., Perry, B. D., Seligman, S., & Tronick, E. (2014). *Infant and early childhood mental health: Core concepts and clinical practice.* American Psychiatric Publishing.

14. Stroud, B. (2012). *How to measure a relationship: A practical approach to dyadic Interventions.* CreateSpace Independent Publishing Platform.

15. Brazelton, T., & Greenspan, S. I. (2000). *The irreducible needs of children: What every child must have to grow learn and flourish.* Merloyd Lawrence Book, DA Capo Press.

16. Greene, R. W. (2008). *Lost at school: Why our kids with behavioral challenges are falling through the cracks and how we can help them.* Scribner.

17. Delahooke, M. (2019). *Beyond behavior: Using brain science and compassion to understand and solve children's behavioral challenges.* Pesi Publishing and Media.

CHAPTER 10

1. Staples, K. E., & Diliberto, J. A. (2010). Guidelines for successful parent involvement: Working with parents of students with disabilities. *Teaching Exceptional Children, 42*(6), 58–63.

2. Graham-Clay, S. (2005). Communicating with parents: Strategies for teachers. *School Community Journal, 15*(1), 117–129.

3. Climie, E., & Henley, L. (2016). A renewed focus on strengths-based assessment in schools. *British Journal of Special Education, 43*(2), 108–121.

4. Climie, E. A., & Mastoras, S. M. (2015). ADHD in schools: Adopting a strengths-based perspective. *Canadian Psychology/Psychologie Canadienne, 56*(3), 295.

Index

CORWIN

A SAGE Publishing Company

CORWIN HAS ONE MISSION: to enhance education through intentional professional learning.

We build long-term relationships with our authors, educators, clients, and associations who partner with us to develop and continuously improve the best evidence-based practices that establish and support lifelong learning.

Solutions YOU WANT | Experts YOU TRUST | Results YOU NEED

EVENTS

>>> **INSTITUTES**

Corwin Institutes provide large regional events where educators collaborate with peers and learn from industry experts. Prepare to be recharged and motivated!

corwin.com/institutes

ON-SITE PD

>>> **ON-SITE PROFESSIONAL LEARNING**

Corwin on-site PD is delivered through high-energy keynotes, practical workshops, and custom coaching services designed to support knowledge development and implementation.

corwin.com/pd

>>> **PROFESSIONAL DEVELOPMENT RESOURCE CENTER**

The PD Resource Center provides school and district PD facilitators with the tools and resources needed to deliver effective PD.

corwin.com/pdrc

ONLINE

>>> **ADVANCE**

Designed for K–12 teachers, Advance offers a range of online learning options that can qualify for graduate-level credit and apply toward license renewal.

corwin.com/advance

Contact a PD Advisor at (800) 831-6640 or visit www.corwin.com for more information

CORWIN